THE MISHNAH BEFORE 70

Program in Judaic Studies
Brown University
BROWN JUDAIC STUDIES
Edited by
Jacob Neusner,
Wendell S. Dietrich, Ernest S. Frerichs,
Calvin Goldscheider, Alan Zuckerman

Project Editors (Project)

David Blumenthal, Emory University (Approaches to Medieval Judaism)
William Brinner (Studies in Judaism and Islam)
Ernest S. Frerichs, Brown University (Dissertations and Monographs)
Lenn Evan Goodman, University of Hawaii (Studies in Medieval Judaism)
(Studies in Judaism and Islam)
William Scott Green, University of Rochester (Approaches to Ancient Judaism)
Ivan Marcus, Jewish Theological Seminary of America
(Texts and Studies in Medieval Judaism)
Marc L. Raphael, Ohio State University (Approaches to Judaism in Modern Times)
Norbert Samuelson, Temple University (Jewish Philosophy)
Jonathan Z. Smith, University of Chicago (Studia Philonica)

Number 51
THE MISHNAH BEFORE 70

by
Jacob Neusner

THE MISHNAH BEFORE 70

by
Jacob Neusner

Scholars Press
Atlanta, Georgia

THE MISHNAH BEFORE 70

©1987
Brown University

Library of Congress Cataloging in Publication Data

Neusner, Jacob, 1932-
  The Mishnah before 70.

  (Brown Judaic studies ; no. 51)
  Includes bibliographical references.
  1. Mishnah--Criticism, Redaction. I. Title.
II. Title: Mishnah before seventy. III. Series.
BM497.8.N4784 1987   296.1'23066   86-31498
ISBN 1-55540-106-6 (alk. paper)

Printed in the United States of America
on acid-free paper

In tribute to

JOEL CARMICHAEL

Editor of *Midstream*

Who gave me a fair and full hearing
when others would have denied it

and so upheld the integrity of
Jewish public discourse in an age
of censorship and repression in Jewish learning.

He is a *Mensch* where and when there are not many.

CONTENTS

Preface ... ix

I. The Method of Correlating Attributions and Sequences of Logical Progression: The Case of Mishnah- and Tosefta-Tractate Makhshirin ... 1
    i. Introduction ... 1
    ii. Attributions ... 1
        1. Unattributed Pericopae ... 1
        2. Attributions ... 3
    iii. The Weaving of the Law: Yavneh and Usha ... 6
        1. Liquids which Impart Susceptibility to Uncleanness ... 7
        2. Imparting Susceptibility to Uncleanness: Intention and Action ... 13
    iv. Makhshirin before 70: The Houses and the Ushans ... 30
    v. A Second Century Tractate ... 48

II. Kelim before 70 ... 53
    i. Definition of the Problem ... 53
    ii. The Yavnean Presuppositions ... 55
    iii. The Houses ... 59
    iv. From Scripture to Yavneh ... 63
    v. "First Cleanse the Inside" ... 72
    vi. Conclusion ... 79

III. Ohalot before 70 ... 85
    i. Definition of the Problem ... 85
    ii. Rules of the Houses and Early Yavneans and their Presuppositions ... 86
    iii. Scriptural Foundations of Ohalot ... 90
    iv. Antecedent Exegetical Traditions ... 91
    v. The Concept of the Tent ... 96

IV. Negaim before 70 ... 103
    i. Definition of the Problem ... 103
    ii. The Givens of the Yavnean Rules: Mishnah and Scripture ... 104
    iii. Scripture and Mishnah, Saraat and Nega ... 108
    iv. Negaim: The Rabbinical Disease ... 126
    v. Two Torahs -- One Whole Torah ... 132

V. Parah before 70 ... 143
    i. The Presuppositions of the Yavnean Stratum ... 143
    ii. Scriptural Foundations of Parah ... 144
        1. Standard of Purity Higher than that Applied to Holy Things ... 144
        2. Labor Spoils the Cow ... 145
    iii. Other Approaches to the Rite of the Red Cow ... 164
        1. The Collections in Apocrypha and Pseudepigrapha ... 146
        2. The Dead Sea Library ... 146
        3. Philo ... 147

	4. Josephus	149
	5. Targumim	149
	6. The Christian Community in the First Century	153
	A. Hebrews	153
	B. The Epistle of Barnabas	154
	7. Samaritans	155
	8. Conclusions	156
	iv. Ritual without Myth: The Meaning of the Laws of Parah	157
VI.	Tohorot before 70	171
	i. Introduction	171
	ii. Removes of Uncleanness, Levels of Sanctification	171
	iii. Conclusion	175
VII.	Miqvaot before 70	181
	i. Miqvaot and Parah	181
	ii. The Scriptural Foundations of Miqvaot	184
	iii. Blood, Spring-Water, and Still Water	186
	iv. Mishnah and Scripture: The Immersion-Pool and the Spring	191
VIII.	Niddah before 70	197
	i. Introduction	197
	ii. Scripture and Mishnah: Oral Torah as the Completion of the Written Torah	198
	iii. Sectarian Views of Menstrual Uncleanness	204
	iv. Conclusion	211
IX.	Zabim before 70	217
	i. Introduction	217
	ii. Attributions	217
	1. Unattributed Pericopae	217
	2. Attributions	219
	iii. The Weaving of the Law	221
	1. Becoming a Zab	222
	2. Transferring the Zab's Uncleanness: Scripture	231
	3. Transferring the Zab's Uncleanness: Unassigned Pericopae Based on Conceptions Clearly Generated by Scripture	240
	4. Transferring the Zab's Uncleanness: Mishnah	248
	iv. The Stages of the Law	257
	v. The Two Torahs: Scripture and the Sources of Uncleanness of Mishnah Negaim, Niddah, and Zabim	260
X.	The Formation of the Mishnaic Law of Purities: The Cases of Kelim and of Ohalot	269
	i. Definition	269
	ii. Introductory Observations	270
	iii. History of Kelim	272
	iv. History of Ohalot	276
	v. Two Torahs -- One Whole Torah	285

Preface

The Mishnah, ca. A.D. 200, contains numerous statements assigned to authorities who flourished in the period before the closure of the Mishnah, and even prior to A.D. 70, when the Temple was destroyed. Its authorship therefore took the position that some ideas in their document (however reformulated by them or their predecessors) reached them from what was to them remote antiquity – two or more hundred years prior to the completion of their document. A history of the formation of the principal doctrines in theology and law of the the Mishnah, therefore of the Oral Torah, of which the Mishnah is the first completed and closed statement, requires a systematic account of the strata of that document that took shape prior to the redaction in 200, specifically before the destruction of the Temple, perhaps long before that time. Not assuming the veracity of attributions of sayings to named authorities but asking how attributions are to be tested and validated or invalidated, I have found it necessary to define the issue and work it out in a fresh way. Specifically, in this book I make available for a wider audience than received the original results a statement of those elements of the Mishnah-tractates in the Division of Purities that, in my judgment, derive from the period before 70. The results derive from the volumes of translation and commentary and systematic literary-analytical and historical-critical reconstruction of the contents of the Mishnah and the Tosefta in my *History of the Mishnaic Law of Purities* (Leiden, 1974-1977: E. J. Brill) I-XXII. (The remainder of my History of the Mishnaic Law, covering the Mishnah and Tosefta, appeared in a further twenty-one volumes). In this book I reproduce the relevant pages of some of those forty-three volumes.

The plan of this book is very simple. In the opening chapter, which derives from my *History of the Mishnaic Law of Purities* . XVII. *Makhshirin,* I give a complete exposition of the method and how it works for an entire tractate over the four periods in the unfolding of the law. Since that tractate contains numerous attributions of sayings to authorities who flourished before 70, and since I am able to demonstrate that these attributions are false, the method of validation, encompassing criteria of invalidation, is fully worked out. In the next chapters I reproduce the discussion of only one topic, the law before 70, as the several tractates of the division yield evidence that some ideas begin in the earliest period of the formation of the Mishnah. Finally, in the concluding chapter, I turn to a systematic statement of the issue of the relationship between conceptions of the Mishnah and those on the same topics of Scripture, showing the point at which the formative and generative conceptions of the later document can intersect with the givens of the Written Torah.

Two issues join together.

First, how shall we move from the point of redaction of the document, in 200, backward to the earliest point at which the document's own attributions claim its materials originate?

Second, how shall we relate the generative conceptions of the tractate at hand to Scripture itself?

The answers to these questions tell us the state of the Mishnah – specifically, its important intellectual principles and legal components of those principles – before 70. The methodological procedure is simple, though working it out in detail is rather protracted and tedious. There are two facts which permit us to test the implicit allegation that a given saying goes "way back."

The first is the claim of the authorship that a given authority stands behind a stated position, along with our general notion that that authority derives from a set period. A correlative fact is that the authorities of the Mishnah are grouped by periods, with authorities A, B, C, and D, whom we can show flourished at a given time, never mixed together with authorities K, L, M, and N, who flourished at some other point. A disputes a point with B, but never with N. Now in the case of the authorities before 70, evidence external to the Mishnah tells us that some of the named authorities of a given group (again, A, B, C, D) flourished prior to the destruction of the Temple, e.g., Gamaliel and Simeon b. Gamaliel. They, and those named as participating in disputes with them, presumably flourished at that time. Other groups of names occurring only with one another but rarely, if ever, with names occurring at the period before 70, flourished from 70 to the war led by Bar Kokhba, a third group thereafter, and a mainly anonymous group stands behind the formation of the Mishnah as a whole. For purposes of abbreviation, I refer to these groups as *before 70, Yavneh*, after the name of a principal center of sages' study after 70, thus from 70 to 130, *Usha*, for the name of an equivalent center after 140, and time of Rabbi [Judah the Patriarch, authority of the Mishnah] thereafter.

The second fact is that the Mishnah's laws take up a limited program of inquiry, and some of them rest upon clearly identifiable premises or principles. One rule rests on another, e.g., a principle of law stands behind a corollary to that same law. To take an example important in my opening chapter, the principle that grain that has been deliberately wet down by water is susceptible to cultic uncleanness, while grain kept dry is not, must come prior to a debate on whether leaving grain out in the rain constitutes a deliberate act of wetting down that grain. That rather arcane instance of the logical sequence of a premise and a secondary syllogism subject to debate – first the principle of deliberation is established as the criterion for effective wetting down, then the issue of what constitutes deliberate, as distinct from accidental, action will come under debate – is only one among many hundreds of sequences from basic premise to secondary corollary.

Now what shall we say if to a later authority is attributed the premise, but to an earlier one a corollary? Then it seems to me on the surface we must wonder whether the attribution is a valid one. And, if to the earlier authority is assigned the premise, to the later authority the secondary issue, we must entertain the proposition that the sequence of attributions – first to an earlier authority the premise, then to a later authority the secondary application of the premise – is entirely plausible. The correlation of the temporal sequence of attributions by generations and the logical progression of principles and their secondary expansion and articulation provides a method for testing the proposition that the Mishnah contains conceptions deriving from generations prior to the one of the authorities who completed and closed the document.

I have done that exercise in detail for the entire Mishnah, exclusive of the Division of Agriculture. Professor Alan J. Avery-Peck, in his *History of the Mishnaic Law of Agriculture* (Atlanta, 1986: Scholars Press for Brown Judaic Study) concluded the work. I devised not only the method, but also a medium for the presentation of the results. In my *Purities* I worked the entire project out in acute detail; in the next four divisions, covering *Holy Things, Women, Appointed Times,* and *Damages,* I did the work in detail but presented the results in a kind of short hand, since readers could readily carry out the analytical steps I had already outlined in such detail.

I was, of course, naive to imagine that people would follow work in such excruciating detail.

First, unless immediately engaged by precisely the same issue and text, colleagues would not likely take the time to follow the matter as I had laid it out.

Second, as I shall explain, the prevailing theological climate rendered the premise of inquiry – testing attributions – unacceptable.

For the generality of Jewish scholars of the history of Judaism in the period at hand have assumed as fact precisely what I wished to investigate: whether or not we have reason to suppose that anything in the Mishnah (hence, in any other, later component of the canon of the Oral Torah) derived from the period in which the document itself was redacted. These scholars, who dominate in the Jewish institutions of Jewish learning in the USA, Europe, and the State of Israel's universities and Yeshivas alike, could not seriously entertain a proposition contrary to the one they took for granted. Hence a systematic demonstration in detail of what might derive from a period prior to redaction of a document, and what probably did not come from that earlier, and determinate, time, hardly enjoyed an enthusiastic welcome. In fact, it got none. I address the present book to the colleagues for whom nothing is yet settled, and who wish to follow in detail the evidence and arguments that stand behind my completed statement, in *Judaism: The Evidence of the Mishnah*, of the history of the Judaism represented by the Mishnah.

The issue of Scripture-Mishnah relationships forms the crux of the matter. For the antiquity of the Oral Torah, the premise of the Judaism of the dual Torah, constitutes not only the definitive theological dogma of Judaism. It also forms a principal topic of debate in contemporary scholarship on the history of Judaism. Important for theological reasons, the issue comes under debate in the academy as well. From the beginning of the intellectual initiative of Reform Judaism in Germany in *Wissenschaft des Judenthums* to the present day, participants in scholarly discourse have framed positions on the matter, announcing that, while, of course, the Oral Torah – meaning the corpus of rabbinic literature – does not (necessarily) derive from Moses at Sinai, it begins with Ezra, or with the Men of the Great Assembly, or with some other determinate point. Taking at face value the attributions of sayings to authorities beyond the pages of the Hebrew Scriptures or Old Testament, scholars have traced the history of the Oral Torah backward to remote antiquity. But what we cannot show, we do not know. No one has demonstrated on rational grounds (thus excluding, "it sounds true," or "our holy rabbis would not lie") that what is assigned to an authority by a document redacted many centuries after the death of that authority was said by him; nor has anyone devised a system to distinguish the things credibly attributed to an ancient authority from those that we must set aside as pseudepigraphic. Many arguments have taken their place, but, not cloaked in the garment of systematic demonstration and detailed testing against evidence, these form a long line of naked emperors. And more than those who offer arguments are those who do not even bother. Invoking the opening sentence of tractate Abot, *Moses received Torah at Sinai,* scholars both within and without the Orthodox camp, in Yeshivas, Seminaries, and Israeli universities alike, simply believe pretty much whatever the sources tell them, inclusive of attributing sayings to the person and time in which late documents place them, and, manipulating the facts at hand, propose to write history.

Common to all of the dispositions of the issue prior to my own is a single trait. Colleagues past and present rarely subject their theses and premises to the systematic test of validation or falsification of the claims of the evidence of concrete documents, worked out in detail and from beginning to end. The Mishnah is the first document of the Judaism of the dual Torah, and one should have expected proponents of the received and Orthodox view to find evidence in the Mishnah for the origin, in remote antiquity (at Sinai?), of sayings or stories, or at least, legal or theological conceptions of that component of the Oral Torah. But while many have assumed that some, or all, of what we find in the Mishnah derives from the revelation of God to Moses at Sinai, or reaches us in a process of exegesis of what was revealed by God to Moses at Sinai, or in a chain of continuous tradition of some sort of other, none has told us, in detail, just how that process works, just what evidence tells us why we should think things began with Moses at Sinai.

Perhaps the proponents of the view (in scholarly form) of the received Judaism do not think they have to, since (as they perceive matters) so many people concur in their premises, arguing only about the consequent conclusions. But we look in vain in the writings of historians of the Oral Tradition, whether of the nineteenth century or of our own day at the end of the twentieth, for sustained and rigorous examination of the documentary evidence forn – or against – their propositions. *Everyone agrees* has substituted for analysis of evidence. To be sure, the earlier generations had the merit of reading works with which they disagreed – if only to condemn them. The current generation does not even bother, rather, like know-nothings, announcing positions they reject without naming those who hold those positions or arguing with them on the basis of a systematic reading of their statements. It is the simple fact that to me is attributed the position that nothing in the Mishnah antedates the Mishnah. Having written a forty-three volume commentary to the Mishnah to prove the opposite, having stated the outcome in several systematic works, in both essay and book form, down to my *Judaism: The Evidence of the Mishnah* (Chicago, 1983: University of Chicago Press), I am not a little puzzled to find imputed to me ideas I do not hold and have labored long and hard to refute. When, moreover, I address these junior colleagues and call to their attention lacunae in their reading, they reply (if they reply at all) that they do not have to read my books anyhow.

Such a sad situation in Jewish learning will inevitably correct itself. If this one does not choose to read a book, that does not stop the other one from doing so. Books do matter and people do read them. There is, moreover, no monopoly that any longer dictates what will be read and what will be ignored. There is a vast world of interested scholars, Jewish and gentile alike, who find important and interesting the sources and problems of ancient Judaism. The monopoly of the Jewish institutions of Jewish learning has been broken; if they will not read or quote or argue with a book, others are not intimidfated. If they do not wish to review books or list them in their bibliographies, the world is full of scholars of integrity and honesty. And, in point of fact, books are read and do make a considerable difference, if not quickly, then in time, and if not everywhere, then in most places. The debate goes forward on legitimate, academic grounds, even though in Yeshivas, Seminaries, and Israeli universities some do not choose to participate. Their systematic effort at murder by silence – *Todschweigen* – of ideas they do not accept and cannot refute, and at discrediting the persons who present those ideas, yields for them little more than frustration. People read books and make up their minds. True, most of the volumes of my *History of the Mishnaic Law* were simply never reviewed at all, for *Todschweigen* does accomplish its goals for a short time, and such reviews as the volumes did get were with few exceptions superficial and (whether or not friendly) essentially uncomprehending. But I am confident that in making available in a cogent statement results widely scattered and not readily accessible beforehand, I shall address a sizable number of interested colleagues.

JACOB NEUSNER

HOSHANNAH RABBAH 5747
October 24, 1986

Program in Judaic Studies
Brown University
Providence Rhode Island 02912-1826 U.S.A.

I. The Method of Correlating Attributions and Sequences of Logical Progression:
The Case of Mishnah-and Tosefta-Tractate Makhshirin

i. INTRODUCTION

The history of the law is the history of the sequence of its paramount conceptions. The sequence is to be recovered with some measure of certainty through the effort to correlate the order of attributions, early and late, with the relationship of ideas which are attributed, primary and secondary or fundamental and derivative. Unattributed materials in all instances contain and develop ideas clearly assigned, in attributed ones, to specific authorities, therefore, for our purpose, to a particular stratum, before 70, Yavneh, Usha, or after Usha. Where attributions fall out of all alignment with the logical sequences of substantive issues under debate is in materials assigned through attributions to the period before 70. We shall observe that Houses' disputes not only contain Ushan attestations, but also exhibit disagreement on principles in fact under debate among diverse Ushans. It is not likely that the Ushans raise issues in fact settled nearly a century earlier. It therefore is highly probable that Ushans assign to the Houses' names positions under debate in their own time. We examine that problem in detail below, pp. 202 ff.

ii. ATTRIBUTIONS

1. *Unattributed Pericopae*

In the following list we consider all items not clearly assigned to specific authorities, as well as those in which the role of a named master is minor and primarily important in helping us locate the larger pericope in a given stratum. Items presented in smaller type and in brackets are included for the sake of completeness, allowing the specification of reasons for assignments of pericope which do not bear clear attribution to some specific authority of the major part of the pericope.

[1. M. 1:1: The rule is unassigned. It is, however, integral to the Houses' (Ushan) dispute of M. 1:2-3 + 4, in that it lays out the parameters within which the dispute is conducted. If the dispute belongs to the period before 70, then M. 1:1 states the primary conclusion following upon the "original" reading of Scripture as to intention in regards liquids. But Joshua speaks to that issue, M. 1:3M, so we cannot take for granted that M. 1:1—and M. 1:2-4—go back before 70.]

2. M. 1:6H-K: If vegetables are wet down under constraint, even though the man then deliberately put water on them, they are not made susceptible. See below, No. 12.

[3. M. 2:1A, 2:2-11: This is clearly a unitary construction, laden with Ushan attestations, e.g., T. 1:7, and glosses, e.g., M. 2:4, 5, 7, 8, 10.]
[4. M. 2:1B-E: Human sweat is clean = M. 6:4-5, which belong *in substance* to Yavneh.]
[5. M. 3:4/T. 2:2: Attested to Usha at M. 3:5A-C, T. 2:3.]
[6. M. 3:8: Attested to Usha at T. 2:4.]
[7. M. 4:1: Attested to Usha by Simeon b. Eleazar's gloss. The principle in any case is the same as M. 3:8. + T. 2:5. T. to M. 5:4 has ʿAqiva cite the pericope verbatim.]
[8. M. 4:2-3: The point is the same as at M. 3:8.]
[9-10. M. 4:6-7: The point is the same on which the Houses agree at M. 4:4D.]
(11. M. 4:8/T. 2:7: (1) A Father of uncleanness alone imparts uncleanness to a clay bowl = M. Kel. 1:1. (2) Water does not clean other liquids = M. Miq. 10:6-8. These principles are not distinctive to our tractate.)

12. M. 5:1/T. 2:12: M.'s point is the same as M. 1:6.

[13. M. 5:2: Attested to Usha by T. 2:13—Meir.]
[14. M. 5:5/T. 2:15: M. carries forward the view of ʿAqiva at M. 5:4.]
[15. M. 5:7/T. 2:16: The principle is the same as that of M. 3:8, etc.]
[16. M. 5:8: The water falls without approval, another illustration of the datum of the tractate.]
[17. M. 6:1/T. 3:2: Attested to Usha by T. 3:1.]
[18. T. 3:6: Surely belongs on the same stratum as T. 3:5, Usha.]
[19-20. T. 3:7-8, 10A: Belongs with the Ushan materials of M. 6:2.]
[21. T. 3:12: The reason fish are susceptible—*re* M. 6:3D, Ushan construction.]
[22. M. 6:4-5: Liquids which impart susceptibility—attested to Yavneh (at the latest) by ʿAqiva, M. 6:8.]
[23. M. 6:6: These impart susceptibility to uncleanness and uncleanness. Attested to Yavneh by Eliezer and Eliezer b. ʿAzariah.]

(24. Sifra Shemini VIII:2: Water lying on the ground is insusceptible, until detached. See M. Miq. 1:1-6.)

The catalogue contains only one item, No. 2 = 12, which bears no evidence of an appropriate point of origination or assignment. That what happens by constraint is null in regard to uncleanness, of course, is an extreme, contrary way of saying that intention is integral in effecting the capacity of liquid to impart uncleanness. But that does not help us to determine whether the items come early or late in the formation of the law. We notice, also, that the diverse exemplifications of the notion that water incidental to one's main purpose does not impart susceptibility to uncleanness do not always bear attributions or attestations. These assignments (Nos. 8, 15, etc.) are not of so firm an order as those which do. Otherwise, the tractate presents remarkably few formal problems in respect to attributions. On the surface, nearly all items are appropriately assigned, with a good measure of confidence, to particular strata. The deeper problem, as I said, is whether later authorities debate principles attributed to earlier ones and then assign the results of the debate to the earlier names.

2. *Attributions*

A. *Before 70*

1. *The Houses*

   (1-3. M. 1:2-4/T. 1:1-2, 3: If a man wants fruit and liquid falls, the liquid is insusceptible, so M. Yosé b. R. Judah: This is under dispute. M.: If a man wants liquid but not all of it falls, etc. See Yosé b. R. Judah, No. 1.)

   (4-6. M. 4:4-5: Splashed and overflowing water, as above. + T. 2:6.)

   7. M. 5:9: House of Shammai gloss the rule.

B. *Yavneh*

1. *Joshua*

   1. M. 1:3M: Liquid imparts susceptibility to uncleanness only when intentionally applied. In the name of Abba Yosé.

2. *Eliezer*

   1. Sifra Shemini VIII:4: Foul liquid is insusceptible (compare M. 6:5-7).

3. *Eliezer, Eleazar b. ʿAzariah*

    1. M. 6:6E-F: Semen of *Zab* does not impart susceptibility to uncleanness, so Eliezer. Eleazar b. ʿAzariah: Blood of menstruant does not impart susceptibility to uncleanness.

    2. M. 6:7J/O: Blood of slaughtering of unclean cattle and of bloodletting for healing—unclean. *Vs.* M. 6:4-6, which also is Yavnean. + T. 3:14H.

4. *Eliezer, Joshua, ʿAqiva*

    1. See Judah, No. 1.

5. *ʿAqiva*

    1. M. 4:9/T. 2:9: Water in swape-bucket which remains after some days.

    2. M. 6:8: Milk of beast imparts susceptibility to uncleanness even if detached without approval.

6. *ʿAqiva vs Ṭarfon*

    1. M. 5:4/T. 2:14: Measuring cistern—status of water on rod.

C. Usha

1. *Yosé*

    1. M. 1:4U/T. 1:4A-C (*vs.* Judah): *Re* status of bottom sack.

    2. M. 1:5/T. 1:5A: Yosé states the Hillelite position of M. 1:2F-G in his own name.

    3. T. 1:5B: Water becomes susceptible to uncleanness not when it is detached but only when it is taken into account.

    4. T. 2:1: Only earthenware absorbs moisture.

    5. M. 5:6: He who beat on wet pelt, etc.

    6. M. 5:11: Steam is not a connector under any circumstances.

    7. T. 3:5: Susceptibility of Sepphoris cucumbers.

    8. M. 6:7K: Blood of still-born child is unclean, so Yosé.

2. *Judah*

    1. T. 1:4D-F: Judah revises the attributions of M. 1:4's issue; not the Houses but Eliezer, Joshua, ʿAqiva.

    2-5. M. 2:4, 5, 7 (= T. 1:8K), 8: Judah glosses M.

    6. M. 3:1: Sack over water, etc.

    7-9. M. 3:5G-I, 3:6, 3:7: Intention is effective only through deed.

    10. T. 2:4D/M. 3:7W-X: Water on feet of man.

    11. T. 3:1: Same point as Nos. 7-9.

    12. M. 6:3: Iltith-fish assumed to be insusceptible, etc.

    13. Sifra Shemini VIII: 4A-C: Wine is a liquid—proof-texts.

3. *Meir*

    1. T. 1:7A-B: Fruit-juice into which any amount [of water] falls is unclean. Sages: We follow the majority.

2. M. 2:10E-I: Storage bin into which gentiles and Israelites put produce.
3. T. 3:8: See Judah *vs.* Meir, No. 1.

4. *Simeon*

1. M. 1:6: He who blows on lentils—not under law, If water be put. He who eats sesame with wet finger—liquid left by finger in his palm is not under law, If water be put on.
2. M. 3:5A-F/T. 2:3: Dampening wheat with dry clay, etc.
3. M. 4:10F/T. 2:11: *Re* unclean fluids absorbed by wood and mixed with sap.
4. M. 5:3: Pieces of fruit wet down by water from roof mixed with dry to hasten evaporation.
5. M. 5:10: He who empties hot into hot, etc.—gloss of rule that a jet is not a connector.
6. M. 6:6G-H: Blood of corpse does not impart susceptibility to uncleanness.

5. *Meir vs. Judah vs. Yosé*

1. M. 3:3: Hot bread over wine.
2. T. 2:13/M. 5:2: He who makes a bird in water—*re* status of water which splashes out and remains inside.

6. *Meir vs. Yosé*

1. T. 2:6: *Re* M. 4:5F-I.
2. T. 3:14: Blood of corpse is unclean in any measure, so Meir. Yosé: Quarter-*log*.

7. *Judah vs. Meir*

1. M. 6:2: On reason vegetables in the market are assumed to be susceptible.
2. T. 3:10B-M/M. 6:3C: Eggs assumed susceptible.

8. *Simeon vs. Meir*

1. M. 6:5I-K: Why sap is like oil [= M. Toh. 9:3].

9. *Simeon b. Gamaliel*

1. T. 3:8: Glosses dispute of Judah *vs.* Meir, M. 6:2.

10. *Simeon b. Eleazar*

1. T. 2:4E/M. 3:7W-X: Water on feet of unclean cattle.
2. M. 4:1F-G: How much rope used by bucket?
3. T. 3:11: Simeon b. Eleazar glosses dispute of Meir, Judah, T. 3:10/M. 6:3.
4. M. 6:7P: Milk of male is insusceptible.

11. *Eleazar*
    1. M. 4:5P-S: If a person must get muddy to dunk utensils, water on feet is subject to the law, If water be put [= M. 4:1].

12. *Eliezer b. Jacob*
    1. T. 1:7C-D = M. 6:3J: If water falls into brine...

13. *Nehemiah*
    1. T. 1:6C: If jars are glazed, they do not absorb moisture.
    2. M. 3:2: Pulse does not absorb moisture. See *Yosé, No. 4*.

14. *Yosé b. R. Judah*
    1. T. 1:2 *re* M. 1:2-3: Yosé b. R. Judah revises the terms of the Houses' dispute.
    2. T. 3:13A: Urine of cattle collected in utensil imparts susceptibility to uncleanness.

D. *After Usha*

1. *Abba Yosé b. Dosa'i and Yosé b. Hammeshulam*
    1. T. 2:1O/M. 4:10: *Re* liquids and rain on wood.

iii. THE WEAVING OF THE LAW: YAVNEH AND USHA

If we were to divide Makhshirin along the lines of the philosophical problems common to many tractates and not distinctive to any one of them, we should ask about the sequence of its rules about mixtures and matters of doubt in connection with mixtures, about the importance of action and practical consequence of action in assessing the weight of one's original intention or plan, and about similar matters not particular to Makhshirin. We might even ask about matters only implied in the several pericopae, e.g., joint ownership of a single object, joint responsibility for a single act of wetting down (one party wants, the other does not want, to wet down an object belonging to both [= M. 2:3]), connection, and topics not introduced into the tractate at all but potentially contained within its logical substructure. But Rabbi chooses to lay out matters neither in accord with philosophical principles cutting across diverse data—facts—of uncleanness, nor, alternatively, in accord with the names of particular authorities, even though among the materials he has in hand is the work of tradents who think that the laws should be set forth along the one or other line of organization, e.g., philosophical principle, as at M. 2:3-11, or the name and distinctive principle of a particular authority, as at M. 3:5-7 (Judah).

Rather Rabbi takes the simple course of organizing tractates around distinctive themes, subject-matter, while he also adds a layer of pericopae whose primary, internally-organizing interest transcends the particular sort of law under discussion.

For Makhshirin, there are two categories in which Rabbi has found room for all his materials, (1) liquids able to impart susceptibility to uncleanness, which subject begins and ends the tractate, on the one side, and (2) the application of the principle that liquids impart susceptibility to uncleanness only when deliberately applied to produce or objects, which theme forms the shank of the tractate, on the other.

1. *Liquids Which Impart Susceptibility to Uncleanness*

The problem of the present unit is to determine which liquids have the capacity to impart susceptibility to uncleanness, on the one side, and to decide how to deal with a mixture of liquids which do, and those which do not, have that capacity at all, on the other. The former matter begins at Yavneh, so far as I can tell, since the most basic questions of defining the liquids under discussion in the process of wetting down are answered in sayings assigned to Eliezer, Eleazar b. 'Azariah, and 'Aqiva, among other Yavneans. Ushans in a derivative way develop rules assigned to Yavneans. It will furthermore become clear that the Yavnean discussion of liquids which can impart susceptibility to uncleanness is shaped by the notion that what is useful or desirable has that capacity, and what is utterly useless and disgusting does not. Hence the Yavnean thought on the present question in its general outlines appears to complement the Yavnean and Ushan inquiry into the role of intention in activating the capacity of liquids to impart susceptibility to uncleanness. The liquid itself must be desired or desirable. The liquid which is desirable also must be applied by intent—two ways of saying the same thing. In this regard, it is difficult to avoid the conclusion reached by Maimonides that a two-stage process of effecting the capacity to receive uncleanness is at hand, as he puts it: 1. detachment with approval, and 2. application with approval. Within the former lies the notion that one must want the liquid, which is even prior to the notion of drawing the liquid by intent.

B. Yavneh[1]

*1. M. 6:4A-C: Seven liquids [to which law, If water be put applies]: Dew, water, wine, oil, blood, milk, bee-honey.
M. 6:5D: Subspecies of water: what exudes from eye, ear, nose, mouth, urine.
M. 6:5F: Subspecies of blood: blood from slaughtering clean cattle, etc., and blood let out of veins for drink [which is desired].
M. 6:7M, N: Blood from slaughtering unclean cattle, etc., blood from blood-letting for healing are clean. Eliezer declares unclean.

*1. At M. 6:8 'Aqiva attests the subspecies of blood, and therefore, I am inclined to suppose, the entire construction. The Eliezer then is probably Eliezer b. Hyrcanus; he rejects 'Aqiva's position on the matter because, so far as he is concerned, one's attitude toward the liquid bears no relevance to whether or not the liquid can impart susceptibility to uncleanness. Either it can, or it cannot, because of intrinsic traits. Had Eliezer and Tarfon stood behind our tractate, its development would have ended at Yavneh, for in the light of their respective principles, there is nothing else to talk about.

M. 6:6F: Blood of menstruating woman does not impart susceptibility to uncleanness, so Eleazar b. 'Azariah.
M. 6:6E: Eliezer: Semen does not impart susceptibility to uncleanness.
Vs. M. 6:6A-D: These impart uncleanness and susceptibility to uncleanness simultaneously: flux of *Zab*, spit, semen, urine; blood of menstruating woman.
See *Usha*, Nos. *1, 2, 3, 4, 6, 7*

The issue is whether menstrual blood is deemed equivalent to all other blood, or is treated as equivalent to excrement.

*2. M. 6:8: Milk of woman imparts susceptibility to uncleanness whether or not it is subject to approval, but milk of beast imparts susceptibility to uncleanness only with approval.
'Aqiva: Milk of beasts imparts susceptibility to uncleanness whether or not detached with approval.
See *above*, No. *1*, *Usha*, No. *5*.

*2. The issue is whether milk belongs on the list of M. 6:4 or 6:6, things which impart uncleanness and susceptibility to uncleanness at one and the same time, along the lines of M. 1:1D. 'Aqiva now raises the issue characteristic of his larger theory of distinguishing essential from accidental applications of liquid, below, p. 188.

The interesting side to the present set is the criterion for the definition of liquids which do or do not impart susceptibility to

---

[1] The * signifies that the pericope is linked conceptually or logically with another in an earlier or later stratum. The † indicates that the pericope bears no relationship to any other in an earlier or later stratum. Items bearing an * also contain an entry on the earlier and later materials. The whole is then summed up under *Reconsiderations*. This obviates devoting a major discussion to the problem.

uncleanness: ordinary usefulness or desirability. The specified liquids all are deemed edible or useful, flowing with approval. This paramount criterion is clearly at M. 6:5F, 6:7M, N, which distinguish wanted from unwanted blood; the former is blood which flows because of an action aimed at serving human needs, e.g., slaughtering clean animals or drawing blood for drink. And this criterion further is blatant at 'Aqiva's pericope, No. 2. 'Aqiva and sages dispute about whether or not cow's milk imparts susceptibility to uncleanness when it is not drawn intentionally or with approval. This means, then, that the Yavneans around 'Aqiva—but not Eliezer— conceive the matter of capacity to impart susceptibility to be affected by one's attitude not only toward the application of the liquid, but even toward the liquid itself. Liquids which one cannot possibly desire, e.g., sweat or pus, do not fall within the system of contamination, whereas those which people do want to use and do produce by intent (as against sweat) have the capacity to impart susceptibility to uncleanness.

Accordingly, the system flowing from 'Aqiva's notion is whole and harmonious: the liquid itself must be wanted by man or useful to man; and the liquid, furthermore, must be applied intentionally and not accidentally or under constraint or in a way peripheral to one's principal purpose. The Yavneans contribute the former conception, the Ushans are the architects of the latter, though, again, on 'Aqiva's foundations. We shall now see that the Ushans carry forward the work of defining liquids capable of imparting susceptibility to uncleanness and introduce an entirely secondary, but not dense, layer of discussion.

C. *Usha*

*1. M. 6:5I-K: Sap is like oil. Attested by Simeon, Meir. See *Yavneh*, *No. 1*.

1. The subspecies of oil is worked out.

*2. M. 6:6C: Quarter-*log* of blood from corpse imparts uncleanness and susceptibility. Simeon: Blood of corpse does not impart susceptibility to uncleanness.

2. The issue is only tangentially relevant.

T. 3:14I-K: Blood of corpse imparts uncleanness in any measure, so Meir. Yosé: In measure of a quarter-*log*.
T. 3:15: All liquid which exudes from corpse is clean, except for

Now the relevance is clear: subspecies of blood.

blood, and anything with the appearance of blood in connection with the corpse is unclean.
See *Yavneh, No. 1*.

*3. T. 3:13A: Blood of boil, blister, and pus squeezed out of flesh; fruit-juice and salt which melted do not receive or impart uncleanness. Urine of cattle does not impart uncleanness or susceptibility. Yosé b. R. Judah: If they collected them in a utensil, they do.
See *Yavneh, No. 1*.

*4. T. 3:13B/E, T. 3:14F-H: Yosé-Onymus: He who slaughters raven for practice—its blood imparts susceptibility to uncleanness. Eleazar: All blood deriving from slaughter invariably imparts susceptibility to uncleanness.
See *Yavneh, No. 1*.

*5. M. 6:7P: Simeon b. Eleazar: Milk of male is insusceptible to uncleanness.
See *Yavneh, Nos. 1, 2*.

*6. M. 6:7I: These do not become unclean or impart susceptibility to uncleanness: Sweat [= M. 2:1], stinking pus [= 3], excrement, blood which exudes with them; liquid excreted with still-born child at eighth month.
Yosé: Except for its blood.
See *Yavneh, No. 1*.

*7. M. 2:1: Sweat of damp walls of houses, pits, cisterns, etc., is clean. Sweat of man is clean. + Secondary issue: If man drank unclean water and sweated, the sweat is clean. If he entered drawn water and sweated, he is unclean, since sweat mixes with water. If he dried himself off and sweated, sweat is clean.

T. 1:6: He who sets up jars in the vaulted chamber, even though they absorbed more than a *log*, the absorbed liquid does not fall under the law, If water be put. Nehemiah: If jars are glazed, they do not absorb water at all.
See *above, No. 6*, and *Yavneh, No. 1*.

*3. The blood is produced by intent but is useless. Fruit-juice is entirely outside the system of contaminable liquids, as the liquid-form of a solid, so too liquid-salt.

*4. This is a gray area of blood produced in slaughtering. The slaughter is valid, but the bird unclean. The Eleazar may be Yavnean, since the rejected principle is.

5. The subspecies of milk is under discussion.

*6. The main point here seems to be that liquid which no one can conceivably want or deliberately produce does not impart susceptibility to uncleanness. The subspecies of water (sweat, pus) and blood is worked out.

7. Sweat is clean, not a subspecies of water.

The Yavnean inquiry is carried forward at Nos. 1, 2, 3, 4, 5, 6 (= 7). In all instances we deal with subspecies of items at M. 6:4. I see no important Ushan innovations in this matter, rather the effort to subject to the established principle a variety of other, derivative liquids.

†8. M. 2:2: If water of bath-house is unclean, sweat is unclean. If clean, sweat is subject to the law, If water be put. Pool in house—if wall sweats on its account, pool is unclean, sweat of walls of entire house produced on account of the pool is unclean. + M. 2:3-11.
T. 1:7: Fruit-juice into which a drop of water in any amount has fallen is susceptible to uncleanness, so Meir. Sages: They follow the status of the majority (+ Eliezer b. Jacob). + M. 2:4-11, T. 1:8.

†8. The main point here and throughout is that in the case of a mixture of clean and unclean, we impose the status of the majority of the mixture. In a case of half and half, we impose the status of the more strict component of the mixture, e.g., uncleanness. Sages' view predominates in the major construction of M. 2:3-11: we follow the status of the majority. The issue is hardly relevant in particular to Makhshirin.

M. 4:10: Pieces of wood on which liquids fall and on which rains fall—if rains were more than the liquids, they are insusceptible. If one took them outside to make the rains fall on them, even though the rains were more than the liquids, the wood is susceptible. If they absorbed unclean liquids, even though he took them outside so rains would fall on them, they are clean. [The rain has not had contact with the absorbed liquid.] But he should kindle them with clean hands alone.
Simeon: If they were freshly cut and he kindled them and the liquids which exude are more than liquids they had absorbed, they are clean (the unclean liquid having been neutralized by the sap). + T. 2:10, 11.

The point that rain-water does not impart susceptibility to uncleanness is secondary to the present unit, primary to that which follows. The relevance of the item to the present unit is in the issue of mixtures of liquids which can, with those which cannot, impart susceptibility to uncleanness. Simeon's point has already been discussed at some length. It is acute and interesting, but not very important in the structure of our tractate.

This entry bears no clear relationship to Yavnean materials. The issue, however, is generated by the notion that some liquids do, and some do not, impart susceptibility to uncleanness. Once we have reached that conclusion, we necessarily ask about the status of mixtures, and the present substantial set follows naturally. Meir's view is ruled out, since all parties at M. 2:3-11 assume we follow the status of the majority of a mixture. M. 4:10 does not change the picture, but refines the conception. It is Simeon's peripheral point which is at the center.

†9. M. 5:9: Any unbroken stream is clean, except for thick honey and porridge. House of Shammai: Also one of porridge made from grits or beans, because it shrinks backwards at the end of the flow.
M. 5:10: He who empties hot water into cold, cold into cold, hot into cold—it [the upper, clean liquid] is still clean. If cold into hot, it is unclean. Simeon: Also he who empties hot into hot, and the force of the lower water was stronger than that of the upper—it is unclean.
M. 5:11: The woman whose hands were clean, and who stirred the unclean cooking pot with a spoon, if her hands sweated—they are unclean. If her hands were unclean and she was stirring the clean cooking pot, if hands sweated, what is in the pot is unclean.
Yosé: If they dripped [sweat] into the pot, then what is in the pot is unclean.

†9. A stream is not a connector. This matter bears no relationship whatsoever to our tractate.

Since the issue here seems to be the uncleanness of the woman's sweat, perhaps the inclusion of the entire set may be accounted for by the pertinence, to our tractate, of the example. Yosé does treat sweat as susceptible to uncleanness, contrary to *No. 7, above.*

D. *After Usha*

No pertinent rulings are attributed to authorities of the time of Rabbi.

E. *Unattributed*

All pericopae bear either clearcut attributions or satisfactory attestations.

Reconsiderations

When we reconsider the diverse character of the bases upon which we assign pericopae to one or the other of the two periods, Yavneh or Usha, we see that the attribution of all Yavnean items is upon firm foundations, in that to Ushans are assigned secondary and contingent rules which rest upon Yavnean items. The matter of mixtures of unclean and clean liquids, by contrast, bearing Ushan attributions only, is not so directly related to, therefore based upon, pericopae assigned to Yavneans. The conception that there are both clean and unclean liquids, to be sure, is Yavnean.

It obviously follows that how we treat mixtures of the two will have to be worked out. Meir will treat the presence of a single drop of liquid capable of imparting susceptibility to uncleanness as sufficient to make the whole capable of doing so, in which case the fundamental conception before us is not Meir's but that of his opposition (but compare M. 2:10!). The nature of the sequences, from Yavneh to Usha, among the first seven Ushan items (omitting the fifth), by contrast, is direct and immediate. Overall, it seems warranted to conclude that the attributions of the several sequences are firm and reliable.

2. *Imparting Susceptibility to Uncleanness: Intention and Action*

The paramount theme of the tractate is the determination of the capacity of the eligible liquids to impart susceptibility to uncleanness. The operative criterion, whether or not the liquids are applied intentionally, obviously is going to emerge in every pericope pertinent to the theme. It is the determination of the implications of that criterion that occupies Yavneans, whose work, moreover, yields numerous Ushan exemplifications of the Yavnean positions, but little development of them. The unfolding of the earlier rabbinic thought on the nature of intention and its affect upon water is complicated by the attributions to the Houses of highly sophisticated conceptions on the subject. We postpone consideration of the Houses' materials until section iv, and, at that point, reconsider parallel pericopae of M. Tohorot and M. Miqvaot, both of which contain allegations that the Houses deal with the same moot point, also with extensive Ushan glosses.

B. *Yavneh*

*1. M. 1:3M: Joshua in the name of Abba Yosé: Be surprised if there is a liquid in the Torah which is unclean before a person actually intends and puts it on [dry produce].

*1. By itself the saying simply maintains that liquid does not impart uncleanness unless a person intentionally applies it.

At the foundations of our tractate as we now have it is the view expressed here. The play on YTN—*water be put, one puts water* (yitten, yūttān)—may be secondary to the law, but its point is unmistakable. Abba Yosé wishes to say that, if produce is wet down unintentionally, it is not made susceptible to uncleanness. Perhaps, as I said, we should take Maimonides' conception at face value and interpret the saying as a dual one: (1) the water must be detached with intention, and (2) the water must be applied with intention. But that is immaterial to the principle. It is hardly necessary to list all the items of Yavneh and Usha which develop and apply Abba Yosé's conception. Abba Yosé stands at the beginning of the matter, and virtually every ruling assigned to a subsequent authority is intended to refine and expand his conception. We must, however, recall that the principle, shared by 'Aqiva but not unique to him, that liquid itself has the capacity to impart susceptibility to uncleanness only if the liquid is produced with approval or serves a human purpose—a notion contained within the distinction, attested by 'Aqiva, between blood produced by slaughter of a clean animal and blood produced by slaughter of an unclean one, or between mother's milk and cow's milk in this same regard—is secondary to Abba Yosé's. Once we insist that liquid imparts susceptibility only when applied by intention, we then ask whether the liquid itself, before application and without regard to application, is intrinsically able to impart susceptibility to uncleanness. If, as seems clear, Abba Yosé's saying stands at the commencement of the tractate, then the position evident in pericopae involving 'Aqiva in respect to the capacity of liquid to impart susceptibility to uncleanness, and the position attributed to 'Aqiva on the importance of intention in the application of liquid (below, *Yavneh, No. 3*), thus limiting the affects of liquid applied only by inadvertance or outside of one's primary intention, are developments of the original and fundamental proposition.

*2. M. 4:9: He who draws water with a swape-pipe—up to three days, water imparts susceptibility. 'Aqiva: If it was dried off, it is insusceptible forthwith, and if not, even after thirty days, it continues to impart susceptibility to uncleanness. + T. 2:9. See *Usha, No. 1*.

*2. The view of the anonymous rule is that water which is detached with approval continues to impart uncleanness until it is dried up, which is assumed to take three days. 'Aqiva's saying uses the *nif'al*, NYGBW, if they—the water(s)—were dried out. If 'Aqiva differs from the anonymous rule, then he asks that *man* dry out the bucket. If he intends to explain it, as T. maintains, then his point is that we simply take into account the presence of water in the bucket. If the water dried up, then it does not impart susceptibility. If it does not dry up, then it does.

The interpretation of 'Aqiva's position is, as indicated, complicated by 'Aqiva's intent: interpretation of the anonymous rule or disagreement with it. The anonymous rule by itself indicates that once water is drawn with approval, it continues to retain the capacity to impart susceptibility to uncleanness even after it has served its function. In the present instance that means that water left in the bucket, which has not served the person's needs—by definition, since it was left in the bucket—remains capable of imparting susceptibility to uncleanness thereafter. That capacity persists for three days, after which we assume the water has dried up. If interpreting that rule, 'Aqiva then holds that if the water dries up forthwith, it of course is not able to impart susceptibility to uncleanness. But if it remains in the bucket, it never loses that capacity. This view seems to me unlikely, because 'Aqiva is represented as saying a rather obvious rule, namely, if there is water, it imparts uncleanness, and if there is none, it does not. If, by contrast, 'Aqiva wishes to disagree with the anonymous rule, then his view must be understood to introduce the action of the person. If the water is dried up deliberately, then the person by his action has indicated that he does not want it, and whatever remains is not subject to his approval. If the water is not dried up deliberately, then the person, by his inaction, indicates that he still wants the water and therefore, even for thirty days, the water continues to impart susceptibility to uncleanness.

If we take this second route in the interpretation of 'Aqiva's saying, then we have to compare his view to that in the following pericope, in which he distinguishes water essential to the person's intention and that which is inessential. The former of course imparts susceptibility to uncleanness, the latter does not. Water remaining in the bucket, in the present pericope, certainly has not served the person. Why not? Because he drew the water in order to use it, and here he has not used it, by definition. Yet that is beside the point. Water remaining in the bucket was drawn for use. The person intended to apply it, but, as it happens, did not apply it. That is an entirely separate matter from what follows, where, to begin with, the person never intended to draw part of the water at all and had no plans for that part, which is incidental. 'Aqiva's point, in this second approach, is that once a person has expressed his intention through a deed, namely, through drawing the water, then that which is subject to his intention, the water remaining in the bucket, remains so until some other deed, such as actually drying out the bucket, effects a different intention. It is hardly farfetched, then, to claim that behind Judah's conception, below,

Usha, No. 1, is 'Aqiva's principle, interpreted, as I said, in this way. But the relationship of Judah's theory to 'Aqiva's is by no means uncomplicated, as we shall see, and other Ushans, who differ from Judah, may well invoke 'Aqiva's views in support, indeed as generative, of their own.

*3. M. 5:4 T. 2:14: He who measures the cistern—whether for depth or for breadth, lo, this water on the rod is under the law, If water be put, so Tarfon. 'Aqiva: If for depth, it is under the law, etc., and if for breadth, it is not. T.: 'Aqiva is given M. 4:1, He who draws water in a jug—verbatim.

M. 5:5: If one stuck his hand or foot or reed into the cistern to know whether there is water in it, it is not under the law, If water be put. If one did so in order to find out how much water is in it, it is under the law, If water be put. If one threw a stone into the cistern to find out whether there is water in it, the water which splashed out is not under the law, If water be put, and that which is on the stone is insusceptible to uncleanness. + T. 2:15.
See, for 'Aqiva, *Usha, Nos. 3, 4, 5, 6, 7, 8*, and, for Tarfon, *Usha, Nos. 9, 10*.

*3. Water intrinsic to one's purpose is detached with approval, but that which is not essential in accomplishing one's goal is not under the law, If water be put, so 'Aqiva. Tarfon's view is that if, in drawing or detaching the water which I need, I draw or detach water which I do not need, that water too is capable of imparting susceptibility to uncleanness. As at M. 1:1A-C, water at one point subject to approval remains capable of imparting susceptibility, even after it was not wanted. The man has drawn water, therefore the water by his action is shown to be wanted. 'Aqiva rejects this view and imposes a narrow conception upon intention. Both carry forward the interpretation of Abba Yosé's principle.

This dispute is of fundamental importance. The positions of both authorities are carried forward at Usha. Indeed, T. to M. 5:4 explicitly assigns to 'Aqiva the citation of M. 4:1. When water is drawn, that which goes up on the outer parts and the rope that is bound about the neck and on the rope needed for using the bucket is subject to the law, If water be put. It is not possible to get at the water without wetting down the outer parts. 'Aqiva, accordingly, maintains that what is essential in attaining one's purpose is subject to the law, If water be put, with the converse position as well, what is not essential or necessary is not subject to the law, If water be put. Tarfon makes no such distinction. So far as he is concerned, once one deliberately puts the rod into the water, whether lengthwise or breadthwise, he thereby detaches water with approval, and this without regard to the ultimate disposition of the water or the purpose in detaching it. Both parties stand on the foundations of Abba

Yosé's view that the water must be detached with approval and used with approval. The issue obviously is secondary to that primary principle, for now we ask, What constitutes approval or defines prior intention?

C. *Usha*

The Ushan materials form a large essay on the interplay between intention and action. Two antecedent items assume a fundamental role. First, Abba Yosé's saying self-evidently supplies the agendum. Water which is not applied intentionally does not impart susceptibility to uncleanness. A secondary and derivative rule, 'Aqiva's distinction, then comes into play: water intrinsic to one's purpose is detached with approval, but that which is not essential in accomplishing one's primary purpose is not under the law, If water be put. What 'Aqiva has done is to carry to its logical next stage the generative principle. If water applied with approval can impart susceptibility to uncleanness, then, it follows, only *that part* of the detached and applied water which is essential to one's intention is subject to the law, If water be put. Ushan items which develop 'Aqiva's improvement of Abba Yosé's principle raise an interesting question: What is the relationship between intention and action? Does intention to do something govern the decision in a case, even though one's action has produced a different effect? For example, if I intend to wet down only part of an object, or make use of only part of a body of water, but then wet down the whole or dispose of the whole, is the whole deemed susceptible? Does my consequent action revise the original effects of my intention? Judah and his son, Yosé, take up the position that ultimate deed or result is definitive of intention. What happens retrospectively is deemed what I wanted to happen. Other Ushans, Yosé in particular, maintain the view that, while consequence plays a role in the determination of intention, it is not exclusive and definitive. What I wanted to make happen affects the assessment of what actually has happened. Yosé b. R. Judah and Yosé furthermore assign their conceptions to the Houses and define the Houses' disputes in terms of their own highly subtle conceptions of the interplay between intention and action, will and result.

*1. M. 3:5G-I, 6, 7: He who brings grain to the mill and rain fell on it en route—if he was happy, it is under the law, If water be put. Judah: It is

*1. Judah's view is that the man's intention is not fully revealed and effective until he does a deed to carry out his intention. Here attitude does

inevitable that he should be happy. But if he stood still. See *Yavneh, Nos. 2, 3.*	not constitute effective intention, because one may always change his mind.

Judah's ruling is not intrinsic to the data of Makhshirin, but a general conception applicable to any appropriate case. On the surface, Judah's reason is that, since the person's attitude in the specific case is unavoidable, he cannot be adjudged except by what he does actually to carry out, and thus give concrete expression to, that attitude. But underneath his ruling is the realistic notion that a person changes his mind, and therefore we adjudge a case solely by what he does and not by what he says he will do, intends, or has intended, to do.

This notion, while secondary to Makhshirin, forms an apt introduction to the other pertinent rulings, because, if we turn Judah's statement around, we come up with the conception predominant throughout: a case is judged in terms solely of what the person does. If he puts on water, that water in particular which he has deliberately applied imparts susceptibility to uncleanness. If he removes water, only that water which he actually removes imparts susceptibility to uncleanness, but water which he intends to remove but which is not actually removed is not deemed subject to the persons's original intention. And, it is fair to add, we know it is not subject to the original intention because the person's action has not accomplished the original intention or has placed limits upon the original intention. What is done is wholly determinative of what is originally intended, and that is the case whether the result is that the water is deemed capable or incapable of imparting susceptibility to uncleanness.

*2. M. 1:5: He who rubs wetness off leek—Yosé: Those that exude are under the law, If water be put, and those that remain are not, because he intends that they exude from its entirety. + T. 1:5A: Even though water descends from top to bottom of leek + not under the law, etc.	*2. Yosé's view, it is obvious, is that the water which the man has removed from the leek is in conformity to his wishes. But water which remains on the leek is not.
T. 1:5B: Water dripping off a *Zab* is clean while it is on him, then rendered susceptible to uncleanness when it falls off—but then it is clean because it is no longer on the *Zab*. See (*Houses, No. 2*) *Yavneh, No. 3* (ʿAqiva).	The case of the *Zab* is secondary. While the water is on the *Zab*, it is not where the *Zab* (presumably) wants it and is insusceptible.

Yosé leaves no doubt on the matter, since the gloss states his reason. Water which has been wiped off is detached with approval. But water which has remained on the leek has not conformed to the man's intention, and that intention is shown by what the man has actually done. Accordingly, the water remaining on the leek is not subject to the law, If water be put. Assigning an asterisk is misleading, because while Yosé takes up the position of the House of Hillel (below, pp. 206-210), in fact, as we shall see, the greater probability is that Yosé assigns to the House of Hillel his position on a conception moot at Usha. Accordingly, it may be wiser to regard the present item as standing without antecedents in conception and formulation, except insofar as both Yosé and Judah depend upon 'Aqiva's fundamental distinction (*Yavneh, No. 3*), with which both are in accord.

*3. M. 1:6A-G: He who blows on lentils to test whether they are good —he who eats sesame with wet finger to pick up sesame grains, liquids in hand—Simeon: Not under the law, If water be put. Sages: Under the law. See *Yavneh, No. 3*, Simeon = 'Aqiva, sages = Tarfon.

*3. Simeon's point is that the liquid in the breath or left on the palm of the hand is not wanted and not necessary to the accomplishment of one's purpose. Sages differ for obvious reasons.

The present pericope states matters with a slightly different nuance. The main point now is that liquid which is not essential in accomplishing one's purpose is not taken into account and does not come under the law, If water be put. Why not? Because water is held to be applied with approval *only* when it serves a specific purpose. That water which is incidental has not been subjected to the man's wishes and therefore does not impart susceptibility to uncleanness. We shall now see that the position assigned to 'Aqiva is applied in diverse cases but not vastly expanded. Stated in this way, the proposition is simply an application of 'Aqiva's position at *Yavneh No. 3*, and so too is Yosé's in the foregoing item, as we saw. In both cases we deem water to have been detached and applied with approval only when it serves a person's essential purpose, and water which is not necessary in accomplishing that purpose is not deemed subject to the law, If water be put. That is why Simeon rules as he does here. Yosé in the preceding ruling states a different aspect of the same conception. Water which actually has dripped off the leek is in conformity with one's intention. But water remaining on the leek in no way has fallen under the person's approval. This is indicated by the facts of the matter, the results of the person's actual deed. The person wanted to squeeze the water off the leek. Water which drips off conforms to his intention, which is expressed by his deed. Water which does not drip off does not conform to his intention and is unaffected by his deed.

*4. M. 3:5-7A-F: He who dampens wheat with wet clay, Simeon: If there is dripping moisture, wheat is under the law, If water be put, and if not, it is not. The case of dew on grass is parallel. + T. 2:3: Augmentation. T. takes Simeon to the position that we take account *solely* of the intention of the man, not of the condition of the liquid at all. See *Yavneh, Nos. 1, 3.*

*4. Simeon's view is that the man's original intention was to wet down the wheat and the wheat in fact was wet down. The sole issue is whether there was water for this purpose.

Why is the wheat considered wet down with approval? Because the man's intent was to dampen the wheat. That is the datum of the protasis. Then the man has put clay on the wheat. All Simeon wants to know is whether there is dripping moisture in the clay. If there is, then, self-evidently, the facts of the case conform to the man's intention. If there is no water, then the man's intention cannot have been to wet down the grain. In any event he has accomplished nothing. The case is parallel to Simeon's ruling at M. 1:6. The continuation of the pericope, moreover, shows that Simeon's distinction, between intention which has actually been realized in action, and intention not realized in action, does *not* bring him into disagreement with 'Aqiva, Judah, and Yosé. Why not? Because (M. 3:5D) he who sprinkles the threshing floor does not scruple lest he put in it grains of wheat and they grow damp. Why not? Because the intention is to sprinkle the floor, not to dampen the wheat. Likewise, M. 3:5E, if one gathers grass when the dew is on it to dampen wheat in it, the moisture is not under the law, If water be put. But if he intended that the *dew* should moisten the wheat, it is under the law, If water be put. It follows that Simeon's pericope leaves no doubt on his position, which conforms to 'Aqiva's, as spelled out at Usha. The case of the dew is most subtle, since we still further limit the matter of intention. One gathers the grass with the idea of dampening the wheat. That is of no consequence. The wheat is still not made susceptible to uncleanness. Why not? Because the *dew* on the grass is not in mind, but only the dampness of the grass itself, parallel to the matter of whether there is dripping moisture on the clay. Merely because the grass is damp is of no account. If, on the other hand, the man had in mind *that very dew* which is on the grass, parallel to the dripping moisture of the opening unit, then of course he has intended to use this *particular* moisture to wet down the grain. And the rest follows.

The next group, which is substantial in size, is not strikingly dense in conception. All we have is a series of illustrations and refinements of the rule of 'Aqiva, just now spelled out: what is primary to one's intention is subject to the law, If water be put. But water which happens, along the way, to be detached or applied has no relationship to one's principal intention or purpose and is not subject to the law, If water be put.

*4. M. 3:8: He who brings wagon wheels and cattle yokes to water at the time of the east wind so they may swell out, lo, this is under the law, If water be put.
He who brings cow to drink—water in mouth is under the law, etc., and what comes up on hooves is not. If he wanted the hooves to be rinsed off, then water on the hooves is under the law, etc.
If deaf-mute, etc., brought down the beast, even intending to wash the hooves, it is not subject to the law, etc.
T. 2:4: Judah: Water which comes up on the feet of man invariably imparts susceptibility to uncleanness. Simeon b. Eleazar: Water which comes up on the hooves of the unclean beast invariably imparts susceptibility to uncleanness.

M. 6:1: He who brings produce to roof because of maggots and dew fell on it—it is not under the law, If water be put. If he intended such, it is under the law, etc. If a deaf-mute, etc., brought it up, even though he wanted dew to fall on it, it is not under the law, If water be put, because they have the power of deed but not intention.

M. 6:2: He who brings bundles to roof to keep them fresh—they are not put under the law, If water be put.

*4. The main point throughout is that if a person uses water for one purpose, what serves a subordinate purpose does not come under the law, If water be put. Water which just happens to be detached as part of the primary use of the water, but which is not subject to the person's original intent, is deemed incapable of imparting susceptibility to uncleanness.

Water which is not applied intentionally does not subject the produce to susceptibility to uncleanness.

The produce is not deliberately wet down.

All bundles of vegetables in the market are susceptible. Judah: Insusceptible in the case of those which are fresh. Meir: The susceptibility is because of the liquid of the mouth. All meal and flour in the market are susceptible, etc. + T. 3:1: He who brings vegetables to roof—it is not under the law, If water be put. If he thought of tying them up, they are under the law, etc. Judah: It is not under the law until he actually ties them, etc., as at M. 3: 5-7, + T. 3:2, 3-10A. T.'s diverse units go over the principle that water applied intentionally subjects produce to susceptibility, giving various local examples.	Judah's view is that fresh vegetables are not wet down. Meir holds that the vegetables are touched by spit when the man ties up the bundle.
M. 6:3: All eggs are assumed insusceptible to uncleanness, except for those of liquid-sellers. All fish is assumed susceptible. Judah: Except various specific sorts of fish, which are kept dry. All brine is assumed susceptible, etc. + T. 3:10B, 11-12. See *Yavneh, No. 3*.	The principle is familiar. If the various items are deliberately wet down, they are deemed susceptible.

All that is new here is the gloss at T. 2:3, which has to do with the judgment on whether the water on the feet is wanted. 'Aqiva presumably may concur with Judah's position. We cannot get at the water unless we walk to it, therefore the water on the feet is detached with approval, just as the water on the rope of the bucket is detached with approval. Simeon b. Eleazar's position is not equivalently clear.

*5. M. 4:1: He who kneels down to drink—water which comes up on mouth and moustache is under the law, If water be put. That on nose and hair is not. He who draws with a jug—water on outer parts and rope, etc. is under the law, and what is wet down not in connection with drawing the water is not under the law, If water be put. Simeon b. Eleazar glosses. + T. 2:5. See *Yavneh, No. 3*.	*5. The principle is 'Aqiva's, explicitly so, since the rule, as noted, is alleged at T. 2:14 to have been cited by him. The reason for citing the pericope among Ushan items is the gloss.
*6. M. 4:5P-S: He who dunks utensil and washes clothing in cave—water on hands is under the law, If	*6. As above, the gloss is the interesting side, but it makes a familiar point.

water be put. Water on feet is not under the law, If water be put. Eleazar: If it is impossible for him to go down without muddying his feet, even water on feet is under the law, If water be put.
See *Yavneh, No. 3.*

Eleazar stresses that if the man cannot get to the water without getting mud on his feet, then the water on the feet is comparable to that on the outside of M. 4:1's jug.

*7. M. 5:2: He who swam in water—water which splashed is not under the law, etc. And if he intended to splash his fellow, it is. He who makes a bird—water splashed out and that which is in it are not under the law, If water be put. T. 2:13: He who makes a bird— Judah: Both this and that are under the law, If water be put. Yosé: Water which splashes out is not under the law, If water be put, and water which is in it, lo, this is under the law, If water be put. Meir: That which splashes out and that which remains are not subject to the law (= M.).
See *Yavneh, No. 3,* and M. 4:4-5, the Houses, below, pp. 211-213.

*7. The principle is not under dispute, only its application to the 'bird.' If we had a clearer idea of what the object is, we might see reasons for the several positions of T.'s stereotype apodosis.

*8. M. 5:6: He who beat on a wet pelt—if he did so outside the water, water which splashes out is subject to the law, If water be put. If he beat the pelt in the water, water which splashes out is not under the law, If water be put. Yosé: Even in the water, what is splashed out is under the law, If water be put, because he intends that it flow out together with the excrement.
See *Yavneh, No. 3.*

*8. Yosé does not differ in principle. The dispute is on the nature of one's intention in this particular case.

There is no difference with 'Aqiva's basic notion, only on how it applies to the case.

The position alternative to 'Aqiva's, that intention governs the interpretation of deed and that the person's purpose imposes its limits upon the consequences of his actions, is Tarfon's, that, whatever one intended, one's actual deeds have their own inexorable affect upon the water and revise the interpretation of the result.

This latter view, as we shall see, is important to the Shammaites, just as 'Aqiva's is expressed by the Hillelites.

*9. M. 3:1: A sack full of pieces of fruit placed on the side of river, or over the mouth of the cistern, etc., and the fruit absorbed water—all fruit which absorbed water is under the law, If water be put. Judah: Whatever is over against the water is under the law, etc., and whatever is not over against the water is not under the law, If water be put.

M. 3:2: Jar made of porous material full of fruit and placed into liquids, and fruit absorbed water—what is absorbed is under the law, If water be put. We speak of absorbable liquids. Nehemiah declares clean in the case of pulse, since pulse does not absorb moisture. T. 2:1: Yosé attests.

M. 3:3: He who took hot bread from oven and put it over a jar of wine—Meir: susceptible; Yosé: insusceptible in case of wheat-bread, susceptible in case of barley-bread, because barley absorbs liquid.

M. 3:4: He who sprinkles water in his house and then puts wheat into it and the wheat is dampened—if it is on account of the water, it is subject to the law, If water be put, and if it is on account of the rock-floor, it is not. + T. 2:2.
See *Yavneh, No. 3* (Tarfon).

*9. What is not directly affected by the water is deemed to be insusceptible, so Judah. The anonymous authorities hold that, even though liquid absorbed by the fruit not opposite the water is slight, the fruit still is susceptible, a view which surely accords with Meir's view of the single drop of water.

The issue is whether bread absorbs wine. It is insusceptible as dough, since it is kneaded with fruit-juice. Does it then absorb wine-vapor?

The issue is clear as stated. We did not sprinkle water intending to wet down the wheat, but, nonetheless, if the water which is sprinkled does affect the wheat and dampen it, then the wheat has been rendered susceptible to uncleanness. Accordingly, what is directly affected by the water is susceptible, and this without regard to the person's original intent. The other cases at M. 3:4 make the same point. Water capable of imparting susceptibility to uncleanness does impart susceptibility whether or not it was originally used for the purpose which it ultimately served. Obviously, the sweat of the walls or floor does not impart susceptibility, in line with M. 2:1.

While on the surface, the issue of M. 3:1-3 seems to be whether or not the fruit absorbs water, in fact that is not primary. The really central criterion of exegesis is Judah's position, which does not depend upon whether the fruit has absorbed water or much water, but upon our view of what the man has done. Judah holds at M. 3:1 that what the man has set against the water absorbs liquid because the man has put it where it is. What he has not placed in such a position that water can be absorbed is not subject to the law, If water be put. Why not? Because if the man wanted to wet the fruit down, he would have placed it in the proper location—that is, he would have put all the fruit over against the water. Again, at M. 3:3, there are easier ways to put wine into the bread. Since the man has not poured the wine into the bread, he by his own deed is not responsible for the presence of the wine-flavor in the bread. Meir, followed by Yosé, takes the position that the bread does absorb wine-fumes, or, in the case of the sack full of pieces of fruit placed on the side of the river, the fruit has been wet down, if by an infinitesimal quantity of water. Meir's position, however, is based upon the conception of the single drop of water's having the capacity to affect the status of the entire amount of water, and Meir's conflict with Judah is for Meir's, not for Judah's, reason.

M. 3:4 is assigned to Usha because of its redactional relationship to M. 3:3D-E, but Tarfon will find it in conformity with his conception.

*10. M. 5:3 + T. 2:13I: Pieces of fruit into which rain dripping from the roof fell, and which one mixed up with dry fruit—Simeon: It is under the law, If water be put. Sages: It is not under the law, If water be put. See *Yavneh, No. 3* (Tarfon).

*10. Simeon now holds that, since one has wet down the formerly dry fruit, it has been made susceptible to uncleanness, even though one intended ultimately to dry the entire quantity of fruit. Sages hold that since one's ultimate purpose was to dry the whole, the means used to reach that end are interpreted in the light of the end.

We clearly do not distinguish between original intention and ultimate deed. If the ultimate purpose in detaching and using the water was not to wet down the wheat, but to wash down the floor of the house, then do we hold that the wheat which is placed in the house thereafter has been wet down with approval? Yes, we deem that it has been wet down with approval. Why? Because the result of our deed is before us: the wheat is wet. Therefore we say that, at this point in the process, the water has been used with approval, even though, at the outset, it was not our original intention to use the water for the purpose for which it ultimately served. Simeon's position is clearly the same as that of M. 1:1A-C.

We recall Simeon's position at M. 1:6A-G, *above*, *No. 3*, and M. 3:5-7A-B, *above*, *No. 4*. In both cases, Simeon differentiates between liquid which is essential to one's purpose and that which is peripheral. In the second, moreover, he takes the most lenient view that if one did not intend to make use of the moisture on the grass to wet down the wheat, the wheat is not deemed susceptible to uncleanness. Here, by contrast, he holds that the fruit has been made susceptible. On the surface, Simeon's present position contradicts that taken in the earlier cases, for we should have expected him to rule that the pieces of fruit are not susceptible. Yet the problem of the case is different from those of the foregoing, and the ruling is not incongruent, or, at the very least, not contradictory. Why not? Because Simeon here stresses that the man has taken formerly dry fruit and wet it down. The ultimate purpose, to be sure, is to dry the whole. But, as in Judah's view, we take account of the man's actual deed. That deed's effects both are determinative of his prior intention and render irrelevant the posterior one. True, the man did not wet the fruit which was dry so that it would be wet, but only so that other fruit, already wet, would dry more quickly. Yet he *has* wet the fruit. Like Judah, Simeon therefore takes account of deed in the interpretation of intention. How does this differ from the dew on the grass? In the former case, the man did not gather the grass to use the dew; it merely happened to be there. Here, by contrast, the man has knowingly and deliberately taken water from wet fruit and put it on dry fruit. Simeon surely would want us to perceive a difference between the two cases. He lines up with 'Aqiva and Judah on the importance of deed, on the one side. But then he carries forward that principle to its logical conclusion, on the other. This brings him to the position of M. 1:1A-C, as we shall see, and, therefore, also to conform to the view of the House of Shammai in the same regard. This explanation of Simeon's diverse positions is not the only possible one. The alternative is that the opinions attributed to Simeon in principle contradict one another. The advantage of this latter approach is that it obviates the need for a certain exegetical acuteness. The disadvantage is self-evident. I am inclined to prefer to deem both rulings to belong to Simeon, therefore, and to interpret his position as somewhat more subtle and complex than that of Judah.

D. *After Usha*

I see no pericopae which originate in the time of Rabbi. The episodic glosses of that period are of no interest. Yosé b. R. Judah, who is generally regarded as a contemporary of Rabbi, is involved in the Houses' materials, cited presently.

E. *Unattributed*

The first group of unattributed pericopae restates principles fundamental to the tractate.

*1. M. 1:1D: Unclean liquids impart susceptibility to uncleanness both with and without approval. See *Yavneh, No. 1.*

*1. The converse is the datum of our tractate: Clean liquids impart susceptibility to uncleanness only when applied with approval.

*2. M. 1:6H-L: He who hides fruit in water because of thieves—water is not under the law, If water be put. + *Ma'aseh*. He who floats fruit in stream of river to bring it along—not under law, etc. See *Yavneh, No. 1.*

*2. Actions done under constraint are not equivalent to actions with approval.

The second group deals with principles familiar in Yavnean and Ushan pericopae.

*3. M. 5:1: He who immersed in a river, and there was before him another river which he crossed—the water of the second renders insusceptible the water of the first. If his fellow in drunkenness pushed him into the second river, the same rule applies. But if the two were wrestling and the man fell into the second river, the second immersion's water is under the law, If water be put. + T. 2:12. See *Yavneh, Nos. 1, 3.*

*3. 1. Water incidental to one's primary purpose does not impart susceptibility to uncleanness.
2. Water applied under constraint is not under the law, If water be put.
3. But water applied through a person's own fault is under the law, etc.

*4. M. 5:7T. 2:16: Water which comes up on hull of ship, bilge, and oars is not under the law, If water be put. Water which comes up on snares, gins, and nets is not under the law, If water be put. And if he shook them, it is under the law, If water be put. He who takes ship onto Great Sea to tighten seams, who takes hot nail into rain to temper it,

*4. The water referred to here is not detached with approval and serves no purpose whatsoever. Therefore it does not impart susceptibility to uncleanness. The important side is *If he shook them*. The point now is that by our deed we have disposed of the water, and what is shaken off has now been detached to conform to our purpose. T.'s dispute on the use

who leaves burning brand in rain to extinguish it—lo, this is under the law, If water be put.

M. 5:8: Covering for tables and matting for bricks—water which falls on these is not under the law, If water be put. And if he shook [these objects off, to get rid of the water, the water which is detached] is under the law, If water be put.
See *Yavneh, Nos. 1, 3*.

*5. M. 5:11J-M: He who weighs grapes in a cup of a balance—the wine in the cup is not susceptible, until one will pour it out into another utensil. Lo, this is like baskets of olives and grapes when they drip.
See *Yavneh, Nos. 1, 3*, and below, pp. 216-220.

*6. M. 4:2: He on whom rains fell, even a Father of uncleanness—it is not under the law, If water be put. If he shook off the rain, it is under the law, If water be put. If he stood under a water-spout to cool off, in the case of an unclean person, the water is unclean, and in the case of a clean person, the water is under the law, If water be put.

M. 4:3: He who puts a dish on end against the wall to rinse it off—water on it is under the law, etc. If he did so to protect the wall, the water is not under the law, etc. Compare M. Miq. 4:2, Part XIII, pp. 101-103.
See *Yavneh, No. 1*.

*7. M. 4:6: Basket full of lupines placed in a pool—one puts out hand and takes lupines from it, and they are insusceptible. If one took them out of the water, the ones which touch the sides of the basket are susceptible.
A radish in cave-water—menstruant washes it off and it remains insusceptible. If she took it out of the water, it is unclean.

of rain-water to extinguish a burning brand, which does not mean the water is used with approval, with M.'s contrary view, is a refinement.

M. 5:8 goes over very familiar ground.

*5. Liquid which is incidental to one's purpose is not capable of imparting susceptibility to uncleanness. If one pours the liquid into another utensil, by contrast, it means that he wants to preserve that liquid, and it now comes under the affect of his intention.

*6. If the rain which is shaken off is only that which fell on the ground, then the Hillelites of M. 1:2 will agree. If we refer also to the water which remains on the man, then the Shammaites alone can concur.

The difference is that, in the latter case, the water clearly is not wanted and does not flow with approval. In any event the water which passes across the dish is secondary to the man's main purpose.

*7. The principles are familiar. One removes the lupine and it remains insusceptible, as at M. 4:4, because the water is not detached with approval but is incidental to getting the lupine. Water on the basket is detached with approval, so lupines touching the basket are affected. The others are not.
The radish in the water is not made susceptible, so is clean, even though

M. 4:7: Pieces of fruit in water-channel—he whose hands were unclean reached out and took them—hands are clean and fruit is insusceptible. If he intended to rinse hands, hands are clean but water on fruit is under the law, If water be put. + T. 2:8.
M. 4:8: Clay dish full of water and placed in pool, and Father of uncleanness put hand into airspace—it is unclean, etc. + T. 2:7. Compare M. Miq. 6:6.

the menstruant touches it. If she takes it out, she makes it unclean. The fruit in the channel is like the lupines in the pool. The Father of uncleanness makes the dish unclean by contaminating its contained airspace. The points are:
1. A clay pot is made unclean only by a Father of uncleanness.
2. It is cleaned not by immersion but by breaking.
3. Water is cleaned in the immersion pool.
4. Someone in the first remove of uncleanness does not contaminate the pot (= 1).

None of the materials of No. 7 presents any surprises; the primary conceptions in any event are not relevant to Makhshirin. The pertinent point, that we distinguish water detached with approval from that not detached with approval, with reference to the lupine and the radish, is entirely familiar, so too the fruit in the water-channel. The issues of M. 4:8 do not pertain.

Reconsiderations

The sequence of rulings, from Abba Yosé-Joshua, through Ṭarfon and ʿAqiva, to the diverse Ushans, is uninterrupted and continuous. *Yavneh, No. 1,* is carried forward throughout the tractate, as we noted. It is difficult to come to a clear notion of the intent of *Yavneh No. 2. Yavneh No. 3,* by contrast, generates a long sequence of exemplifications and also some developments, all given in the names of Ushans. We have already dwelt at some length on the interpretation of the views of Judah and Simeon in relationship to those of ʿAqiva. Accordingly, it suffices to state that all of the attributions in this second division of the materials of Makhshirin are firm, since what is attributed to Ushans depends upon, and in important ways is secondary to and derivative of, what is attributed to Yavneans. I do not know of a single item which stands outside of established sequences of thought. As with Miqvaot and Niddah, so far as the history of the law of Makhshirin depends upon the correlation of chronological attributions to earlier and later authorities with logical sequences of generative principles and derivative, contingent ideas, the history is both comprehensive and reliable.

iv. Makhshirin before 70: The Houses and the Ushans

In regard to imparting susceptibility to uncleanness, Yavneans know two fundamental principles: first, wet produce is susceptible to uncleanness only if it is deliberately made wet; second, we may or may not distinguish between water one really wants, essential to his purpose or intention, which imparts susceptibility to uncleanness, and water one does not want, peripheral to his purpose or intention, which does not. ʿAqiva's and Ṭarfon's positions, we have just observed, at Usha both come under significant development and receive substantial restatement. Let us now turn to the important complexes of materials attributed to the Houses and ask about the relationship between principles at issue between them, on the one side, and the conceptions of Yavneans and of Ushans, on the other. In this regard we notice that Ushans invariably attest to, and, as we shall see, participate in, all Houses' disputes of our tractate. The real question, therefore, is whether or not the Houses in fact are merely made to express opinions on issues live only at Usha. The data for answering this question are located in the protases of the disputes, since the apodoses are fixed and stereotype, with the Shammaites' perpetually maintaining, "It is under the law, If water be put," and the Hillelites' alleging the contrary. We shall now see that all Houses' disputes not only bear Ushan attestations, but, as formulated, address themselves to issues which both are vivid and moot at Usha and are secondary developments of conceptions assigned to Yavneans, particularly Ṭarfon and ʿAqiva (*Yavneh, No. 3*). It follows that, in regard to the affect of liquid on dry produce, the tractate contains no ideas both attributed to authorities before 70 *and* clearly prior to, and generative of, conceptions assigned to authorities thereafter. Whatever is given in the names of the Houses is cited in those names presumably for literary-mnemonic reasons, perhaps because of the powerful force of the fixed apodosis, *It is* (+/— *not*) *under the law, If water be put*, which invites the use of the names of the Houses, nearly always served by such an acutely disciplined apodosis. In any event the generative conception of the shank of the tractate is contained in the notion attributed by Joshua to Abba Yosé: water does not induce susceptibility to uncleanness unless it is deliberately applied. Whether or not that notion goes back before 70 depends upon the time at which Abba Yosé lived, which we do not know. But the tractate as a whole does not exhibit a trace of significant development before Eliezer, and, indeed, it is only at the dispute of Tarfon and ʿAqiva (*Yavneh, No. 3*) that serious attention to the nature and meaning of intention comes into evidence. The bulk of the Ushan materials, we know, carries forward and relates to that single dispute. The dominant conception of Makhshirin may begin at Yavneh, but its articulation is nearly wholly the work of Ushans.

There is another way of seeing things, and that is characteristic of such history of Mishnaic law as has been attempted to this time. It is to maintain that the Ushans had access to an oral tradition, deriving from the original, "historical" Houses of the period before 70, and that theories attributed both to Ushans and by Ushans to the Houses in fact originate with the Houses themselves. The theory of an oral fundament, upon the basis of which the Ushans assign opinions to the Houses and indeed formulate their own diverse views of matters, runs parallel to an equivalent approach to the history of ideas attempted in connection with the study of Plato and Aristotle. Cherniss (1945, p. 17) states matters as follows:

> They adopt the hypothesis of an oral doctrine which was set up to explain how Aristotle can ascribe to Plato a theory which is not to be found in the latter's writings...

Further, he observes (1945, p. 29):

> This oral doctrine, a hypothesis set up to save the phenomena of Aristotle's testimony, has come to be treated as if it were itself part of the phenomena to be saved... The only healthy and reasonable course... is to discard this hypothesis and try another: to accept that part of Aristotle's testimony which agrees with the Platonic writings, and, since this testimony is at variance with the identification of ideas and numbers, to see whether that identification may not have its origin and explanation in Aristotle's own critical interpretation of Academic thought rather than in any supposititious oral exposition of Plato's own.

Accordingly, Cherniss takes seriously the possibility that "Aristotle was capable of setting down something other than the objective truth when he had occasion to write about his predecessors" (1935, p. ix). The reason is that "Aristotle was so consumed with the ideology of Platonism and the new concepts he had himself discovered or developed that it was impossible for him to imagine a time when thinking men did not see the problems of philosophy in the same terms as did he...We know that certain concepts and theories were introduced by Aristotle and others by Plato. If a Presocratic theory is presented in a way which involves such a notion, there is clearly something wrong with the statement" (1935, pp. x-xi). Aristotle uses theories "as interlocutors in the artificial debates which he sets up to lead 'inevitably' to his own solutions" (1935, p. xii). This is Cherniss's solution to the problem posed by Aristotle's ascription of Plato to "a form of the theory of ideas which does not appear in Plato's dialogues" (Cherniss, 1944, p. xii). Cherniss's success is based upon "taking into consideration all the evidence" and not merely relying upon general impressions. It follows that he has found it necessary "to interpret Platonic and Aristotelian texts... and to interpret them furthermore in their full philosophical intention; but there is no automatic canon in any case, and it is certainly unreasonable to disregard part of our evidence on the supposition that we are thus eliminating the danger of misinterpretation" (Cherniss, 1944, p. xxii). And, with Cherniss, we too have to confess: "This may seem to make a tedious business still more tedious; but there can be no approach to common agreement on more general issues until scholars stop passing by in silence the discordant interpretations of specific passages on which any sound decision of those larger issues must depend" (Cherniss, 1944, p. xxii).

The importance of Cherniss's work for ours is both substantive and methodological.[1] As to the latter, we follow his example in our stress on treating the later authorities, the Ushans, as active participants in the process of the formation of tradition. Ideas attributed by Ushans to the Houses may or may not have been held by the Houses, but most certainly were held by the Ushans. When, as we shall now observe, the Houses are made to debate matters under discussion at Usha, we must ask whether Ushans invariably attribute the issue to the Houses or discuss it also in their own names. It will be clear that the latter is the case, even within the narrow limits of the present tractate, all the more so when we consider disputes on the same moot principle found in other tractates. This approach, moreover, seems especially called for when we notice that the Yavneans know nothing about the fundamental principles allegedly debated by the Houses, do not address themselves either to those principles (e.g., the Hillelite position) and do not take up and develop them. On the contrary, the Yavnean stratum is remarkably uninformed about the conflicted roles of intention and action in the interpretation of the effects of a deed.

---

[1] Professor E. J. Bickerman kindly drew my attention to Cherniss.

A gap of nearly a century is curious, especially so when we recall close interrelationships characteristically discerned between Yavnean conceptions and Ushan ones, or between those assigned to authorities before 70 and Yavnean ones. Where we have disputes between the Houses on the most primitive and fundamental issues of a tractate, e.g., at Niddah and Miqvaot, we also have disputes among Yavneans about the consequences of the prior disputes, development, in one line, of thought inaugurated before 70; we further find among Ushans still tertiary developments of the same linear sequence of logical issues, problems, and principles. But here that is not the case, and I think the reason is clear.

This leads to the substantive importance of Cherniss's results for our own, which may be stated very succinctly. Just as, Cherniss shows, Aristotle could not imagine a time at which thinking men did not see the problems of philosophy in the same terms as did he, so the second-century authorities, in the mode of ahistorical, logical thinking natural to philosophers, likewise could not imagine that the Houses did not define and debate problems of moral philosophy in the same terms as did they.

*1. M. 1:1A-C: Any liquid which is put on with approval, even though it ultimately is not wanted, or *vice versa*, is under the law, If water be put.

*1. The process is indivisible and inexorable. Once, at any point, a person has shown that he wants the water or approves its being detached, the water has the capacity to impart susceptibility to uncleanness.

It is difficult indeed to see how Simeon, Yosé, and Judah can agree with this proposition, and it is easy to claim that 'Aqiva will reject it. Why? Because all of the later authorities are clear that if liquid is ultimately not wanted—e.g., if it is extrinsic to the accomplishment of a person's primary purpose—then that liquid is *not* under the law, If water be put. We want the liquid in the bucket; we have to wet down the rope as well; but liquid on parts of the bucket not necessary for use in drawing the water is not wanted and therefore insusceptible. The instance of the wheat wet down on a floor which we have washed is even clearer. Here is a case in which the remaining water is not wanted. Yet we wet the wheat down. Is the water ultimately wanted? Of course it is. Yet because it originally was not pertinent to the principal reason for detaching and using the water—washing the floor—the water does not impart susceptibility to uncleanness to the wheat. Țarfon assuredly can agree with the position of the present rule, and, as we shall see, so too can the House of Shammai. But 'Aqiva and his successors and the House of Hillel will find it difficult to harmonize their rulings with this principle. Still, in a moment we shall see matters in a different light.

*2. M. 1:2-4A-C: He who shakes the tree to bring down fruit and water falls—water is not under law, If water be put. D-G (= T. 1:1): If he shakes tree to bring down water—Shammaites: Drops which fall and drops which remain in the tree are under the law, If water be put. Hillelites: Drops which remain in the tree are not under the law, If water be put, because the man intends that all the water should fall from the entire tree.

H-L: He who shakes tree and water fell from one branch to another—as above.

N-P: He who shakes a bunch of herbs and water fell from top to bottom of the bunch—as above.

T. 1:3: T. augments the debate of M. 1:4S.

T. 1:4: Yosé: The law for one sack and for two sacks is the same. Judah: Eliezer says that the law is the same for one and for two sacks: It is under the law, If water be put. Joshua says the law is the same, as above: It is not under the law, etc. 'Aqiva says the lower one is under the law, and the upper is not.

T. 1:2: Yosé b. R. Judah: The Houses agree that if one shook the tree to bring down liquids, what fell on detached pieces of fruit in the tree and on unplucked produce on the ground is under the law, If water be put. They agree that if one picked the fruit after it dried, it is not under the law, If water be put. They differ about shaking the tree to bring down fruit, and moisture fell from one part of the tree to another + the usual apodosis.
See iii.2: *Usha, No. 2.*

*2. The water is incidental to one's purpose and is insusceptible, as 'Aqiva would agree.
The water which is shaken down has conformed to one's intention, that which remains has not. Yosé is explicit on this matter.

Yosé b. R. Judah has the Houses differ on M. 1:2A-C, shaking the tree to bring down fruit, and is indifferent to the dispute of M. 1:2. In his view, the dispute is on the fundamental, not the secondary, issue of M. That is, moisture not shaken when the man shakes the tree to bring down fruit—without regard to the moisture at all. The Shammaites deem the water to be under the law, If water be put.

Let us begin with the last rule, Yosé b. R. Judah's. In his conception the issues have been wrongly stated at M. Why? Because the disagreement between the Houses is on the fundamental matter of whether water which falls only incidentally to one's main purpose is subject to the law, If water be put. The Hillelites, like 'Aqiva and the major Ushans, are in entire agreement that water which falls when I want the fruit is *not* subject to the law, If water be put. Why not? Because the man shook the tree for fruit and never intended to shake the water out of the tree at all. It has never been subject to his intention. The disagreements alleged in M. are resolved differently in Yosé's view. The Houses agree that if one shakes down water from the tree, whatever falls as a result has been subject to his intention. How do we know it? Because the man shook the tree, and without regard to where the water falls, it falls because he wants it to. Like his father Judah, Yosé therefore maintains that what one *does* is decisive, and not only so, but retrospectively imparts meaning to what he originally *thought* of doing. Accordingly, the deed is ultimately and exhaustively determinative. The deed is to shake down the tree to get moisture from it. Wherever the water falls, the man's original action has made it fall. Why should the Houses differ on that point? They indeed do not, Yosé b. R. Judah maintains. Parenthetically, they also do not dispute about detaching the fruit formerly attached to the ground. It is not susceptible to uncleanness. Why not? Because the water dried up before the fruit was susceptible to its affects. Self-evidently, had the fruit been detached while still wet, the Houses would have agreed that the fruit *is* susceptible to uncleanness. Accordingly, Yosé b. R. Judah concedes nothing in this last matter, which is peripheral to his main point. In summary, in insisting that the Houses differ on the fundamental matter of shaking the tree to get the fruit, Yosé, Judah's son, imposes the conceptual principle of Judah, that action, and action alone, retrospectively is determinative and definitive of intent.

Let us return to M.'s (= Yosé's) conception of the dispute. All parties agree, M. alleges, that if one shakes the tree for the fruit and water falls, the water is not subject to the law, If water be put. Why not? Because one's action never was intended to bring down water. Judah's view that the deed is determinative of the intent, the result paramount in interpreting the means, is rejected. 'Aqiva's position clearly is behind the notion that all parties agree water which comes down along with the fruit is insusceptible. But what if one brings down the water, but only part of it? Here we come to Yosé's view at M. 1:5, which is verbatim that of the House of Hillel. And why not—since Yosé's consistent position, as given at M. 1:5 and M. 5:2, is that water which does not ultimately and wholly conform to my intention is not susceptible! Why not? Because Yosé differs from Judah on the determinative role of action in defining prior intention. He wishes to preserve a balance between what one ultimately does and what he to begin with wants to do. These matters must be interpreted in a balanced way. If one wants the water to fall, that is not the end of the matter. He wants it to fall in a particular place. It falls both there and elsewhere. Just as 'Aqiva distinguishes between what serves one's purpose, which is susceptible, and what is extrinsic to his purpose, which is not, so Yosé distinguishes between what *has* served one's purpose, which is susceptible, and what has ultimately *not* served his purpose, which is not.

Where does Simeon fit into this pattern? Is there a third position? Simeon assuredly agrees that water not subject to one's intention is not able to impart susceptibility to uncleanness (*Usha, No. 3*). If one intends to wet wheat and there is water for that purpose, then the wheat is susceptible (*Usha, No. 4*). How does Simeon stand in the (from his perspective) decidedly subordinate matter at issue between Yosé and Judah? M. 5:3 (*Usha, No. 10*) places Simeon squarely on Judah's side. If one has wet fruit and spreads out the water to dry, so that the whole will evaporate more rapidly, Simeon declares the fruit susceptible to uncleanness. The action, wetting down formerly dry fruit, is determinative. Even though one's ultimate intention is that the whole dry off, that is of no consequence against the actual deed. One actually has wet down dry fruit. One may or may not allow the process of evaporation to proceed. M. 1:1A-C is not invoked, but could be. Simeon's underlying conception accords with Judah's. Yet, it is obvious, even though both take up a position congruent to a principle agreeable to Ṭarfon, their basic reasoning is 'Aqiva's, and they stand in direct line after him, debating a secondary and subordinate matter with Yosé. This is a striking result, since it places both Simeon and Judah behind the gloss, *If he shook it off*, e.g., at M. 5:7-8. The water originally was not wanted, but, by a deed, a person has imposed a definition even on his prior intention.

We now return, *via* this rather circuitous route, to T. 1:4. Yosé maintains that the Houses equally dispute one sack and two sacks. Why? Because, in line with his principle, there is no basis for making any distinction between the case of one and that of two sacks. As at M. 5:6, if one beats the pelt in the water, it is to get fresh water to flow over the pelt. If he beats it outside of the water, it is to get rid of the water. In both cases, for different reasons, the disposition of the water conforms to one's intent. Yosé has no basis for making a distinction between one sack and two sacks. The Shammaites in all instances—just as at M. 1:2—will maintain that, however the water flows, it has been subject to one's intention, because he did leave the sacks in juxtaposition with one another. The Hillelites have a different position, *but* for a different reason. In all instances one wants only that the liquid flow out and disperse. Therefore what flows from the upper sack to the lower is not wanted, even though it wets down the lower sack—contrary to Simeon's and Judah's view—and what flows out of the two is not wanted, self-evidently, since one has by his action indicated that the water is wholly unwanted.

Judah's three positions, by contrast, develop a different line of thought. Eliezer sees both sacks as affected by the water. Why? Because the water *ultimately* conforms to one's intention that it flow out. This is a purely Shammaite conception, shown at M. 4:4-5. If in any way one disposes of the water, then we invoke the principle of M. 1:1A-C. What is unwanted at the end but wanted at the beginning imparts susceptibility, and, for a time, one does want the water. The reason is, of course, transparent. Wetting down the fruit is to one's advantage, as M. 3:1-2 indicate. Judah's Joshua takes the purely Hillelite position. Since one's action results in the water's flowing out, he does not want the water. In both cases, therefore, the Yavneans conform to Judah's conception of the paramount and exclusive importance of one's action, which is determinative of the interpretation of one's prior and primary intention. The net difference is in how one assesses the role of the water. That is, Judah's Eliezer holds that in all cases the action is determinative, in that one wants to wet down the fruit, while Judah's Joshua holds that in all cases the action is determinative, in that one wants to get rid of the water. Does 'Aqiva differ? Yes, Judah states, he does, *but* for the same reason agreed upon by all three parties. The upper sack is left to drain off. The lower sack is left to receive the water. Accordingly, we make a distinction in the matter, but only because of the *action* which one has taken. Placing the upper sack above the lower, one indicates that he wants the water to leak out of the upper sack. Therefore it is not susceptible to uncleanness. Action is determinative. Placing the lower sack below the upper, he indicates that he wants to wet it down. Therefore, once more, action is determinative. All parties thus agree to interpret the case in terms of what one actually *does*, not in terms of what one supposedly intends to do. But while the interpretation of the determinative deed is diverse, for the reasons given, all parties agree on Judah's principle.

We know that M. differs from Yosé b. R. Judah. But how will Yosé and Judah see M.? Clearly, Yosé will be happy with M. 1:4, which has the Hillelites accord with his conception. Self-evidently, Judah must reject M. Why? Because, as just noted, its attributions are all wrong. If Judah were to construct the cases of M., he would give them a tripartite apodosis. In his opinion, M. 1:2A-C should provoke a disagreement, as his son has told us, with the authoritative party—let us assume, the House of Hillel—in the view that water which falls is not under the law, If water be put, *because* of the priority of ultimate, practical result over primary and prior intention. The Shammaites should disagree, since they must take up the (false) position that water which happens to come down along with the fruit is subject to the law, If water be put. (Tarfon maintains exactly that, as we know.) But, to fill out Judah's picture, we should have a third position, one which maintains that water which falls has conformed to the person's action, if not his original intention, and water which does not fall has not been subject to his intention at all—that is, 'Aqiva's position in T., but no one's position at M. 1:2A-C. Judah in respect to M. 1:2D-G certainly cannot be happy. Yosé of course has his way. How would Judah want to construct M. 1:2D: *If one shakes the tree to bring down from it liquids*—then what? In Judah's view, all the drops have been shaken. All have been subjected to the man's will. But some have fallen, some have not. Here is a fine dispute, Judah will say. All that he will want to omit is M. 1:2G. His reason is not the man's prior intention. The dispute is possible solely because of the ambiguity of the ultimate result which generates three possible positions, not two, and therefore for formal (as well as substantive) cannot be served by the Houses.

*3. M. 4:4-5: 1. Jug into which water leaking from the roof came down—House of Shammi: It should be broken. House of Hillel: It is emptied out. But man can put his hand in and take out fruit.
2. Trough into which rain dripping from roof flowed—water in trough and drops of water that splashed out and overflowed are not under the law, If water be put. If he took the trough to empty it, House of Shammai: It is under the law, If water be put. House of Hillel: It is not under the law.
3. If one intentionally left trough out to collect water—drops of water that splashed out and those that overflowed—House of Shammai: They are under the law, etc. House of Hillel: Drops are not under the law. If one took it to pour it out, they agree that the water is wholly under the law, If water be put.
4. T. 2:5-6: Meir *vs.* Yosé: Clean *vs.* unclean trough.

*3. If I pour out the water, I indicate that, for a time, it was where I wanted it, and in line with M. 1:1A-C was subject to approval and then not subject to approval, so is susceptible. No. 2 is a rerun of No. 1.

Drops which splash out are not where I want them, so are insusceptible in the Hillelite view. No. 3 is a rerun of M. 1:3. T.'s revision of M., No. 4, is discussed below. In fact, it goes over the ground of M. Miq. 4:1.

This unit deals with three cases and two sorts of water, water one has never wanted and only wants to get rid of, and water he has deliberately collected but now wants to get rid of, this last producing the third of the three cases. At the first two the issue, as I said, is how to get rid of unwanted water. The distinction is between breaking and merely emptying the jug. Certainly Judah will agree with the Hillelites: the ultimate result of one's deed determines the original intent. Therefore if he picks up the jug—thus shifting it from its original position and indicating that, for a time, he wanted it where it was—and pours it out, the ultimate disposition of the water is determinative. I do not say, as at M. 1:1A-C, that what was wanted for a time but then unwanted is deemed capable of imparting susceptibility to uncleanness. Judah will of course disagree with the Shammaites, but so what? M. 4:5F-J repeat this same viewpoint.

If one deliberately gathered the water by contrast, then he produces a quite separate case. It is, as noted, exactly the problem of M. 1:2's water which is shaken out as against that which remains in the tree. Does Judah have a solution to this problem? No, it is not even relevant to his principle. The issue is not what the man has done at all. Yosé, by contrast, will find M. 4:5K-N highly congenial, since it conforms to his conception of what is at issue at M., and, once more, leaves the Hillelites in Yosé's position: the man wanted all the water to flow into the trough, just as, at M. 1:5, he wanted all the water to flow off the leek. That which remains, or, in the present case, that which splashes out, has not conformed to his wishes. Accordingly, the ultimate result is tempered by the original intention.

T. 2:6 shows that M. 4:5F-I conform to Yosé's conception, as we surmised, but for a quite different reason. Here Yosé rejects Meir's distinction between the clean and unclean trough. Meir maintains that if the trough is clean, then the House of Hillel rule that, if the man took the trough in order to pour it out, the water is not subject to the law, If water be put. But the reason is that the trough is *clean*. The water has not had an opportunity to become unclean. What if the water falls into an unclean trough? Then, Meir maintains, the water is under the law, If water be put, if the man takes the trough to pour the water out. Why? Because, as soon as the man moves the trough, the water becomes susceptible to uncleanness—and unclean!

Accordingly, does Meir agree with Judah? Hardly. Judah will regard the water as insusceptible to uncleanness because of the man's ultimate disposition of the water. The deed is finally determinative. Meir cannot take that position. Yosé disagrees with Meir, T. maintains, but not because of the matter of the clean or the unclean trough. No, Yosé's reason is his own and does not meet Meir's head-on. The reason that the water in the trough which the man took and poured out is not under the law, If water be put, so far as the Hillelites are concerned, has nothing to do with the status of the trough, but solely with the interplay of intention and action. This brings us back to where we started, leaving only Meir.

So far as Meir is concerned, water in the unclean trough *is* under the law, If water be put. The view of all parties is that the water has been deliberately collected and therefore is outside of the purview of our tractate. The water to begin with *is* susceptible to uncleanness. This brings us to the peculiar reading of T. 2:6A-B, *A trough into which water dripping from the roof has fallen—the drops of water which splash out and those which overflow are subject to the law, If water be put.* If one took it to pour it out, Meir continues, the water (of course) is subject to the law, If water be put, so far as the

Shammaites are concerned. The Hillelites differ only in the case of a clean trough. Water dripping from the roof into a trough indeed has been collected with approval, which accounts for the view that drops in the trough and those which splash out *are* subject to the law, If water be put. To be sure, if the trough is clean, the water has not been made unclean, and on that account the Hillelites rule, T. 2:6E/H, that the water is *clean.* That must be Meir's intent, since B's reading does not permit Meir to maintain that the water in the trough cannot be subject to the law, If water be put. He has already maintained that it *is* under the law, If water be put.

Accordingly, Meir claims the Hillelites agree in the case of a clean trough that, if one takes the trough to pour the water out, the water is *clean*—and why should they not maintain the water is clean? For what is there to make the water unclean? In the case of an unclean trough, however, Meir maintains that the Hillelites rule the water indeed is unclean, just as do the Shammaites. T.'s reading at B therefore is sound, and we have to read the remainder of the pericope in accord with Meir's distinction between *unclean* and *clean,* not between *If water be put* and *not.* Meir's ruling, therefore, really is about a quite separate matter, to which neither Judah nor Yosé attend: the status of the water which has dripped into the trough. Meir maintains all parties agree the water is subject to the law, If water be put. What is the basis for his ruling? We have to turn to M. Miq. 4:1 to find the answer.

At M. Miq. 4:1 Meir maintains that the Houses ultimately agree that water collected in utensils under a waterspout is deemed gathered in a utensil and useless for an immersion-pool, which requires water gathered naturally upon the ground. Passage through the utensil spoils the water. The issue is whether leaving utensils under a waterspout is equivalent to forgetting them. At the outset the Shammaites declare that that is the case, and the Hillelites hold that if one forgets the utensils, water is not spoiled for use in the immersion-pool. Meir maintains that the Houses took a vote and the Shammaites prevailed. Accordingly, as in the present case, *all parties agree that water which merely happens to drip from the roof into a utensil*—there, the jug, here, the trough—*has been deliberately collected.* It will follow, for Makhshirin, that the water *is* subject to the law, If water be put. Therefore, as I said, the only moot point is whether the water is contaminated, and all parties must agree that if the trough is unclean, the water is made unclean thereby!

Let us go over the details of the *locus classicus* (Part XIV, pp. 125-126).

M. Miq. 4:1: He who leaves utensils under the water spout [to collect rain-water in them] spoils the pool.
All the same is one who leaves and one who forgets, so the House of Shammai. House of Hillel declare clean in the case of one who forgets. Meir: Took a vote and House of Shammai won. Yosé: No vote, no decision.

The Houses are in agreement that mere passage of the water through the utensils spoils it. But the reason is intent. Since the person left the utensils under the spout, what could he expect, except that the utensils would fill up? And so his action testifies to his intent, which was to gather rain-water in utensils. The water is invalid.
The secondary issue is whether forgetting the utensils is of the same character as leaving them with intent. The Shammaites hold that it is. Action testifies to prior intent. The Hillelites hold that is not so. Forgetfulness is not the same as intent, and the subsequent result does not prove the original fact.

As we see, it follows that Meir's version of M. 4:4-5 requires the Houses to agree that the water dripping from the roof into the trough *is* subject to the law, If water be put. Only Yosé can maintain M.'s conception of the matter, and T.'s testimony on that point is unambivalent, since it assigns M. verbatim to Yosé.

It remains to examine M. Miq. 2:7-9, because the apodosis of the Houses' dispute at M. Makh. 4:4 is reminiscent of that of the dispute of Eliezer and Joshua at the former pericope and its point is relevant to M. Miq. 4:1. The issue is the status of rain-water collected in jars on the roof. If it is deliberately collected, then it cannot be used for the immersion-pool. If not, then it can. In that case, how do we get at the water? We may not raise up the jugs, for that is tantamount to drawing the water. We break them, which allows the water naturally to flow into the pool. Eliezer holds that if one left the jars during the rainy season, then he expected water to collect; he has deliberately gathered it by his action; the water is unfit for the pool, and one does not break the jugs and allow it to flow into the pool. Joshua says that, whether or not it is the rainy season, the water is not deemed deliberately gathered, and therefore the jugs may be broken and the water used for a pool. The details of the item are as follows (Part XIV, pp. 127-131):

M. Miq. 2:7-9: He who leaves wine-jars on top of roof and they filled with water—Eliezer: rainy season/if

This pericope is to be interpreted in its original version, not as it is developed in line with M. Miq. 2:4's

there is in it as little water as is in cistern—breaks them. If not, does not break them. Joshua: One way or the other, he breaks.

Plasterer who forgot lime-pot in cistern, etc.

Eliezer. And then the issue is the affect upon the rain-water of passage through the jars. Eliezer's position is that if the jars are left on the roof and are filled with rain, it is deemed drawn water. Why? Because mere passage through the jars suffices to turn rain-water into drawn water. The man's action, as in Judah's view, is determinative, and he has left jars on the roof in the rainy season. Since it has rained, the intent of the action is defined by its result.

Joshua's position is that since the man did not intend to gather the water in the jars, his purpose having been to dry them, the fact that the rain-water collected in the jars does not change matters. He rejects Judah's principle. The rain-water remains rain-water. Accordingly, as to Yosé, so to Joshua, the issue of prior intention is paramount. So long as the man did not intend to collect the water in the jars, what happens in the natural course of events does not change the picture. Self-evidently, the man is not to lift up the jars. Joshua will agree that if he removes the water by pouring it out, emptying it into the cistern, he indeed turns the rain-water into drawn-water. Accordingly, Joshua will not reject the view that one's deed in connection with the water is paramount. Yosé, T. Miq. 3:2B, explains Joshua's opinion in exactly these terms: one must not pick up the jar and turn it over. Accordingly, to Joshua the water is fit, and the only concern is that by our *action* we not render it drawn-water.

Certainly Joshua and 'Aqiva will concur: what is incidental to one's main purpose is not taken into account, and this, Joshua must add, is without regard to the ultimate consequence of one's deeds. 'Aqiva proposes to distinguish between what one intended and what actually happened, thus between water on the rope or the outer part of the jug essential in dipping the jug into the cistern, and water on parts of the rope not essential in dipping the jug into the cistern. Equivalently, Joshua maintains that one's intention was to dry the jugs. If rain-water falls in, that is not within one's original plan. The water is valid for a pool. One line of thought therefore goes from Joshua through 'Aqiva to all the Ushans who distinguish primary from secondary aspects of the wetting down. The other flows from Eliezer through Tarfon to those Ushans who make no such distinction, on the one side, and to Judah and Simeon, who, for quite separate reasons, maintain that the deed is determinative of the prior intention, on the other. Just as Eliezer maintains that, having left the jars on the roof in the rainy season, one cannot disclaim responsibility for the rain which falls into them, so Tarfon rules that we cannot distinguish among the drops of water on diverse parts of the jug and rope. He has, after all, let the whole down into the cistern. And Judah, though in appropriate instances in agreement with 'Aqiva's conception, nonetheless stands with Eliezer in maintaining the ultimately determinative force of deed. It goes without saying that the Hillelite apodosis at M. Makh. 4:4 has to be interpreted in its own terms, and not in relationship to M. Miq. 2:7-9, to which it is not pertinent (just as MA maintains, *ad loc.*). The breaking of M. Miq. 2:7 is necessitated by the facts of the law of Miqvaot; the pouring out of M. Makh. 4:4 is permitted because of the givens of Makhshirin.

The final question in relationship to the Houses of Makhshirin arises at M. Tohorot 9:1, which on the surface sets the Houses into dispute on exactly the issue we have argued stands outside of the purview of their theory, the intent of a person in respect to the use of liquids. The positions of the Houses at that pericope are generally understood to depend upon one's assessment of the owner's intent in respect to olives: the liquids—oil—become susceptible to uncleanness, the Houses are supposed to agree, from the time that the owner wants the oil. A second glance at the matter (Part XII, pp. 133-137), however, shows us that the issue of intention is secondary and imposed, and that the primary consideration is primitive and undeveloped.

M. Toh. 9:1: Olives—from what time do they receive uncleanness?
Shammaites: After they exude sweat of vat, but not sweat of basket.
Simeon: Measure is three days.
Hillelites: After three olives stick together.
Gamaliel: After the work of preparing them is completed.
+ T. Toh. 10:1-2A.

The principle, all commentaries agree, is, When is the liquid desired?

The Shammaites say that once the olives exude sweat in the vat, the moisture is desired. But that of the basket is allowed to run out and is shown not wanted.

The Hillelites say that once there is moisture enough for three olives to stick together, the moisture is wanted, even in the basket.

METHOD OF CORRELATION 45

Gamaliel says that when the owner is ready to bring the olives to press, he wants the slime and liquid; they are now prepared to receive uncleanness. Maimonides: "Because the presumption is that they have been made susceptible by their sap, since the owner approves its presence so that the olives may be easier to press. But before their preparation is finished, sap that issues from them does not make them susceptible, since the owner does not approve its presence."

Accordingly, on the surface, the issue is, as I said, When is the sap or liquid desired? The several parties agree on the principle and differ on the facts. The Shammaites say the sap is desired once the olives are in the vat. The Hillelites say that (even in the vat) only after they are squashed together do the olives produce desirable liquid. Gamaliel places the time of desired liquid at the moment that the farmer is ready to put the olives in the vat. At that time his intention to press them for liquid is clear, when he plans to add no more to the vat.

M. Toh. 9:2-3: If one has finished gathering olives but plans to buy more, the ones already in the vat are not yet susceptible. Even if unclean liquid falls on them, it affects only what it touches. Sap which comes from the olives at that point is clean. When the work of preparing them is complete, then, but only then, are the olives susceptible, and if unclean liquids fell on them, the whole is unclean.

Gamaliel's view is taken for granted. The point of the set is to explain the difference between insusceptibility and susceptibility.

M. Toh. 10:4: He who places grapes into press from what is stored in baskets (which do not preserve the liquid) and from what is spread out on ground—House of Shammai: He places with clean hands, and if he did so with unclean hands, he has rendered them unclean.
House of Hillel: He places with unclean hands.

The issue is whether the grapes are susceptible once they are cut, or only when they are put into the vat for pressing. The Shammaites say they are rendered susceptible when brought for pressing, even before they are in the vat. The Hillelites hold that cutting grapes for eating does not render them susceptible to uncleanness, so they may be put into

But he separates heave-offering in cleanness.
He who puts grapes into press from grape-basket or from what is spread out on leaves—all agree he puts them in with clean hands.
(b. Shab. 15a: Grapes cut for vat—Shammai: Susceptible to uncleanness. Hillel: Not susceptible.)

the vat with unclean hands. The owner's putting them into the vat indicates his intention. Now the liquid is preserved and so is desired, before rendering the grapes susceptible.
(The main point is that as soon as grapes are taken up for the wine press, they are made susceptible.)

The rather substantial set of materials attributed to the Houses at M.-T. Tohorot, with or without the participation of Yavneans and Ushans, read as a unity, makes a single point. In connection with olives and grapes, liquid which is desired renders the produce susceptible to uncleanness, but that which is not desired does not. That point is shared by all parties; the disagreements between the Houses and among later authorities are understood to devolve its application. The principle itself therefore depends upon intention, assessing the likely wishes and intentions of people.

If we had no idea that the major issue of the pericopae before us is the desirability of liquid, however, how should we have interpreted the materials attributed, rightly or wrongly, to the Houses? M. Toh. 9:1 gives several answers to the question, When do olives receive uncleanness? The Shammaites say this comes when the olives in the vat have exuded slime or sweat. The Hillelites simply say that this comes when three olives stick together—*whether or not this takes place in the vat*. The Shammaites mnemonic is *vat/not basket*, yielding *vat and basket*. Gamaliel, after 70, tells us the susceptibility begins when the work of preparation is complete. Does Gamaliel know anything about exuded liquid? Obviously not. He supplies the simplest definition, which is that, once the olives require no further preparation, they become susceptible. It is possible to do all the work in a state of uncleanness. Only when the work is complete do the olives enter the category of uncleanness. This opinion is self-evidently separate from that of the Houses, who are interested in the liquid exuded by the olives and agree that, once the olives begin to exude liquid, they become susceptible. They differ only on the location of the olives when the exuded liquid is taken into account. Do olives stick together before they go into the vat? Of course they do—in the basket! Does this definition, on the face of it, have anything to do with one's attitude toward the exuded liquid? Obviously not. The Houses in fact differ on the issue of the location of the olives, as I said: *vat, not basket* vs. even *basket*.

True, it is "self-evident" that the basis of the difference is in the owner's intent. Once the vat contains the olives, we clearly plan to preserve the liquid, therefore obviously desire it. But that is not intrinsic to the dispute. It is, rather, a layer of meaning added to it. The Houses really differ on whether, during the process of cutting the olives, before the olives are brought to the vat, the work must be done in a state of cleanness. The Hillelite position yields the rule that work must be done in a state of cleanness. The Shammaites will allow the work to be done in a state of uncleanness, until the olives are actually in the vat. Does Gamaliel differ from the Hillelites? Of course he does, since, so far as he is concerned, all the work is done in a state of uncleanness, as he states explicitly. Does he differ from the Shammaites? Hardly, since the work is not done before the olives are in the vat, and it is only then (if slightly later in time) that the olives exude susceptible sweat.

This brings us to the story about Shammai and Hillel on this very question:

> He who cuts grapes for the vat—
> Shammai says, "It is made susceptible to uncleanness."
> Hillel says, "It is not made susceptible to uncleanness."
>
> b. Shab. 15a/17a

> Said Hillel to Shammai: "Why do they cut grapes for the vat in purity but not gather olives in purity?"
> He said to him, "If you anger me, I shall decree susceptibility to uncleanness even on the process of gathering olives."
>
> b. Shab. 17a

What is the opinion of both authorities? It is that when olives are being cut down and prepared for the vat, they are *not* susceptible to uncleanness. If, therefore, I had to explain the Houses' dispute without reference to the issue of the desirability of liquids, I should interpret it as a dispute on *the point at which the process of gathering olives is complete*. Since we know the process may be done in a state of uncleanness, we have to place a limit on it. The limit is, after the olives have been in the vat, not after they have been in the basket, so the House of Shammai. The House of Hillel hold that the point at which olives, in the basket, exude moisture and stick together, the work of gathering is complete, since the work of producing the oil begins.

M. Toh. 10:4 brings us to the dispute of Shammai and Hillel. Shammai is clear that he who cuts grapes for the vat has rendered them susceptible; Hillel holds that he has not rendered them susceptible to uncleanness. What about cutting grapes not for the vat, but for eating? Grapes stored in the sort of baskets which do not hold in the liquid and spread out on the ground are eating-grapes, not for vintaging. The House of Shammai hold that these grapes, too, are susceptible to uncleanness. The House of Hillel say that these grapes are not susceptible. Is the issue of the owner's intent in respect to the liquid necessarily to be located in the dispute? Hardly. All we have is a refinement of the protasis of the dispute between Shammai and Hillel:

He who cuts grapes for the vat—

What about him who cuts grapes not *for the vat*? The unanimous agreement at the end again introduces the preservation of the liquid, therefore its presumed desirability. But this too is to be understood as referring to grapes cut for the vat, the liquid of which naturally is preserved, as against grapes cut for eating, which are spread out to dry. The issue of liquid obviously may be invoked in the interpretation of the dispute. But the dispute, without the matter of intention, is perfectly clear. Accordingly, the earliest problem is to work out the implication of the distinction between the harvesting of grapes, which requires cleanness, and olives, which does not. The secondary issue of the intention of the owner in regard to the liquid is not essential in the interpretation of the primary stratum of the Houses' disputes at M. Tohorot.

v. A Second-Century Tractate

If we now summarize the central and generative theme of our tractate, we may state matters as follows.

First, liquids are capable of imparting susceptibility to uncleanness only if they are useful to men, e.g., drawn with approval, or otherwise subject to human deliberation and intention. The contrary view is that all liquids without distinction impart susceptibility to uncleanness.

Second, liquids capable of imparting susceptibility to uncleanness do so only if they serve a person's purpose, are deliberately applied to produce, or otherwise irrigate something through human deliberation and intention. The contrary view is that however something is wet down, once it is wet, it falls within the rule of Lev. 11:34, 38 and is subject to uncleanness.

If the tractate derived from Eliezer's circle, we should have no discussion of the matter of which liquids impart or do not impart susceptibility to uncleanness. Since he says that the matter of why a beast is slaughtered, or whether the beast is clean or unclean, is irrelevant, he is apt to regard the origin—usefulness, intentional drawing, and the like—as irrelevant. If the tractate came to us from Tarfon's circle, it is at least plausible to suppose that the matter of intention in wetting down produce would have been deemed peripheral, if not irrelevant. In any event, if the opposition to Abba Yosé-Joshua had had its way, there is no doubt that we should have no tractate of Makhshirin at all. For what law is needed to develop the simple proposition that what is wet, whatever the source of wetness may be, and however the wetness may happen to come upon produce, is susceptible to uncleanness. Accordingly, our tractate's first principle, its distinction between liquids which do and do not impart susceptibility to uncleanness, derives from circles including 'Aqiva, and its second principle, the distinction between intentional and unintentional wetting down, assuredly comes to us from 'Aqiva, in a direct line from Abba Yosé-Joshua. The tractate as a whole begins its major conceptual development with 'Aqiva. What forms its center and unifies its diverse pericopae into a single, remarkably coherent document is the thought of 'Aqiva on the principal role of human intention in activating the supernatural forces of uncleanness.

The upshot of our inquiry is to locate the primary conceptual development of the first five chapters of Makhshirin—the dominant theme of the interplay of intention and the capacity of liquids to impart susceptibility to uncleanness—among Ushan followers of 'Aqiva. The Yavnean stratum, however, is so remarkably slight—a single saying attributed by Joshua to Abba Yosé, and one dispute of Tarfon and 'Aqiva—as to render rather uncertain the theory that the Ushans inherit and carry forward Yavnean conceptions. On the contrary, what we find in Usha in the main is the repetition of the two contrary conceptions on an essentially secondary matter, attributed to Yavneans, 'Aqiva, and, alongside, Tarfon. It may be even that that single stray item is of the same pseudepigraphic sort as the pericopae attributed to the Houses by Ushans. That is, it may in fact also be the creation of Ushans. Of this we cannot be sure. The net result is that the conceptual shank of the tractate Makhshirin begins its history, at the earliest, at the turn of the second century, formed of five layers of conception, in sequence:

1. Dry produce is insusceptible, a notion which begins in the plain meaning of Lev. 11:34, 38.

2. Wet produce is susceptible only when intentionally wet down, a view expressed in gross terms by Abba Yosé as cited by Joshua.

3. Then follow the refinements of the meaning and effects of intention, beginning in 'Aqiva's and Tarfon's dispute, in which the secondary matter of what is tangential to one's primary motive is investigated.

4. This yields the contrary views, assuredly belonging to Ushans, that what is essential imparts susceptibility and what is peripheral to one's primary purpose does not; and that both what is essential and what is peripheral impart susceptibility to uncleanness. (A corollary to this matter is the refinement that what is wet down under constraint is not deemed wet down by deliberation.)

5. The Ushan dispute on the interpretation of intention—is it solely defined by what one actually does or modified also by what one has wanted to do as well as by what one has done—belongs to Yosé and Judah and his son Yosé and is attributed by them to the Houses.

In point of fact, of course, the difference of opinion begins in the gross principle assigned to 'Aqiva. We do not vastly exaggerate, therefore, in declaring that Makhshirin is a second century tractate, with roots in the later strata of Yavnean thought, and is, in the main, the work of 'Aqiva and his Ushan successors and continuators. In conclusion, we observe that a tractate devoted to the issues predominant in Makhshirin therefore is possible only within the suppositions of 'Aqiva. Significant development, not merely restatement, of those suppositions, moreover, is conceivable only within the subtle conceptions of Judah, Judah's son, Yosé, Simeon, and Yosé. Had the problematic of the tractate been subjected to the development of Eliezer, for the one part, of the opposition to Abba Yosé, and possibly even of Tarfon, for the other, there would have been no Makhshirin at all.

II. Kelim Before 70

i. Definition of the Problem

The final question is, What was the state of the law about Kelim before 70? What we want to know is not *whether* there were laws or exegeses of pertinent Scriptures. We take for granted there were. Our problem is, To what degree are the earliest Mishnaic laws before us founded on an antecedent heritage, and to what degree do they appear to have begun their development primarily after the destruction?

The answer to the question, Were there laws about utensils before 70? is obvious. The Temple cult was based upon Leviticus and priestly interpretations thereof, so one can hardly doubt the availability, and enforcement, of a substantial corpus of rules on the cleanness of utensils. On the other hand, no evidence known to me describes the shape and detailed substance of those Temple laws, with the possible exception of M. 25:9; but this too comes to us from rabbinical, not from pre-70 priestly, tradents.

The Mishnaic laws we have examined seem to have been the work mainly of Yavneans and Ushans. Anonymous sayings exhibit not a hint of coming from authorities prior to the Yavneans or, more commonly, prior even to the Ushans, whose principles and modes of formulation predominate in most instances of unassigned sayings. We cannot, therefore, postulate that what is without attribution derives from some very old source, which has been vastly augmented by the addition of named sayings and disputes. The contrary is the case. The absence of attribution in our tractate seems to mean anything but that the law is very old, from the period before 70.

The question therefore is, to what degree do the rules of Kelim seem to be based upon the work of Yavneans, and to what degree to they seem to continue principles, if not exact formulations, laid down at some point, discernible or otherwise, before 70? Here the absence of evidence necessitates a bit of conjecture and speculation. Yet the limits of conjecture may be clearly stated.

We shall first consider those principles which clearly lie at the foundations of the Yavnean rulings and dispute and which also do not seem to have been at issue among Yavneans. These, we may postulate, come at the very beginning and may go back to pre-Yavnean times.

Second, we shall ask about the laws attributed to the Houses. We cannot take for granted that attribution to the Houses means a law goes back before 70, or even before 140. Ushans quite systematically made use of the names of the Houses for mnemonic and pedagogical purposes (they are the same). It will therefore be important to examine the disputes between the Houses one by one and to ask, Are issues at hand primarily characteristic of Ushans, in which case pseudepigraphic use of the Houses' names cannot be ruled out? Or are the issues fundamentally in accord with the Yavnean or even earlier principles, demonstrably so on the basis of other evidence?

Once we have a clear picture of the principles which lie at the very foundations of our Mishnah, we shall ask, To what degree do these principles depend upon Scripture's plain meaning or obvious exegetical requirements, and to what degree do they rest upon a substantial antecedent tradition both of Scriptural exegesis and of legal thinking? We already have seen how much the tradition changed, how new and sophisticated conceptions were introduced, between Yavneh and Usha. We therefore have some sense for the potentialities of the nurture and development of legal traditions over a period of less than a century, that is, from 70 to 170 at the outside, but, more likely, from ca. 100 to ca. 150, from the time of ʿAqiva's ascendency to the time of Meir's, Judah's, and Yosé's activity. If we see evidence of a substantial development from the legal principles and ideas revealed in Scriptures to the legal principles and ideas taken for granted at Yavneh, then that period of development may be assumed, at least hypothetically, to have taken a considerable number of years. On the other hand, if we do not locate evidences of substantial change and, particularly, development from the rules of Leviticus and Numbers to the fundamental conceptions of Yavneh, we shall be unable to show a long period of legal change to have taken place from Scripture to Yavneh. Claims to the contrary will have to be accompanied by evidence and arguments to account for the evident absence of indications of a long period of gestation and growth, parallel to what took place in the century before us. For at any point it was possible to turn to Scripture and apply its laws to the table-fellowship, including the utensils, of a current sect. But once those laws *were* applied, much new legal theory and many new rulings would be generated even in the very process of their application, let alone in study and reflection.

It now becomes necessary once more to stress the pertinent issue. It is not, Were the Levitical rules studied and obeyed from the redaction of Leviticus, let us say in about the fifth century B.C., to 70? We suppose that in the Temple they were. We readily concede, furthermore, that some sort of exegetical tradition, carried forth by the Temple priests, the Sadducees, or whoever else, did develop. Our problem is the history, specifically, of the *Mishnaic* law of Kelim. We seek evidence for the antiquity, before 70, of *our* particular laws, not of laws about utensils in general, let alone about traditions of the elders, oral traditions, exegeses of Scriptural traditions, or *The Oral Torah*. The point made above (p. 327), that a striking correspondence is to be discerned between the Levitical conception of the sources of uncleanness and the Mishnaic conception of objects susceptible to the uncleanness imparted by those sources, changes nothing. Insight into the meaning and dynamic of the Levitical rules (if it is not our eisegesis of the laws to begin with) can have been the work of anyone, at any time, and hardly requires a hypothetically long period of gestation and nurture.

Once we have answered these questions, we turn, finally, to the evidence of the controversy-sayings, having to do with utensils in particular, supplied by the Synoptic Gospels. We can hardly draw upon such sayings to help us solve problems intrinsic to the Mishnaic law and its history. But we shall have both to test our conclusions against the extra-Mishnaic evidences, on the one hand, and to attempt to apply them to the illumination of that evidence, on the other.

ii. The Yavnean Presuppositions

The earliest attributed law, coming before 70, concerns the division of clay utensils into an outside and an inner part. Hezekiah testifies before Gamaliel the Elder that any clay utensil which has no inner part has no outer parts. Underlying that statement—or equivalent to it—is the conception that whatever has a receptacle is susceptible, and whatever does not is insusceptible. A third, closely related conception is that the contained airspace of a clay utensil is contaminable as part of the inner space. The pertinent pericopae are as follows:

A. Inside-outside

1. Attributed to Hezekiah before Gamaliel the Elder (Sifra Shemini Parashah 7:5: Whatever has no inside has no outer parts among clay utensils (= M. 27:1G).

56   THE MISHNAH BEFORE 70

2. M. 25:7-8: Utensils have an outer part, an inner part, and a holding place, which are regarded as separate from one another.

[3. M. 2:1E-F: Clay utensils are made unclean from the contact of uncleanness with their inner space but not with their outer sides. This rule is not attested at Yavneh. It is, however, the opposite of the implication of M. 25:1A/25:7-8, that utensils are divided and their parts do not affect one another. M. 2:1E-F cannot come before Hezekiah's saying, No. 1, because it spells out the implications of that saying—but so does No. 2.]

[4. M. 10:1-3: The finger-hold is part of the utensil. This is the Temple rule of M. 25:9. + Houses, M. 9:1 vs. M. 10:1.]

B. *Receptacles*

1. Any sort of receptacle is susceptible (M. 17:16). The nature of receptacles and the uncleanness of utensils which have them is a given for Yavneans.

2. M. 30:2: All parties agree a receptacle is susceptible. The issue is whether it is a normal one.

3. M. 8:9D-H, M. 12:3.

4. The further implication of M. 17:16 is that flat (wooden) utensils are insusceptible.

5. M. 12:3: Gamaliel says a domestic metal basket cover is susceptible, because it forms a receptacle.

6. M. 26:2E-F: That receptacles are susceptible is taken for granted.

C. *Clay Utensils are susceptible through the contamination of airspace:*

1. M. 2:8C-E: Comb of water-cooler (Eliezer).

A second group of Yavnean presuppositions concerns the susceptibility of any sort of utensil. The stress is on the traits of utensils in general, not on characteristics of specific substances, which, overall, is not a predominant concern among Yavnean rulings. The principle may be stated as follows: A susceptible utensil is one which is useful and which has a distinctive trait or quality or character of its own. An insusceptible utensil is one which is useless, that is, broken. What therefore is taken for granted is that a utensil is susceptible, a non-utensil is not. Yavneans furthermore take for granted a development of this last point, a perforated utensil is regarded as broken and insusceptible.

A. *What is permanently used or kept is susceptible. What is discarded is not.*

1. M. 17:2.

B. *An autonomous, useful object is susceptible, one which has no distinctive character is not susceptible.*

1. M. 11:8H-I; M. 11:4F-K; M. 11:7C-E.

2. M. 12:5A-E: What makes a nail a distinctive utensil? Takes for granted the fundamental principle.
   3. M. 20:4: Same issue for a trough, this time turning a trough into a bench.
   4. M. 22:9A-C: A wooden block, same issue. + T. B.B. 2:4.
   5. M. 22:10: Occasional use *vs.* distinctive function.
   6. M. 27:5: Same issue for sifter.
   7. M. 12:3: Autonomous utensils are susceptible.
   8. M. 12:4-5.
   [9. M. 5:10D-F: The oven of Ben Dinaʾi has to stand by itself.]
   10. T. B.B. 4:5: ʿAqiva and the sages take for granted a normal utensil is susceptible.

C. *A perforated or broken utensil is insusceptible.*

   1. M. 7:1: The principle is taken for granted. The issue is solely, how large a perforation?
   2. M. 2:2: A sherd which serves in the way it did before breaking is susceptible. This seems a qualification of the fundamental principle that breaking is purifying.
   3. M. 2:4C-E: All parties agree receptacles are susceptible.

The third important presupposition of Yavnean rulings concerns the relationship of metal to wood. If wood is subsidiary to metal, it is susceptible as metal, and even the presence of a single part made of metal, which carries out a significant function, renders the entire utensil susceptible. The presupposition is that a flat wooden object normally is insusceptible, while a flat metal object is susceptible. The evidence is as follows:

A. *Wood subsidiary to metal is susceptible as metal.*

   1. M. 13:7C: Joshua says he cannot explain the inherited ruling that a single metal tooth makes a wooden comb susceptible. Accordingly, a flat wooden object is normally insusceptible.
   2. M. 11:4: Wood plated with metal is clean.
   3. T. B.M. 1:5: Halafta, ʿAqiva. + M. 11:6.

We have two further principles taken for granted in Yavnean rulings.

The fourth is that what is used for sitting or lying is susceptible to *midras*. What is not used for sitting or lying is susceptible to corpse- and other uncleanness. The cases are at M. 26:5D-F and M. 28:2.

The fifth and final principle is that a damaged clay utensil in the tent of a corpse does not afford protection. Eliezer's view, that we do partition clay utensils (M. 8:6, against the sages of M. 8:1) is probably new to him; the sages, I think, carry forward an inherited rule, or, rather, affirm an inherited anomaly.

Let us now contrast the established principles with those which seem to have been created to begin with in the Yavnean period. These raise quite fundamental issues:

A. *How to render an oven susceptible to uncleanness or insusceptible?*

1. M. 5:10A-C + 5:8C: If one cut an oven into rings and removed the plaster, it is clean. Eliezer says it is not clean.

2. M. 5:1/4:4E: Making an oven susceptible to uncleanness is a dispute between Judah and Meir, based upon a disagreement between Eliezer and ᶜAqiva. It is difficult to see that the issue had been raised and settled before Eliezer and ᶜAqiva, whose argument is wholly exegetical and cites no antecedent rules or precedents, let alone established cases.

B. *Does an inverted, sealed jar afford protection in the tent of a corpse?*

1. M. 10:1: Eliezer's view and that of the sages shows no principle common to both opinions.

C. *The meaning of connection*

1. M. 23:1 does not suggest that an established, antecedent opinion was available to both parties.

2. T. B.Q. 3:4 likewise does not appear to have been based upon an established principle about connecting pitch to wood, or even about how connections were to be effected.

3. M. 28:7, by contrast, affirms for all parties that a patch must be firmly attached to form a connector.

To the degree that the principle of connection was taken for granted at Yavneh and may have derived from pre-70 times, it consisted solely of the proposition that objects connected to one another in a very firm way would convey uncleanness to one another. The modes of purification of connected objects, by contrast, cannot have been raised before Ushan times.

D. *Whole Utensils and Broken Utensils*

While it is clear that all Yavneans took for granted a broken utensil was clean, the issue is raised by Eliezer and Joshua about whether susceptibility and purification applies also to broken ones.

1. M. 14:7 + M. 18:9: Eliezer holds susceptibility and purification pertain only to whole utensils. Joshua says sherds are also subject to uncleanness. I do not see how the antecedent law can have raised the question.
2. M. 17:1: The size of a perforation which renders a utensil insusceptible.

E. *The Beginning and End of Susceptibility*

1. The question of unfinished metal utensils and whether they are susceptible seems first raised by Gamaliel + ᶜAqiva (M. 14:1, 14:5). + M. 12:6.
2. M. 28:2: Is throwing out a cloth an act of purification? Is discarding equivalent to breaking?

While it may be reasonable to suppose that from pre-70 times came rulings on the susceptibility of numerous specific objects, in point of fact we are unable to find a Yavnean attestation for major *lists* of such objects. The Yavnean discussions of individual items, it already is clear, involve just a few general principles, in the main, about the autonomy and distinctiveness of a utensil. So it cannot be shown that in the tradition before 70 were rulings on many individual items, from which general principles were deduced. On the whole, the contrary seems to have been the pattern. This is an unexpected—if very tentative—result.

iii. The Houses

It generally is supposed both that the Houses go back to the time of Shammai and Hillel, ca. A.D., and that their traditions attest the state of the law in at least the last fifty years before 70. But this cannot be taken for granted, for the names of the Houses are routinely used as mnemonic devices for the recording of opinions on controverted matters. Ushans, for example, do not hesitate to supply to the Houses a more complex problem, for their established opinions ("unclean," "clean") than is originally given. They will supply the Houses' names to disputes on principles first under discussion long after 70. We cannot, therefore, take for granted that the attributions to the Houses invariably supply firm evidence of the relative antiquity of sayings, for the criterion employed above (pp. 237-243), to show the relative reliability of attributions to Yavneans, then Ushans, does not apply without variation or exception. That is to say, while opinions attributed to Ushans, where relevant to matters covered in opinions attributed to Yavneans, nearly always in substance and reasoning follow upon Yavnean sayings, taking for granted and augmenting their conclusions, the same is not so for the Houses. Indeed, we have observed in at least one instance, M. 18:1, that we have opinions on the same matter both in the names of the Houses, and in the names of Ushans in behalf of the Houses, and in the names of Ushans without reference to the Houses at all. The same matter, moreover, depends on a dispute between Meir and Judah in M. 15:1.

In order, therefore, to make use of the Houses' disputes in assessing the state of the law before 70, we have to reconsider each item and ask whether it seems to refer to Ushan issues and modes of inquiry or whether it seems ignorant of them. Only in the latter case will it be possible with some certainty to assign the substance of the Houses' opinion to the period of Yavneh or even earlier. For, obviously, if the Houses debated an issue, and the decided law was assigned to the Hillelites, then the Ushans should not have faced and worked on the same matter or principle. The cases, following our list on pp. 249-251, are as follows.

1. M. 9:2/M. 10:1: Does a tightly-fitting cover afford protection to a metal object or only food, liquid, and other clay objects?

2. M. 11:3: The susceptibility of nails. The context requires the issue to concern nails the origin of which we do not know. But by itself, the issue is simply nails—as with Ṣadoq, M. 12:4-5, with the criteria of autonomy and distinctiveness taken for granted.

3. M. 14:2E-H: Again, the context imposes a complex issue. But by itself, the Houses' dispute concerns when a siphon ceases to constitute a susceptible object. The principles at hand, on which all parties agree, are 1. autonomy and 2. usefulness. These assuredly are Yavnean at the latest. The Shammaites require damage, the Hillelites, attachment. It will naturally follow from this dispute that an object which is damaged or loses its independent status becomes insusceptible, and other disputes which take for granted the same principle will be equally authentic to Yavneh, if not earlier.

The Ushan attestation in T. B.M. 4:5 does not introduce new principles. It does, however, indicate that the two established ones may be assigned to either House. That means the Ushans had no tradition assigning usefulness as the primary criterion for one House, autonomy to the other (as with Judah/Meir materials)—surely a sign of the authenticity of the dispute. But, as often, the Ushan redefinition of the issue hardly tells us what was the problem to begin with.

4. M. 20:2: The issue is whether the trough is used for sitting. The Hillelites say it is not, therefore is susceptible only to corpse-uncleanness. The Shammaites say it is, so is susceptible to *midras*. Accordingly, on the surface the Yavnean (and Scriptural) principle

that that which is used for sitting is susceptible to *midras* is applied to an intermediate item. The remainder of M. 20:2 assumes the correctness of the Shammaite view. Here we cannot suppose Meir's stress on form (M. 19:9-10) is necessarily behind, or to be read into, the pericope. + T. B.M. 11:3.

5. M. 20:6: A sheet used for lying loses its susceptibility to *midras* when it is no longer available for lying. This takes place, all parties agree, when it is no longer a sheet but is turned into a curtain. The only issue is when that takes place. ᶜAqiva participates in the structure, as well as issue, of the pericope.

+ But T. B.M. 1:8 ignores the Houses entirely. Yosé b. R. Judah and Eleazar b. R. Simeon debate whether the sheet, after being made into a curtain, is susceptible at all. The Houses take for granted that it is susceptible. T. B.M. 11:8E assumes "purification" means complete insusceptibility, not merely from *midras*. + T. B.M. 11:9.

6. M. 22:4E-H: A chair affixed to a trough is susceptible to *midras*, the Shammaites say. It remains an autonomous object. The Hillelites say it is insusceptible, having lost its identity. Shammai says even if it is carved into the trough, it is susceptible. I do not see how the Houses' dispute differs from M. 20:3. An unclean chair attached to a post is unclean—it retains its autonomy. One made on a post is unclean—Shammai's position. Here again we have the Shammaite view without a dispute. M. 20:5 relates in the same way.

7. M. 26:6: The issue is whether the bag will be used for sitting.

8. M. 28:4: If "susceptible" means, to *midras*, then the issue is as above. The Shammaites hold the wrappers will be used for sitting. The Hillelites hold those which are ornamented will not be used for sitting. Gamaliel is internal to the structure of the pericope. Yosé and Simeon attest. The reading of *Simeon b.* Gamaliel is difficult.

9. T. B.B. 5:7-8: A belt made out of the side of a garment needs no hem, the Shammaites hold. The Hillelites say it needs a hem. I am not sure what principle is at hand. Perhaps it comes down to whether the belt is an autonomous object without some hem. Ushans attest.

10. T. B.M. 4:16/M. 14:8: The principle taken for granted by both Houses is that a utensil to be susceptible must serve its normal purpose.

The disputes between the Houses which do not seem to concern problems unfamiliar at Yavneh at the latest thus take for granted the following principles:

1. The effects of a tightly-fitting cover: No. 1.
2. A susceptible object is one which is a utensil, that is, autonomous and of distinctive character: Nos. 2, 3, 6, 9 (?), 10.
3. The difference between *midras-* and corpse-uncleanness is whether or not an object is used for sitting: Nos. 4, 5, 6, 7, 8.

We have, in addition, several items which seems to involve principles otherwise unattested for Yavneh, as follows:

1. M. 15:1: Judah and Meir debate the susceptibility of vessels which hold more than forty seʾahs etc. Meir says they are susceptible, Judah says they are not. Meir will not care when a utensil reaches the specified volume or how we know that volume. It makes no difference to him. Only to Judah is this a significant issue. Accordingly, the debate, M. 18:1, on how we measure a utensil's volume is important only to Judah and depends on his opinion. M. 18:1 is probably pseudepigraphic. The silence of Yavneans on the question probably means it is Ushan to begin with. Underlying Judah's and Meir's dispute is the issue of form (Meir) *vs.* function (Judah), and that same issue *may* be discerned in M. 14:2 (use *vs.* autonomy). So it is possible, but I think highly improbable, that both Houses' regarded use as a primary consideration, and so, early and independently, came to the second-level issue debated here. Overall, however, I think the version of M. 18:1 is pseudepigraphic. M. 18:1 is attested by Yosé who shares Judah's view of the centrality of function, and Simeon Shezuri, whose opinion on the larger issue we do not know.

2. M. 22:4A-D: The Houses debate the susceptibility of a bride's chair which cannot be used for a bride. The Shammaites hold it is still susceptible as a container. The Hillelites say it is clean. Here the issue can only be secondary purpose, with the Shammaites in accord with Meir's view in M. 19:9-10.

3. M. 29:8: The length of various remnants. We do not have a single Yavnean ruling on this matter. The mnemonic purpose is self-evident; Yosé gloss marks it as Ushan at the latest. Perhaps it also is an Ushan mnemonic.

4. T. B.M. 3:8: Nathan b. R. Joseph assigns Meir's principle to the House of Shammai.

[5. T. B.Q. 6:18: Eleazar b. R. Simeon phrases as a Houses' dispute M. 9:6's rule that new peat may be clean. But old peat may not be unclean. M. is not relevant to Kelim, and I do not know what principle is at hand.]

Of these items, No. 1 is the most likely to represent pseudepigraphic use of the names of the Houses for mnemonic purposes. It looks as though the names of the Houses are used either in support of Judah's position, with both Houses agreeing with him, as in No. 1, or in contradiction to Meir's, with Meir represented as Shammaite, hence rejected, as in Nos. 2 and 4. The mnemonic value of the Houses names to preserve the sequence, seven through ten, is obvious in M. 29:8, but the primary reason for supposing that the item is Ushan is the otherwise unknown issue of the pericope, the lengths of remnants. Without a single Yavnean allusion to that matter, we can hardly suppose the item to be accurately attributed to the pre-Yavnean Houses. No. 5 is difficult only because it is not a problem of Kelim, so we cannot assess the state of Yavnean opinion on it.

We thus are on firm grounds to assign to the period before 70 three very fundamental issues.

First is an effort to work out the effects of a tightly-fitting cover on clay utensils in the tent of a corpse, with the problem of deciding the result of such a cover for metal.

Second, on the definition of a utensil, all parties are in agreement that an object constitutes a utensil and is susceptible when it is autonomous and exhibits distinctive character and use.

Finally comes the view that *midras*-uncleanness affects things used for sitting, with the concomitant principle that when something formerly employed for that purpose ceases to be useful it ceases to be susceptible to *midras* uncleanness.

When we review the principles clearly assigned to Yavnean authorities, we find these same three principles or issues, and in addition, the matter of the division of utensils, receptacles, breakage as purification, the relationship of metal to wood. Of these items, only the last two look to be important innovations of the Yavnean thinkers, for the division of utensils and the closely-related matter of the division of utensils are issues attributed to the time of Gamaliel the Elder and, in the latter instance, Yohanan b. Zakkai. Both are contemporaries of the Houses.

Let us now consider the relationships between these principles and their Scriptural foundations, to see which of them is apt to have required an extensive antecedent exegetical tradition or indeed to have been generated by exegesis of Scripture at all.

iv. From Scripture to Yavneh

Two issues are before us. First, to what degree are the several earliest laws or principles based upon the plain meaning of Scriptures? Second, in what measure do the statements of principles either presuppose or make explicit a considerable, antecedent exegesis of Scriptures? For example, if a Yavnean law is worked out primarily through reasoning, without reference to Scriptural support, then we may hardly imagine that an ancient exegetical tradition, long under development, stands behind the result of the reasoning or, indeed, that the sages had in hand any sort of tradition at all.

Let us now review those Scriptures pertinent to the laws of utensils, observing also the Scriptures which seem to have generated no laws at all. The relevant passages are as follows:

> Lev. 11:29: And these are unclean to you among the swarming things that swarm upon the earth...
>
> 11:31: These [afore-named] are unclean to you among all that swarm. Whoever touches them when they are dead shall be unclean until the evening.
>
> 11:32: And anything upon which any of them falls when they are dead shall be unclean, whether it is an article of wood or a garment or a skin or a sack, any vessel that is used for any purpose; it must be put into water, and it shall be unclean until the evening. Then it shall be clean.
>
> 11:33: And if any of them falls into any earthen vessel, all that is in it shall be unclean, and you shall break it.
>
> 11:34: Any food in it which may be eaten, upon which water may come, shall be unclean; and all drink which may be drunk from every such vessel shall be unclean.
>
> 11:35: And everything upon which any part of their carcass falls shall be unclean; whether oven or stove, it shall be broken in pieces; they are unclean, and shall be unclean to you.
>
> Lev. 15:4-6: Every bed on which he who has the discharge lies shall be unclean; and everything on which he sits shall be unclean. And any one who touches his bed shall wash his clothes and bathe himself in water, and be unclean until the evening. And whoever sits on anything on which he who has the discharge has sat shall wash his clothes and bathe himself in water and be unclean until the evening.
>
> Lev. 15:9-12: And any saddle on which he who has the discharge rides shall be unclean. And whoever touches anything that was under him shall be unclean until the evening; and he who carries such a thing shall wash his clothes and bathe himself in water and be unclean until the evening. Any one whom he that has the discharge touches without having rinsed his hands in water shall wash his clothes and bathe himself in water and be unclean until the evening. And the earthen vessel which he who has the discharge touches shall be broken; and every vessel of wood shall be rinsed in water.
>
> Lev. 15:19-24: When a woman has a discharge of blood which is her regular discharge from her body, she shall be in her impurity for seven days, and whoever touches her shall be unclean until the evening. And everything upon which she lies during her impurity shall be unclean; everything also upon which she sits shall be unclean. And whoever touches her bed shall wash his clothes and bathe himself in water and be unclean until the evening. And whoever touches anything upon which she sits shall wash his clothes and bathe himself in water and be unclean until the evening, whether it is the bed or anything upon which she sits, when he touches it he shall be unclean until the evening.
>
> Num. 19:14-15: This is the law when a man dies in a tent: everyone

who comes into the tent, and everyone who is in the tent, shall be unclean seven days. And every open vessel, which has no cover fastened upon it, is unclean.

Num. 31:19-24: Encamp outside the camp seven days; whoever of you has killed any person, and whoever has touched any slain, purify yourselves and your captives on the third day and on the seventh day. You shall purify every garment, every article of skin, all work of goats' hair, and every article of wood. And Eleazar the priest said to the men of war who had gone to battle: This is the statute of the law which the Lord has commanded Moses: Only the gold, the silver, the bronze, the iron, the tin, and the lead, everything that can stand the fire, you shall pass through the fire and it shall be clean. Nevertheless it shall also be purified with the water of impurity; and whatever cannot stand the fire you shall pass through the water. You must wash your clothes on the seventh day, and you shall be clean; and afterward you shall come into the camp.

Without further ado, we may eliminate from further consideration three Yavnean or pre-Yavnean principles.

1. *Midras-uncleanness affects something which is used for sitting or lying.*

This matter is made explicit in Lev. 15:4-6, 9-12, and 19-24. No one had to look further than these verses to find the view that things used for sitting are susceptible to *midras*-uncleanness. This applies both for sitting (*moshav*) and for riding (*merkav*), as we saw. What lies behind the concept of pressure, or *midras*, however, is not to be gainsaid; but it is not, at present, our problem.

2. *The effects of the tent over the corpse-uncleanness are nullified by a tightly-sealed cover.*

Num. 19:15 is simply turned into an affirmative statement. Every closed vessel, with a tightly-sealed cover, is clean. The Houses' debate (M. 9:2) on clay utensils' protection for metal is phrased entirely in terms of rational analysis, without a hint as to an antecedent tradition based on Scriptural exegesis.

The proper location of the cover seems also to be a point first raised by Eliezer.

3. *Breaking a clay utensil cleans it.*

Lev. 11:33 is simply completed: All that is in it shall be unclean, and you shall break it *and then it is clean*. All issues on breaking as purification depend upon that simple allegation. All are Yavnean or later, based on rational inquiry into the meaning of breaking, investigated in accord with the principle that a susceptible object is one which is useful—a utensil. So breaking means rendering useless. It goes without saying that, since Scripture is clear, no one will have had to engage in elaborate processes of reasoning or argument to conclude that a perforated or broken—thus useless—utensil is insusceptible.

The central issue of utensils, however, concerns normal use, distinctiveness, autonomy, and the whole range of conceptions intimately related to use. Without finding that fundamental conception in Scriptures, we shall have to look for, or at least postulate, a very substantial layer of exegesis, conceptual innovation, or both. How would a legal philosopher, whenever he lived, have come to the conception that a random object becomes a utensil, therefore is susceptible, at the point at which it is useful, and ceases to be a utensil, therefore becomes insusceptible, when it is useless?

It seems to me the answer is simply that, opening Scripture, anyone at any time will have found the following at Lev. 11:32: "Any vessel that is used for any purpose," KL KLY ʾŠR YʿŠH MLʾKH BHM. The point is that, since there are some objects, also referred to as KLY, which are not "used for any purpose," after listing various materials, Scripture adds, "every utensil." This must function as an inclusionary phrase, followed by "used for any purpose," a limiting one—and the rest follows. That very simple process of reasoning, governing the answer to the question, raised throughout our study, "when is a KLY a utensil?" begins in a not very close reading of Scripture. So much for an object as *utensil*, that is, as something useful.

Now let us ask about autonomy and distinctiveness? These, I think, are the clear intent of the construction in inclusionary, then exclusionary, clauses: "Every KLY made of any material" will include any object whatsoever. Then, "any KLY used for any purpose" excludes the just-stated proposition, for we no longer have in mind *any* KLY, meaning any object, but now refer explicitly to any KLY meaning any *useful* object. In other words, as soon as we refer to use, autonomy and distinctiveness will, in the nature of the Scripture, follow in its wake. Indeed, it is entirely possible that the categories of autonomy and distinctiveness ("having a name of its own") are Mishnaic ways of rephrasing the primary Scriptural statement, "with which work is done."

Add to this the view that an insusceptible utensil is one which is broken, and the matter of usefulness is reenforced. Restatements of the same matter will include the issue of permanence, on the one side, or perforation and breaking on the other. In this matter we then include the oven. Everyone will agree breaking an oven purifies it, since Lev. 11:33 says so. The only question is, What is breaking?

The conception of Eliezer in M. 5:10A is that breaking the oven and then reconstructing it so that it is useful, but not in its former form, does not constitute breaking. So Eliezer's notion, carried forward by Judah, is that "breaking" means "rendering useless," with stress on function, and not merely altering the primary form. If the oven still functions as before, despite the alteration of its form, it will be susceptible. What is important in this instance is the primary and unmediated resort to Scripture, the spelling out of matters directly consequent upon the open-endedness of the Scriptural statement.

Let us now ask about the matter of receptacles and the closely-related issue of the division of a utensil into inner and outer parts. Lev. 11:33 speaks of "falling into its midst" (ʾL TWKW), and we have seen the exegetical result: "That which has a 'midst'" against that which does not. Clearly, the interpretation of TWK to mean "that which has an inside, a receptacle," is not going to require a great many intervening stages of reasoning. Once we are told "whatever falls into the midst," it is going to be a short step indeed to a negative formulation, "what has no 'midst'" is not going to be subject to the susceptibility of an insect in contained air space. So far we are in close accord with the simple meaning of the verse.

The saying of Hezekiah before Gamaliel the Elder, and the conception attested to, but hardly originated by, Yoḥanan b. Zakkai that that which has a receptacle is susceptible, simply make explicit what Scripture makes quite clear to begin with. There is, however, an important qualification. Lev. 11:33 speaks of clay utensils, and so too does Hezekiah. Yet by the time of the saying attributed to Yoḥanan b. Zakkai, "the midst" of a clay utensil has been extended to all utensils. And this is central to the interpretation of Yoḥanan b. Zakkai's materials in M. 17:16, therefore to M. 17:15 as well: Whatever has a receptacle—*of any sort*—is susceptible. The key words must therefore be MKL MQWM, of any sort, with the qualification as to permanence and use of secondary importance. The distance from "TWK of clay utensils" to TWK of any sort of utensil has been covered, so to speak, from Gamaliel the Elder to Yoḥanan b. Zakkai, who comments on a secondary effect of the larger rule, concerning all receptacles.

I tend to think that some time between the point of Hezekiah's testimony—let us say, ca. 40 A.D.—and the observation of Yoḥanan b. Zakkai—let us say, 75 A.D. (to speak in unrefined terms for the moment, for Yoḥanan, after all, was a contemporary of Gamaliel the Elder), the conception of receptacle was applied to all sorts of utensils made of all sorts of materials. Obviously, this sort of guess relies upon many infirm presuppositions, first, about the accuracy of attributions, also about the correctness of our interpretation of the meaning of the two sayings. But, assuming for the moment we are right, what will have taken place between Gamaliel the Elder and Yoḥanan b. Zakkai?

I think all that has happened is a reading of Lev. 11:33 in the context of 11:32. Lev. 11:32 speaks of objects made of any material, limited by the insistence that they be useful. Lev. 11:33 then speaks specifically of any earthen vessel, but its point is not that the vessel has to have 'an inside'—that is Hezekiah's point. Lev. 11:33 simply states that if a creeping thing falls into any earthen vessel, the vessel's contents will be susceptible. All the exegete has to have done is take at face value the reference to the "inside," at the same time correctly interpreting that reference to be tangential to the point of the law. That is, the law does not state, "clay utensils alone have an inner part," which is contaminable through its airspace (the falling of the creeping thing into the contained space). The Scripture takes for granted there is a contained space, explaining the effects of a creeping thing's falling into it. The exegete then will have taken for granted that anything which in like manner forms a receptacle is going to be susceptible. What Lev. 11:33 will have told him is that only clay utensils' *airspace* is susceptible, excluding the airspace of utensils made of other materials.

Two important ideas have been ignored, first, the division of utensils, second, the relationship of wood to metal. I am unable to see any basis in Scripture for that latter issue, let alone for the way in which it is resolved. If, as I suppose, it is a Yavnean contribution, then it stands to reason it is a point raised at Yavneh specifically because settled issues involving utility and serviceability raised secondary ones, concerning the primary surface which is used. I tend to think the conception of wood as secondary and of metal as primary simply is based upon the recognition of the primary function of the metal object attached to a wood handle. The specific problem, for example, the spinner adjudged by ᶜAqiva (either susceptible or insusceptible, depending on the tradition we prefer), hardly seems important. It is the Ushans who showed the conceptual profundity of the issue. Joshua's simple observation that he cannot explain the inherited ruling certainly shows, I think, that some sort of rules came down to Yavneh on the subject; Joshua cannot fully explain the anomalies. In this minor matter, the relationship to Scripture cannot have been clear to Joshua, and the probable reason is that there was none.

Before proceeding to the division of utensils, however, let us test our conception of the earliest exegesis of Scripture against the evidence of Sifra. Our interest is to see whether Sifra preserves exegeses, properly assigned or not, which accord with our conception of what should reflect issues fundamental to the Yavnean and pre-Yavnean corpus of rules.

1. Sifra Shemini 7:3: Simply cites M.-T.
2. Sifra Shemini 7:5: Hezekiah before Gamaliel: "into its midst —that which has a 'midst' is susceptible to uncleanness, and that which does not is not." The importance of this exegesis is already clear.
3. Sifra Shemini 10:5-6: Eliezer vs. ᶜAqiva on the beginning of susceptibility of ovens: Is heating required?
4. Sifra Shemini 10:10: "Will be for you"—"whatever is for your needs, to include the handles of utensils." This exegetical basis for connection is forthwith tied to Judah's rule, M. 5:2. Whether the exegesis comes before Judah, even in Yavnean times, we cannot say. But "to include..." cannot come before Judah, simply because it alludes to his case. What remains, however, is stress on the usefulness to man, excluding, I suppose, utensils. Judah alleges ᶜAqiva will not have been surprised by that rule, and perhaps from "will be for you... whatever...," the principle of connection was spun out. That seems to me possible, if far-fetched. But a rule founded on the exegesis available before 70, hardly is self-evident. No effort is made to link "for your needs" to any early-Yavnean issue.
5. Sifra Shemini 10:2-3: It will be unclean: The whole oven is unclean, the divided (broken) one is clean. This is the plain meaning of Scripture: "breaking is purifying." It is cited in connection with Meir's view of purifying an oven.
6. Sifra Shemini 10:4: Same exegesis as above, different Mishnah.
7. Sifra Shemini 10:7-8: It will be overturned...clean. That which can be overturned is susceptible, that which cannot be overturned is not susceptible...except for an oven of stone, etc. The importance of 'overturning' is linked to M. 5:11, to which it is only marginally relevant. But no Yavnean or pre-Yavnean rule at its foundation depends on this exegesis, so far as I can see. The importance of the exegesis seems to me exactly what the redactor tells us—that is, to prove Judah's case in M. 5:11.
8. Sifra Shemini 10:9: The same exegesis as above, to prove another point for Judah, this time M. 6:2.
9. Sifra Shemini 7:10-11: Re M. 8:1, merely cites debate. No clear exegetical link to M.
10. Sifra Shemini 7:8: "All which is in it will be unclean, and not that which is inside its inner part." This is the basis for the subdivision of ovens, M. 8:2, which continues the discussion of M. 8:1 from the sages' viewpoint. Perhaps the exegesis therefore is pre-70. The relevance of No. 5 is obvious. The whole set stands behind the

tradition maintained by the sages and rejected by Elieezr. This group furthermore is to be linked to Hezekiah's saying, for when one distinguishes the outer from the inner part, then, but not before, one will also distinguish the "inside" from the "inside of the inside" as is done here.

11. Sifra Shemini 9:1: Utensils are not made unclean through the airspace of a clay utensil. This is to be expanded to, "clay utensils do not render clay utensils unclean. Only a Father of uncleanness renders a clay utensil unclean, not something unclean in the first degree." This rule is one of the primary principles of our tractate, everywhere taken for granted and nowhere spelled out in M. I should be inclined to regard the rule, and the underlying exegesis, as part of the pre-70 tradition, even though it is nowhere important in the Yavnean part of the law. This surmise is supported by the fact that the rule clearly operates in M. 8:3, part of the extended discussion of the sages' position *vis à vis* Eliezer in M. 8:1.

12. Sifra Shemini 7:2: That one of them may fall—there are among them those which render unclean, and there are among them those which do not render unclean, to exclude + M. 8:5.

13. Sifra Shemini 6:5-6: Cites M. 15:1, Judah's and Meir's dispute. The direct Scriptural exegeses are pertinent only to proving the points of the dispute and do not seem to have generated the dispute.

14. Sifra Shemini 6:7: Cites T. B.M. 5:1.

15. Sifra Shemini 6:4: Just as sacking serves man and things which serve man, etc. While linked to T. B.M. 6:7/M. 16:7, the exegesis is independent of both and may stand behind the rule attributed by Judah to ᶜAqiva, just as with No. 4 above. But if this is so, the original exegesis has been submerged into the language and issues of M.-T.

16. Sifra Meṣoraᶜ Zabim 2:4-5: Restates M. 19:1.

17. Sifra Meṣoraᶜ Zabim 2:3-4 and 2:3: Cites M. 20:1.

18. Sifra Meṣoraᶜ Zabim 3:2: The exegesis proves that an empty utensil on which a *Zab* might sit is regarded as equivalent to a full one. This principle is simply an extension of Scripture's stress on what can be used as a seat as something susceptible to *midras*. The principle seems to me important, but I do not see close relationship to any rule before us.

19. Sifra Meṣoraᶜ Zabim 2:6: Cites and backs up M. 20:2.

20. Sifra Meṣoraᶜ Zabim 3:9-11: *Merkav* is different from *moshav*. The distinction is important for M. 23:2, which is cited. But it plays no role in a single pericope attested at Yavneh or in the disputes probably rightly attributed to the Houses. The Houses here know no such distinction. But the matter is so unimportant to Kelim as a whole that that fact is not decisive in assessing the origin of the exegesis.

The important items are as follows: No. 2, already considered; Nos. 4 + 15: what is susceptible is something which serves man; and Nos. 5, 9, 10, 11, 12 (and, as noted, No. 10 depends on No. 2), all of which relate in one way or another to M. 8:1ff., Eliezer's and the sages' consideration of what we posited to be an anomaly in inherited laws. This set probably does provide insight into the state of exegesis before the time of Eliezer b. Hyrcanus. The rules based on that exegesis are 1. utensils are viewed as divided in various ways; 2. clay utensils do not render clay utensils unclean, a secondary development of the issue of airspace. (I think items 16-20 had best be considered in the context of M. Zabim. The relationship to our tractate is tenuous.)

It follows that the saying of Hezekiah to Gamaliel the Elder marks the earliest phase in the formation of an exegetical tradition on the matter of the cleanness of utensils. When, as shown here, we separate the exegeses from the attached citations of M., we find pretty much the same principles attested at Yavneh or by the Houses: first, usefulness is decisive, with the further point, perhaps Yavnean, that usefulness is determined by human needs; second, utensils may be divided and subdivided; third, breaking ("overturning") purifies ovens. It therefore is clear that whatever "very ancient" exegeses are preserved in Sifra, when separated from the Yavnean and Ushan materials to which they are attached, all seem to relate to the principles we are able to posit as under development from the time of Gamaliel the Elder to early Yavnean times. Nothing generated by exegesis is apt to reflect issues or principles important at some unknown time before the last decades of the Temple's existence and the first years of Yavneh. Over all, it is very difficult to suppose that the fundamental issues and principles which underlie the development of Kelim depend upon an exegetical tradition beginning at any point before the first century. To be sure, anyone might have opened Scriptures and learned that an object forms a susceptible utensil when it is used for some work—that is, when it is useful. But if that obvious conclusion was drawn, it produced no result whatsoever before the mid-first century at the earliest. The same is so of the other exegeses of Scripture pertinent to the earliest parts of the laws of Kelim.

We have left to the end the matter of the division of utensils. This is to be considered in connection with the Synoptics' controversy-saying pertinent to Kelim. But at the outset it must be clear that the importance of dividing utensils can have been assessed only after utensils were held to be divided for purposes of uncleanness, that is to say, after the importance of a receptacle for the containing of uncleanness was established. Without the requirement of a receptacle, one has, after all, no "inner part" to be distinguished from the "outer part," or non-receptacle.

v. "First Cleanse the Inside"

The matter still outstanding concerns the division of utensils into inner and outer parts for the purpose of assessing susceptibility and uncleanness alike. Here we come to the one pericope in the Synoptic tradition directly relevant to Kelim. Luke 11:39 is in the setting of a controversy with a Pharisee, so at the outset it is taken for granted the issue is sectarian law. The Pharisee is surprised that Jesus did not wash before dinner (Lk. 11:39):

> "And he Lord said to him, "Now you Pharisees cleanse the outside of the cup and of the dish, but inside you are full of extortion and wickedness (11:39). You fools! Did not he who made the outside make the inside also (11:40)? But give for alms those things which are within, and behold, everything is clean for you (11:41)."

The passage in Matthew (23:25-6) omits the narrative setting, adds the *woe*-preamble, and then provides a more apposite homily:

> "Woe to you, scribes and Pharisees, hypocrites! For you cleanse the outside of the cup and of the plate, but inside they are full of extortion and rapacity. You blind Pharisee. First cleanse the inside of the cup and of the plate, that the outside also may be clean."

The original Q saying, Professor Wayne Meeks observes, is evidently garbled in some fashion in the extant versions. Neither the Lukan version nor the Matthean can make much claim at representing the original, Mt. because the figurative 'contents' of the cup or plate, "robbery and extortion," do not fit the context of purity-questions nor the proposed remedy, "first cleanse the inside." Luke's "give what is inside to charity," however, seems even more jarring in context, while the "inside" becomes "what is inside you." Professor Meeks proposes that originally there was a simple aphorism, like Mt. 23: 25b-c: "You cleanse the outside of the cup and plate, but not the inside. Hypocrites! First cleanse the inside and then the outside will be clean." This may have been intended for a moralizing, anti-ritual interpretation, as in Mk. 7:15. One stage of the moralizing is to name the contents as vices, which Mt. merges with the original saying, with somewhat irrational results, while Lk., by carrying through the notion to underline that it is the inner man that is meant, destroys the form. The only versions we actually have, Meeks comments, presuppose that inside/outside is to be interpreted metaphorically.

I shall now propose that when its aphorism was coined, the debate over the priority of inside *vs.* outside was a live issue. We begin by noting that the point of both versions of the saying presupposes that a distinction is made between the inside and outside of a cup or plate. Second, the saying takes for granted Pharisees first or only cleanse the outside. If the contrary was taken for granted, that is, that Pharisees cleanse the inside of the cup before they cleanse the outside, or do not cleanse the outside at all, then the homily is utterly without meaning. One is not going to score points against people who first do clean the inside by saying to them—in however metaphorical a sense—"first cleanse the inside." That is what they do anyhow; the metaphor is useless.

The value of these saying for the consideration of the pre-70 state of the laws of Kelim is not obvious on the surface. For we cannot take for granted Jesus really said these things, nor do we know at what point in the early years of the formation of the Synoptic traditions the sayings were attributed to him. So we shall have to take the sayings as evidence that, at some point before the redaction of Matthew and Luke, and very likely, at some point early in the formation of Q, it was clearly taken for granted that Pharisees divide cups and plates for the purposes of uncleanness, on the one side, and cleanse the outside (without regard to the inside—this point is unclear) on the, second, and more difficult, side.

We may forthwith supply a *terminus ante quem* for the sayings. M. 25:1A is clear that one distinguishes the inside from the outside of a utensil (without regard to the substance of which it is composed.) But the Ushan dispute on the matter is little help. What is of much greater help is the saying attributed to Hezekiah. If we rely upon the attribution, then we may assign to the period before Gamaliel the Elder's death, at about 50, but after his estimated time of authoritative activity, at about 20, the accepted view that distinctions *are* made in the parts of utensils. That is the point at which the "inside" is seen as separate from the outside. If one part is made unclean, another part is not made unclean. So the datum of the saying attributed to Jesus also forms the datum of the saying of M. 25:1A.

M. 25:7-8 adds the matter of the holding place, and the attestations of Tarfon and ᶜAqiva leave no reason to doubt that consideration of the division of utensils in general had by their time reached the point at which still a third part was distinguished. Indeed ,their perplexity as to its effects is not to be taken lightly. What it seems to me to mean is either that a new principle has not been understood by them, or that an old principle's meaning already is no longer clear to them. I think the latter more likely.

The real problem comes not with the making of distinctions, which we may with some confidence regard as a given in mid-first century consideration of Kelim. The real problem is the question of which of the two parts of the clay utensil is prior and predominant in the receiving of uncleanness. At what point in the history of Pharisaic and later rabbinic conceptions of utensils is it taken for granted, as in M. 2:1, that if the outside of a clay utensil is unclean, the inside is unaffected, but if the inside is unclean, the outside also is affected? At that point, the saying of Mt.-Lk. is no longer possible.

Now one thing is perfectly clear, and that is, M. 25:1A and 25:7-8 know no such rule. On the contrary, the supposition of those statements is the opposite. Later, all parties agree, if the outside is unclean, the inside is not unclean. But if the inside is unclean, what is the status of the outside? M. 25:1A and M. 25:7-8, strikingly, do not tell us. M. 25:1A simply says that all utensils have outer parts and an inside. M. 25:7 announces a gloss: All utensils have outer parts and an inside—*and they have a holding place.* It is this gloss which is further glossed by ᶜAqiva and Ṭarfon. Strikingly absent from M. 25:1 and 7 is the consequence: If the outer part is made unclean, what of the inner part? And vice versa? We have no notion. As I shall show in a moment, even the later Ushan exegesis of the law omits one important point. It simply knows nothing of the inevitable uncleanness of the outer parts of an object whose inside is unclean. So I think the silence of M. 25:1 and 7 is to be interpreted as evidence that no one took for granted the principle that the outside is made unclean automatically upon the contamination of the inside.

It is M. 2:1 which so phrases matters as to interpret the distinction between the outer parts and the inside as a substantive difference: "They are rendered unclean from airspace and are made unclean from their outer parts but do not render unclean from their GB." The exegesis of this sentence seems to me nearly impossible, as indicated when I attempted to explain it. Whatever it does mean, it clearly does not mean that when the outside is made unclean, the inner part is made unclean. It may mean that when the inside is unclean, the outer part also is unclean—but it does not say so. It is the exegetical tradition which interprets the law as just now indicated. We cannot take for granted that that is what it meant to begin with.

Whatever meaning we assign to M. 2:1, one thing is certain. The passage is post-Ushan, for reasons already stated. It therefore cannot on the face of it be adduced in evidence of the meaning of M. 25:1 and 7. Indeed, whenever we date M. 2:1 and however we interpret its meaning, we shall have to ask, At what point is M. 2:1 taken to mean that the status of the inside of a utensil governs that of the outside, but that the status of the outside has no affect upon that of the inside? Or, to put it differently, on what basis have we ourselves interpreted M. 2:1 to distinguish the inside from the outside in the way just now stated? M. 2:1F says the clay utensil becomes unclean and conveys uncleanness from the contained airspace, and imparts or receives uncleanness from the outer sides. The issue of M. 2:1F is that of the contained airspace; that is the point of the saying of Hezekiah to Gamaliel. Who, therefore, has said anything at all about the uncleanness of the inner part of the utensil? Where do we have evidence that anyone supposes the inner part affects the outer parts? The answer is—no where.

Having a rule on the affects of the contained airspace, *we* were the ones who then took for granted the issue is the inner *part* in general. But the point of Hezekiah's saying has to do with the interpretation of Lev. 11:33, explaining that TWK of Scripture refers not only to the inner *surface*, but also to the contained *airspace*. And, to return to M. 2:1F, the further point has to do with the distinction between ʾḤWR and GB (or GB explains ʾḤWR).

What has happened? We have, in point of fact, read M. 2:1F in the light of M. 25:1A and 7A, and, *vice versa*, we have read M. 25:1A and 7A in the light of M. 2:1F. That is, in the former instance, we have seen M. 2:1F as referring to the carefully distinguished inner and outer parts, so we have understood the point of M. 2:1F to be not the matter of airspace, to which it refers, but the matter of *inner parts vs. outer parts*, to which it does not refer. And then we have read M. 25:1A and 7A in the light of M. 2:1F, and so taken for granted that the force and effect of the distinction are to declare that if the inner part is made unclean, the *whole* utensil is unclean, but if the outer parts are unclean, the inner part—which is distinguished from the outer part—is not unclean. That, it is clear, is reading into M. 25:1A and 7A what simply is not there.

Why should we not have interpreted matters in this way, however, since Yosé and Meir seem to? That is, in M. 25:7 and 8, it is taken for granted that if one's hands are clean and the outer parts of the utensil are unclean, then one who takes hold of the cup by the holding place need not worry about the condition of his hands. They are clean. That is to say, Yosé's view (with which Meir explicitly concurs) is that the division of the outer side of the cup into the holding place and the remainder of the outer side means uncleanness affecting the one part does not affect the other. And then who will have assumed otherwise than that the status of the inside is similarly governed by the same distinctions? If the outer part is made unclean, the inner part is unaffected—for all utensils have outer parts and an inside. But, relying on M. 2:1F as just now interpreted, we further suppose that if the inner part is affected, the whole is unclean. So we forget the division just now postulated!

To put is differently, M. 25:1 and 7 certainly are early-Yavnean or pre-Yavnean, assuming that 25:7 glosses 25:1 and itself is glossed by ʿAqiva and Ṭarfon. This progression would place M. 25:1 at the threshold of Yavnean development. The distinction between outer and inner parts bears no relationship to the relative susceptibility of the one over the other. If the one is unclean, the other is not unclean. That is the very point of the distinction. Then, as I said (1) M. 2:1F bears no relationship to M. 25:1, because it makes a point unknown to M. 25:1. Or (2) M. 2:1 contradicts M. 25:1. Or (3) M. 2:1 is intended to add to and work out the implications of the division of utensils in a way unimagined by the people who to begin with recognize those distinctions, by saying the inner division affects the outer, but not the contrary.

Before we return to the consideration of the saying attributed to Jesus, let us now ask, What of the Houses? Is it possible that the *inside/outside* relationship is at issue between them? To answer the question, we shall now consider M. Berakhot 8:2 as interpreted by y. Berakhot 8:2, in which the relationship of the Houses to the opinions of Yosé and Meir in M. 25:7-8 is spelled out. Relying upon the Amoraic interpretation of the supposed relationship between the two Ushans and the two Houses, we may at the end offer our final point.

> 8:2. *Mishnah*: The House of Shammai say, They wash the hands and afterward mix the cup. And the House of Hillel say, They mix the cup first and afterward wash the hands.
> *Gemara*: A. What is the reason of the House of Shammai?

So that the liquids which are on the outer side of the cup may not be made unclean by his hands and go and make the cup unclean.

What is the reason of the House of Hillel? The outer side of the cup is always unclean [so there is no reason to protect it from the hands' uncleanness].

Another matter: One should wash the hands immediately before saying the blessing.

B. R. Biban in the name of R. Yoḥanan [said], "The opinion of the House of Shammai is in accord with R. Yosé, and that of the House of Hillel with R. Meir, as we have learned there [Mishnah Kelim 25:7]:

"[In all vessels an outer part and an inner part are distinguished, and also a part by which they are held.]

"R. Meir says, 'For the hands they are unclean and clean.'

"R. Yosé said, 'This applies only to clean hands alone."

Meir says that if hands are unclean and touch the outer side of the vessel, they do not make the holding place unclean. If hands are clean and touch one part which is clean, another part, which is unclean, has no affect on the hands. The hands still are clean. Yosé says this distinction among the elements of the cup applies *only* if the hands are clean.

Both Yosé and the House of Shammai therefore hold that the outer part *may* be clean, even while the inner part is unclean. If, obviously, the outer part is unclean, the holding place may still be clean. So Yosé says the outer side of the cup is *not* always unclean. And this is contrary to the Hillelites' claim—and the view of M. 2:1F. If the hands were clean and liquid was dripping on them, and the outside of the cup was unclean, one may nonetheless hold the cup with the holding place and not fear lest his hand may be unclean by the unclean outer part of the cup. We do not suppose, according to the Hillelites, that the liquid on the hands will be made unclean by the outer part of the cup and then go and make the hands unclean.

Yosé says this rule applies only to clean hands. That is, if the hands are clean, and the outer part of the cup is unclean, we do not have to worry about uncleanness. But if the hands are unclean, we have to take precautions lest the liquid touch the unclean outer part of the cup and go and make the whole cup unclean.

Yosé and the House of Shammai thus are concerned about unclean hands' not touching the liquid on the outer part of the cup, which then will go and make the cup unclean. And the House of Hillel and Meir do not take account of that possibility *even* in the case of unclean hands' touching the liquid on the *outside* of the cup and making the whole cup unclean. It follows that the Hillelites regard the state of the inner part as decisive (as does the homily assigned to Jesus). The Hillelite position does not take account of the consideration important to the Shammaites because the outer side is deemed always to be unclean. It necessarily follows that the condition of the outer part has no affect on the inner part. So why can the cup ever be clean? Because the state of the inner part determines that of the cup as a whole. Thus "first cleanse the inside"—so that the cup will fall into the status of cleanness. The outer part can never be clean, so why bother to cleanse that part first—or at all? To the Hillelites' position, instruction first to cleanse the inner part, so the outer part may be clean also, is absurd, because the inside to begin with is determinative.

If Yoḥanan's interpretation of the parallels between the Houses' opinions in M. Ber. 8:2 and Yosé and Meir in M. 25:7-8, is correct, two important results follow.

First, even by Ushan times, the matter of the affect of the inside upon the outside could not have been settled. That is why Yosé could take a position declared by the decided law of M. 2:1F as (mis)interpreted in the light of M. 25:1A and 7A to be rejected.

Second, and far more important, the opinions assigned to the Houses in M. Ber. 8:2 yield this fact: The House of Shammai hold that one does not have to cleanse the outer part before the inner part or the inner part before the outer, because there is no affect of the one upon the other. And the House of Hillel do rule that one cleanses the inner part first and then (if at all) the outer part, because the inner part is susceptible and will then render the outer part unclean by virtue of its own uncleanness.

It is only from the perspective of the House of Hillel that the saying assigned to Jesus, which surely is to be dated some time between 40 and 75, is meaningless. If the Shammaite rule—the outer part is not governed by the inner—predominated at that time, as we have surmised was in general the case on moot points between the Houses and as is the clear implication of M. 25:1A, then the saying is meaningful. The metaphor built upon it is evocative, because it rests upon and criticizes current practice (or confusion). And it further follows, I think, that the issue of the status of the inner and outer part, which cannot have come before Hezekiah's saying before Gamaliel, also was a matter of concern long afterward, surely to the end of the first century. The place of the controversy-saying on the cleaning of the inner part first of all seems to me to testify to an issue which, if it was current at all before 70, should be regarded as nascent in the antecedent decade or two. Whether other sayings in the same pericope indicate that the moot issues—washing hands before eating, purity at meals—also were current and controversial because the Pharisees' practices represented innovations we cannot say. What may be the case is that the homily assigned to Jesus took up a debate current in Pharisaism and did two things. First, it turned the debate into a moral matter, so showed its true implications. Second, it assigned to Jesus, in accord with stress probably known from earlier, and more authentic, sayings, the position that the inner traits of man are what matter. The Pharisees' interest in purity laws is therefore made into a polemic against them. They do not understand the true meaning of the law, therefore debate "outer/inner" of utensils, while the law really refers to moral character. If it is doubtful that the saying is authentic in the sense that Jesus "really" said it, I think it very likely that the sense of more authentic teachings has generated this wry comment on a matter of some importance to late pre-70 or early post-70 Pharisaism.

vi. Conclusion

Relying on remarkably few conjectures, excluding the matter of the saying attributed to Jesus about cleansing the inside first, we have come to a number of clearcut perspectives on the state of the laws of Kelim before 70.

We saw, first of all, that the Yavnean rulings were based upon a number of important, presupposed principles, which were apt to derive from the period before 70. The most important of these was that an object which is useful is susceptible, and one which is useless is not. In like manner, it was a given for Yavneans that a broken utensil is insusceptible, merely a corollary of the former.

The second principle, directly attributed to authorities before 70, was that a clay utensil without an inner part has no outer parts; this is either restated by, or itself generates, the further data of Yavnean law, first, that a utensil with a receptacle is susceptible, and one without is not, and second, that utensils are divided, for the purpose of assessing their status as to uncleanness, into inner and outer parts.

Two further principles, assuredly pre-70, were, first, that what is used for sitting or lying is susceptible to *midras*-uncleanness, other things being susceptible only to corpse-uncleanness; and, second, that a partitioned clay utensil in the corpse's tent affords protection. All of these rules, we have seen, derive directly from the plain meaning of Scripture; no extensive intervening exegetical tradition can be located.

It became possible, moreover, to show that some of these principles were taken for granted in rulings evidently reliably attributed to the Houses. That means that the materials taken for granted at Yavneh very likely go back at least for about half-a-century before that time. The principles involve a tightly fitting cover, the susceptibility of useful, and the insusceptibility of useless, objects, the susceptibility to *midras* of something used for sitting, and the insusceptibility to *midras* of something not used for sitting (or lying). All three principles derive directly from Scripture; none, it hardly needs repeating, rests upon a considerable exegetical tradition. If the attributions to the Houses are authentic and if the Houses formed historical entities dating from the early decades of the first century, then these three matters will have marked the beginning of the laws of Kelim.

When we tested this conception against the exegesis preserved in Sifra, we found a somewhat more complicated picture. But the main part of the exegeses in Sifra which pertain to other than Ushan matters concern M. 8:1ff., developing the main lines of thought behind the issues faced by Eliezer and the sages. It may be that the view attributed by Judah to ᶜAqiva, that what serves man is susceptible and what does not is not, develops the issue of usefulness and is secondary to the plain meaning of the Scriptural view that a utensil is something with which one does work. But the exegesis hardly appears to derive from the earliest period of the Houses, or even from the period immediately before 70. The matter of dividing utensils into insides and outsides seems to bear no clear relationship to an antecedent exegetical tradition, apart from Hezekiah's saying. The state of the law at that point seems fairly clear.

We have found no evidence, therefore, that Kelim rests upon four or five hundred years of antecedent Scriptural exegesis. We have, indeed, found remarkably little evidence of an intensive development of the law from the Houses to Yavneh through either Scriptural exegesis or through reasoning. If the state of the earliest law is accurately represented by the Houses, then it seems not unreasonable to suggest that the matter of Kelim began with them or with their masters. From that point the main lines of legal development before

70 probably involved the matters represented by Hezekiah's saying, on the one side, and by Eliezer's dispute in M. 8:1, on the other. That is, the direction of legal development was in terms of dividing utensils—for both matters come back to the effects of doing just that. Obviously, the principle that a susceptible object is one which is useful could have led to a great many specific rulings, and perhaps it did, but we cannot demonstrate it. What I think more likely is that the first fifty years of legal development, from ca. 20 to ca. 70, were marked by the laying forth of the most fundamental points on usefulness, on the one side, and division, on the other, in addition to the simplest issues of the status of a utensil in the tent of a corpse.

To what degree rules primarily prevailing in the Temple supplied the Pharisees with their conceptions is difficult to say. I tend to think that both the division of utensils, which did not apply to Temple vessels (as the later code maintains), and the affects of the tightly-sealed cover of a clay utensil as to metal contents, on which contrary traditions seem to have been available, may have been worked out in contrast to Temple rules. This will mean that the Temple law provided the model, with the Pharisees doing the opposite. But no speculation on that matter presently can be fruitful.

Our firm result is that the laws of Kelim could have begun their development at any point, from the redaction of Leviticus onward, at which someone opened the pertinent Scriptures and decided to apply them to utensils not involved in the cult, part of a larger intention to keep purity laws outside the Temple. No considerable exegesis was then required to demonstrate that the Torah required pretty much what the authorities before 70 and immediately afterward took at face value. While, as I said, the laws of Kelim could have begun their development any time from the completion of Leviticus to the first century, the greatest probability is that the laws of Kelim began their development shortly before the Houses. It is only then, as we saw, that the traces of a secondary exegetical tradition are to be found, resting on something more complex than the simple and plain meaning of the Scriptures themselves. What was accomplished in the century from 70 to 170 is already clear. The results of the period from ca. 20 to ca. 70 should not seem meagre by contrast, for it was then that the most fundamental and original conception of all took shape: utensils not in the Temple and not used for the cult to begin with should be subject to uncleanness. That, after all, is what is taken for granted even by the Houses' rulings. And neither Scriptures nor exegesis of Scriptures will have generated such an original and revolutionary conception. The mere passage of time accounts for nothing. I think it likely that some one person or a small group of people effected the most profound development of all, laying the foundations for our tractate, as for much else in the Order of Purities.

III. Ohalot Before 70

i. DEFINITION OF THE PROBLEM

Our task is to trace the line extending backward, from the laws attributed to the Houses and masters at the beginning of the Mishnaic process, and toward (but not to) the Priestly Code of Numbers 19. In this work we rely upon no conjecture whatever; there is no need. Working systematically, we sift and resift the materials, replacing conjecture with orderly description and routine analysis of facts. This process permits description of the history of the law in two synchronized patterns: (1) by the order of attributions, from the Houses onward, and (2) by the order of laws revealed or imposed by logic. Our history consists, therefore, in the unfolding of the ideas and laws of Tents in terms of the necessary and uncontingent logic of the laws, on the one side, and of the order of the authorities to whose times these ideas and laws are attributed, on the other. The one aspect of history we shall be unable to explore is the specific time in which these intellectual events took place. I shall show pretty well what came first and what came afterward. But whether the logical process lasted for a day, a week, or a century, we cannot say, nor, of course, shall we know which century (let alone which week) set the stage for the process, all or in part.

First we again turn to the laws attributed to the Houses and to Yavneans, this time listing the most basic principles upon which those laws are constructed. We thereby reckon the degree to which the Mishnaic laws attributed to the earliest authorities are founded on an antecedent heritage, and the degree to which they begin their development primarily after 70 (or at the time of the Houses somewhat before 70).

Second, we review the pertinent Scriptural verses, to eliminate from our catalogue of principles and presuppositions those items which certainly derive from the Written Torah.

Third, we examine the relevant, extant exegetical heritage, seeking those items which do not cite, therefore cannot be assumed to know about, our Mishnah, and which do contain principles upon which our Mishnah clearly is founded. This will allow us to isolate those elements which underpin our Mishnah's laws, yet which are likely to come before the earliest laws before us.

Fourth, seeing those elements, we shall recognize the contributions to Ohalot made in the period between the conclusion of the Priestly Code and the later part of the first century.

To state the result at the outset: that contribution consists in the conception upon which the entire tractate rests. A Tent, a handbreadth in its three dimensions, has nothing to do with a tent, let alone with a house. The Tent means something quite different from what we have to this point suggested, yet something subsumed by, and taken for granted in, nearly every law we have examined. The Tent is *the new house, the container, in place of the body, for that which exudes from the body upon death.* In Philo's language (*Special Laws* 3:207), to which we shall return by a circuitous route, "For a man's soul is a precious thing, and when it departs to seek another home, all that will be left behind is defiled, deprived as it is of the divine image." The Tent is that 'other home,' and the standard measure, the handbreadth, is the space required for the passage of that which exudes from the body upon death, and which I think Philo (among other Hellenists) would have called the soul, and which our Mishnah calls by the homogeneous circumlocution—applicable to so much else—"uncleanness" or "corpse-uncleanness."

ii. Rules of the Houses and Early Yavneans and their Presuppositions

In making use of pericopae assigned to the Houses we have always to ask whether these items serve primarily mnemonic purposes or indeed contain traditions going back to the Houses themselves. A fair criterion is whether later generations debate the same issues in pretty much the same terms. If they do, then it seems improbable that the historical Houses of Shammai and Hillel debated and settled the disputed point. If they had, then the question ought no longer to have been moot for the Yavneans or Ushans. Since the tradental and redactional framework of the Houses self-evidently is the same as that prevailing later on (there being no sign of independent redaction and transmission of Houses' materials), we can hardly imagine that matters settled by the Houses were open to the Ushans only because the Ushans did not know what the Houses had debated (or, what the House of Hillel had decided). More likely, the correct explanation for the matter is that the Ushans phrased matters in the names of the

Houses for purposes of formulating and transmitting "classic" disputes of principles.

A review of the materials before us (following the presentation above, p. 151), shows that a major problematic item is M. 11:7, the dog on the threshhold. At first glance, it would seem that Meir holds the dog may form a Tent for the transmission of uncleanness, against Judah and Eleazar. Since Meir accords with the Hillelites of the preceding pericopae, we ought then see Judah and Eleazar as in accord with the Shammaites. Yet perhaps the issue is not whether or not the dog gives passage to uncleanness, as with the Houses' debates of M. 11:3-6, but the *criterion* by which the problem, to begin with, is to be solved: Tent *vs.* point of egress. That is a typically Ushan conundrum. M. 11:7 then would fall into that category of pericopae which pose problems for solution, rather than present rules for memorization. Further, the pericope's literary traits hardly suggest a unitary origin, therefore a single dispute as to whether or not dogs give passage to uncleanness through the (theoretical) Tent formed by their necks. The literary aspect of the pericope strongly suggests we have quite separate rulings on separate aspects of a single problem, not a classic "dispute." Meir's opinion, after all, has nothing to do with those that follow. Yosé's dispute is not with Meir, but with Eleazar, and Judah b. Betera's opinion can be seen to dispute with either Yosé and Eleazar or Meir. Accordingly, it was *our* interpretation, powerfully signaled, to be sure, by the ultimate redactor, who placed M. 11:7 after the House's disputes on what looked like the same problem, which led us to suppose we have a duplicated debate of a single principle, in which, then, the names of the Houses serve as mnemonics. In any event at no other point do I discern evidence that an issue debated by the Houses remained open at Yavneh, let alone at Usha (but see below, p. 251).

ᶜAqiva's partcipation in M. 5:1-4 in fact is a secondary layer, revising the terms of argument *only* if we treat ᶜAqiva as part of the debate. Removing his contribution we get a quite separate, simple and classic discussion of the role of the pot in protecting its contents.

Let us now turn to the presuppositions of the Houses and Yavneans, those points agreed upon by all parties, or, of still greater probative value, taken for granted by all parties without the need of articulate agreement at all. They should allow us accurately to describe the heritage of rules, principles, and fundamental conceptions going back to the period before 70 and before the Houses, to whom, for convenience' sake, we may assign a date of 40-50. These presuppositions seem to have been the following.

I. *Houses*

Modes

1. A Tent spreads contamination when it overshadows a corpse (M. 2:3) or the excretions or remains of a corpse (M. 2:1). A corpse and things like a corpse contaminate in a Tent.

Sources

2. A grave-area is assumed to contain corpse-matter (which may be removed). (M. 16:4, 5, 18:1, 18:4.)
3. A dwelling of a gentile in the Land of Israel is unclean (M. 18:7).

Tents

4. The standard measure is a handbreadth (M. 3:6, M. 15:1-3, 11:1-3).
5. If one door is open by a handbreadth, the uncleanness will exude from that door, so what is subject to other doors is now unaffected (M. 7:3). The same principle is in M. 11:1-2.
6. Compressed uncleanness is that in a space of less than requisite size. It spurts up and down, but is not spread to the sides (M. 15:3).
[7. Holes give passage to uncleanness if they are adequate to their own purpose (M. 13:1-2). This may not be early, see below, p. 251.]
8. A Tent consists of an enclosed, empty space of a cubic handbreadth (M. 11:3-7). = No. 4.
9. Diminishing the space open in a hatchway by means of a pot prevents the passage of corpse-uncleanness (M. 5:1-4). The suppositions are (1) corpse-uncleanness passes through a handbreadth and through no lesser space; (2) the pot does diminish, so interposes. The principle of conjoining with the walls of the Tent is assumed by the Houses in M. 11:8. + T. for M. 15:9.

II. *Yavneans*

Modes

10. A human being who touches a corpse becomes unclean for seven days. A utensil becomes unclean in the same degree as the corpse itself (M. 1:1-3, M. 15:10).
11. Movables contaminate by overshadowing if they are a handbreadth in size. (M. 15:10, 16:1-2.) The standard measure of a Tent applies to movables.
12. Blood contaminates (M. 2:2).
13. Dirt from a grave-area and dirt from abroad contaminate (M. 17:5).

Sources

14. Limbs and other parts of the body contaminate (T. 2:7-8).
15. Things which have exuded from a corpse contaminate (M. 2:2, 3:5).
16. Things connected with the grave (stones) contaminate (M. 2:4, 16:3).
17. Dirt which may contain bone matter contaminates (M. 17:2).

Tents

18. Utensils afford protection along with walls of Tents (M. 5:5-6).

If we now further reduce these presuppositions to the simplest and most comprehensive propositions, what do we have?

1. Tents spread contamination produced by corpses and things similar to corpses (1, 2, 10, 12, 13, 14, 15, 16, 17). It is particularly striking that the several Yavnean preconceptions here stand close to, but develop in some small way, the givens of the Houses' rulings.

2. Gentiles' land and dwellings in the Land of Israel are unclean (3, 13). This is not an important aspect of Ohalot.

3. A Tent is a handbreadth in surface area (whether or not we require sides, doors, etc.) (4, 8). The point is that corpse-uncleanness requires a space of a handbreadth for its passage. If, therefore, we have egress of a handbreadth, corpse-uncleanness will exude. If we have a cover or protection on the upper surface of a handbreadth, corpse-uncleanness will not descend in the covered area (7, 8, 9 + 5).

4. Corpse-matter in a space of less than a handbreadth in cubic measure is regarded as compressed. It spurts upward and downward, but is not spread to the sides, since we do not have a Tent to accomplish the spreading (6).

5. The converse of No. 4 is that corpse-matter in a space of a handbreadth which lacks adequate egress (a handbreadth) is regarded as in a sealed tomb, contaminating on all sides. The point is that here we do have a Tent to spread the uncleanness, but we do not have a door to release it. All parts of the enclosed space are going to produce contamination, on the one hand, but we do not have interposition, on the part of the Tent, on the other (No. 5).

6. Space for the transfer of corpse-uncleanness is adequate if that space serves some useful and intended purpose (No. 7, contradicts Nos. 4, 5, 6, 8, 9).

To come to a still simpler formulation: Corpses contaminate and Tents interpose. Tents are made up by surfaces of a handbreadth's width, breadth and height.

Let us now turn to Scripture once again, seeking those points at which the written Torah, requiring no explanation or exegesis whatsoever, certainly supplies the presuppositions upon which the laws of Ohalot have been constructed.

iii. Scriptural Foundations of Ohalot

The first important principle of Ohalot is that corpses contaminate for seven days, and this, of course, comes to us from Num. 19:11: "He who touches the dead body of any person shall be unclean for seven days." The same verse, moreover, tells us that corpse-contamination is conveyed through contact (touching). The person who touches the corpse is unclean with the seven days', or corpse-uncleanness. Contamination by the mode, or means, of Tent is declared in Num. 19:14: "This is the law when a man dies in a tent: every one who comes into the tent, and every one who is in the tent, shall be unclean seven days." The tent thus (so to speak) serves as a Tent, that is, whatever is overshadowed by the tent is made unclean through overshadowing, the Tent's affect, which is to spread the corpse uncleanness to all beneath its shadow, as if the person in the tent has touched the corpse itself. The Amoraim who read *contact* as equivalent to *Tent* were on perfectly firm grounds indeed.

What about utensils in the Tent? Num. 19:15 says, "And every open vessel, which has no cover fastened upon it, is unclean." The contrary is that every closed and sealed vessel is clean. That can mean only, the contents of the vessel, not the outer surface.

Num. 19:16 intends to tell us about a corpse not in a Tent, "Whoever in the open field touches one who is slain with a sword or a dead body or a bone of a man or a grave shall be unclean seven days." One would not have to be a very clever exegete to learn from this verse that things which are like the corpse or grave—the bone, the grave-area itself—produce corpse-contamination. Further, we learn that touching out of doors is equivalent to overshadowing in or by the Tent.

What about touching a utensil affected by a corpse? Num. 19:22 states, "But whatever the unclean person touches shall be unclean and any one who touches it shall be unclean until evening." This verse surely meant in the first place that whatever object the person unclean with corpse-uncleanness touches will be unclean in the same way as the person who has touched it. The converse—the rule about someone who touches that unclean object—is clearly stated. But outside of our opening chapter, M. 1:1-3, this matter is of no interest to Ohalot.

Now if we ask, upon what foundation do the opening and closing parts of Ohalot, that is, the discussion of modes and sources of uncleanness, stand? the answer is very clear: Scripture, the Written Torah, supplied with remarkably little exegesis, gives the laws pretty much as Mishnah—the Oral Torah—presents them. To return to the presuppositions of modes and sources of uncleanness, Nos. 1, 2, 10, 12, 13, 14, 15, 16, 17, all may be readily discerned as the implications of Scripture itself. The sole item which clearly is not based upon the Pentateuchal law is No. 3. So it is difficult to see the materials in M. 1:1-3:5 and 16:3-18:10 as much more than useful supplements to what Scripture makes clear.

What about Tents—M. 3:6-16:2? When we pass the presupposition that Tents spread corpse-contamination, we have left the Scriptural domain entirely. Not a single concept or presupposition before us seems to derive directly or indirectly from the exegesis of Scripture. Let us now ask, Did the later rabbinical exegetical tradition contain materials developing Scriptural rules and thus bridging the remarkable gap between Scripture and Mishnah, Written and Oral Torah? The answer is mostly negative.

iv. Antecedent Exegetical Traditions

While the evidence compiled in the collection of legal exegeses attributed to Tannaitic authorities in Sifré on Numbers and in Sifré Zutta obviously reached its final redaction in later times, we nonetheless must look for exegeses deriving from the earlier period. Do we find any materials which seem capable of having generated the ideas now contained in Mishnah-Tosefta?

The criterion for answering that question is this: Does the exegetical pericope contain a hint that Mishnah in its present formulation or something close to it stands before the authority represented in the exegesis. If it does, then it is hardly likely that the exegesis comes before and stands behind Mishnah, but more probable that the exegesis links an available Mishnah (Oral Torah) to the written Torah. To answer the present question, we review the whole of Sifré Numbers on Num. 19:11-12 and rapidly resurvey Sifré Zutta, much of which has already been given in translation in Part IV (pp. 52, 69, 70, 136, 276, 322). Sifré Numbers follows.

1. 125A: Num. 19:11 proves that the corpse renders unclean through contact.

2. 125B: Alludes to M. 2:2, ʿAqiva's opinion that the blood of a child less than a *log* which has entirely exuded contaminates. Assigns the opposing opinion to Ishmael.
3. 125C: The corpse contaminates for seven days.
4. 125D: Not relevant.
5. 125E: Not relevant.
6. 125F: Num. 19:13 proves there is no contamination before death = M. 1:6.
7. 125G: Not relevant.
8. 125H: Not relevant.
9. 125I: Not relevant.
10. 126A: This is the Torah. When a man dies in the Tent, whatever comes to the Tent and whatever is in the Tent will be unclean seven days.
    1. Issi b. ʿAqiva *vs.* Ishmael *re* exegesis.
    2. How do we know to treat whatever overshadows like a Tent? Said R. Yiṣḥaq: Just as the *meṣora*...
11. 126B: Whatever comes into the Tent: Thus refers to something which comes only in part (= M. 3:4).
    R. Aḥai b. R. Josiah: To treat the ground of the house to the nethermost deep just like it (the house) (= M. 15:5).
12. 126C: Whatever comes into the Tent—through its door does it render unclean, and it does not render unclean on all its sides when it [the door] is open. On the basis of this Scripture you may reason with regard to the tomb. If the Tent, which is susceptible to uncleanness, does not render unclean on all its sides when it is open, a tomb, which does not receive uncleanness, all the more so should it not render unclean on all its sides when it is open.
    Or perhaps the opposite: If the tomb, which is not going to receive uncleanness, lo, it renders unclean on all its sides when it is open, a Tent, which does receive uncleanness, is it not logical that it should render unclean on all its sides when it is open?
    Scripture says, Whatever comes to the Tent—through its door it renders unclean, and it does not render unclean on all sides when it is open... (M. 3:6/7:3).
13. 126D: Not relevant.
14. 126E: Not relevant.
15. 126F: Not relevant.
16. 126G: And every open utensil: On this basis they have said, Utensils afford protection with a tightly-sealed stopper in a Tent of the corpse, Tents with a cover (= M. 5:6).
17. 126H: Cites M. Kel. 10:1 verbatim.
18. 126I: Not relevant.
19. 126J: Not relevant.
20. 127A: Whoever in the open field touches one who is slain with a sword or a dead body or a bone of a man or a grave shall be unclean seven days (Num. 19:16).

R. ᶜAqiva says: To include the rolling stone and the buttressing stone (M. 2:4).

21. 127B: Slain with a sword: Scripture comes to teach concerning the sword that it is unclean for seven days and he who touches it is unclean seven days. Cites M. 1:2.
22. 127C: Slain with a sword or a dead body: But the corpse is also in the category of one slain, and lo, Scripture excludes it from its category, to make the person who separates from him (after touching the corpse) like him (in the same degree of uncleanness as the corpse), the words of R. Josiah.

    R. Jonathan says, The corpse is not in the category of the slain one, because we find that it (Scripture) treats the corpse by itself and the slain person by himself. How do we know to treat even the one who separates from it (the corpse) like it (in the same degree of uncleanness... etc.)

    Rest not relevant.
23. 127D: Or the bone of a man: This refers to the limb of a living person. Or perhaps it refers only to a bone the size of a barley corn. When it says, And whatever touches a bone—lo, the referent is the bone the size of a barley corn. Why does Scripture say, Or a bone of a man? This refers to a limb from a living person... (M. Ed. 6:2-3).
24. 127E: Or a grave—This is a sealed grave. You say this is a sealed grave? Or perhaps it refers only to an open grave. Have you thought so? It is an argument *a fortiori*. If the Tent, which is susceptible to uncleanness, does not render something unclean on all its sides when it is open, a tomb, which does not receive uncleanness, ought logically not render something unclean on all its sides when it is open...
25. 128A: Not relevant.
26. 128B: Not relevant.
27. 128C: Not relevant.
28. 129A: Not relevant.
29. 129B: Not relevant.
30. 129C: Not relevant.
31. 129D: And he shall sprinkle on the Tent (Num. 19:18): Scripture comes and teaches concerning the Tent that it receives uncleanness... (M. 7:2).
32. 129E: And upon him who touched the bone (Num. 19:18): See 127D.
33. 129F: Not relevant.
34. 129G: Not relevant.
35. 129H: Not relevant.
36. 130: And whatever the unclean person touches shall be unclean (Num. 19:22): Why is it stated? Because it says, "One slain by a sword"—Scripture comes and teaches concerning the sword that it is unclean for a seven days' uncleanness and one who touches it is unclean for a seven days' uncleanness. Thus have we learned for utensils and man, etc. (M. 1:1-3 cited).

Relevant materials in Sifré Zuṭṭa are as follows:

37. 19:11: Epstein, p. 62, Horovitz, p. 306, ls. 11-13: He who touches the corpse: excluding one who touches its teeth, hair, and nails when they are separate (M. 3:3-4).
38. 19:11: Epstein, p. 63, Horovitz, p. 307, ls. 5-10: M. 3:5 *re* mixed blood. T. is cited.
39. 19:14, Epstein, p. 67, Horovitz, p. 309, ls. 9-17: When a man dies in a Tent... That it will render unclean like a complete corpse. What do I include? The backbone and the skull and a half-*log* of blood and a half-*qab* of bones, etc. = M. 2:1, 2 cited.
40. 19:14, Epstein, p. 68, Horovitz, p. 309, ls. 22-3, p. 310, ls. 1-4: See Sifré Num. 127E: A sealed tomb is like a sealed Tent and contaminates on all sides.
41. 19:14, Epstein, p. 68, Horovitz, p. 310, ls. 4-13: *Re* M. 3:7, 8:1-5.
42. 19:15, Epstein, p. 71, Horovitz, p. 310, l. 25, p. 311, ls. 1-17: Cites M. 13:1ff.
43. 19:16, Epstein, p. 72-5, Horovitz, p. 311, ls. 18-19: How do we know that if the corpse overshadowed someone, he is unclean? P. 311, ls. 19-20: *Re* M. 2:4. P. 312, ls. 2-16, p. 313, ls. 1-21 = M. 2:4, 17:2.

The important items in Sifré Num. are Nos. 12, 16, 24 (= 12), 31, and 36. The others are either not relevant to Tents or explicitly refer to extant Mishnahs.

No. 12 is striking in its distinction between the sealed tomb and the Tent, regarding the sole difference as the possibility of egress for the contamination. Further, "Through its door does it render unclean" surely stands behind M. 7:3/3:6, the attributions of which place the passage at the beginning of the Mishnaic law of Tents. Accordingly, the conception behind No. 12 is prior to the conception behind items bearing the earliest attributions.

No. 16 is no less clearly part of the foundation of our tractate. The distinction between the Tent and utensil—taken for granted everywhere and never spelled out—is laid before us in No. 16. Yet how much easier our exegetical task would have been with such a straight-forward conception applied throughout.

There is no important difference between No. 12 and No. 24.

No. 31, like No. 16, is of the most fundamental order, for it holds that a Tent is susceptible to uncleanness and thus is the datum behind M. 7:1-2.

No. 36 stands behind M. 1:1-3, but it is not cited there; its conception is taken for granted by M.

By contrast to the afore-cited pericopae, nothing in SZ does more than allude to extant Mishnaic law, most commonly citing Mishnah as we have it (though providing important variations in readings). Perhaps No. 43 is important, but as we now have it, it does nothing more than bring us to M. 2:4.

If we now return to the most profound presuppositions of our tractate, we find the following: (1) a Tent requires egress. This, logically and concommitantly, links to (2) the sealed tomb. But that presupposition should not obscure the conception upon which these statements, in their turn, depend. *Corpse-uncleanness passes through handbreadth of open space. Its passage may be prevented, therefore, by a handbreadth of closed space.* In other words, our entire tractate is founded upon a single conception, to which we have referred, for the sake of convenience, as the standard measure.

And what imposes that "measure" is the trait of corpse-uncleanness. Everything else in one way or another is logically spun out of that single, fundamental trait of that which exudes from the corpse.

In no way is that concept related to Scripture. No exegete even tried to find some Scriptural foundation for it. And, as we recognize, what is at issue is not merely the measurement of a handbreadth, but all which is expressed by that simple measurement.

For what the "handbreadth in breadth, depth, and height" means is that the Scriptural tent, a place where people live, obviously has been left far behind us. The Tent of the Oral Torah, culminating in Mishnah, is anything but a place in which people dwell. So, while Sifré Num. seems to preserve important exegeses which originate before the earliest laws of Mishnah-Tosefta Ohalot, it contains no hint that that tradition begins with the exegesis of Scripture, the discovery *in* the Written Torah of the foundations of our tractate. At the outset to be sure we saw the Talmud's own statement to the same effect (IV, p. 1): little Scripture, many laws. What, then, is the conception of Tent laid out in the Oral Torah?

To give the answer in advance: The Written Torah speaks of a tent or a house in which people, whole and healthy in body and soul, live. The Oral Torah speaks of a Tent capable of containing that which exudes from the body at the moment of death, a Tent which takes the place of the body. It goes without saying that the laws of Numbers 19:11ff. were not understood in this way by others who make reference to them. The Zadokite Documents (CD 12:16-18) refer to the uncleanness of ahouse in which a corpse is found as follows (in the translation of Chaim Rabin, *The Zadokite Documents* [London, 1958], p. 62):

> And all wood and stones and dust which are defiled by the uncleanness of a dead human being shall be reckoned like them (i.e., men) for conveying defilement; according to their uncleanness shall he that touches them become unclean [= M. 1:1-3].
>
> And every utensil or nail or peg in the wall that are with the dead person in the house shall become unclean in the same manner as any working tool [= M. 16:2].

What we have here is little more than a reprise of the rules of Numbers. 19:11ff. What is in the house with the corpse is made unclean. M. 16:2 will not have been surprised by the rule that a peg in the wall is contaminated. Josephus' reference (*Against Apion* 2:206) to the uncleanness of the house in which a corpse has lain is routine and casual.

v. The Concept of the Tent

What has the Oral Torah contributed? On the surface, as I just said, we have nothing more than a useful definition, a filling out of the Scriptural law with some necessary additional information. What is this tent, referred to in Num. 19:11? It is simply an enclosed space of a certain dimension. And what is that dimension? A handbreadth of space. If this were the primary conceptual contribution of Mishnah, then our notion of the Oral Torah should be stated as follows: The role of Oral Torah—of Mishnah—is to fill in some unimportant gaps in Scriptural law, to supply some needed definitions.

But a closer look at the basis of Mishnah's contribution requires a revision of our conception of the Oral Torah. For that handbreadth which is at the foundation of everything else is nothing other than a brief and elliptical way of referring to the space through which the effects of the corpse will make their way. We have observed time and again that "a corpse is assumed to pass through four such handbreadths, its contaminating effects through *one*." When, therefore, we define a Tent as a handbreadth in height, breadth, and depth, what have we said? We have defined a Tent not as a house or a building in which people can live or even in which a corpse will fit. We have defined a Tent as the space occupied by the gaseous effusion of the corpse. This self-evidently has nothing to do with the house or building which people see and use. It has much, I think, to do with the house or building in which the person *has* existed, the body.

Now to spell this out: when we say a Tent must measure a handbreadth, either to prevent uncleanness from entering its enclosed space, or to keep uncleanness within its enclosed space (without regard to the nature of the enclosure—walls or no walls), what is the meaning of such an allegation? What is this Tent to which reference is made in Ohalot? (Even if we substitute house for Tent, when *house* is used in Ohalot, the referent at some points seems to be burial niche, *kokh*, as much as a real house.) And what is it that can be contained in the Tent of which Ohalot speaks? The answer is not the body, for a whole body by definition is four times larger than a handbreadth, and therefore a body cannot be contained in a Tent. The terms of the answer, moreover, have to include that invisible viscuous gas which is uncleanness, because it is everywhere taken for granted that uncleanness cannot penetrate a closed area of a handbreadth or less, on the one hand, or will be prevented from exuding by that same closed area, if it is enclosed by it.

Corpse-uncleanness is something which can be contained by a Tent. A Tent is something which can contain or interpose against corpse-uncleanness.

The one has—in the nature of things—to be defined in terms of the other. Our definition of a Tent is curiously out of phase with the simple meaning of Scripture. The issue of Scripture is drastically revised, indeed, when Tent becomes "that which can contain what exudes from a corpse." When, therefore, we define Tent as we do here, and as is taken for granted throughout the Mishnaic laws which depend upon the simple definition before us, we mean something entirely different from what Scripture means.

If the conception of death is that at death something leaves, exudes from, the body, then the Tent serves as the functional equivalent to the body, for it is able to receive and contain that which exudes from the body. The Tent, therefore, takes the place of the body, makes a place for that which, in the body, leaves at the point or moment of death. The Tent is to be understood as a surrogate for the body, restoring the order which has broken with the leaving of the body by that which exudes from it. Death has released this effusion. The Tent then contains it. We have avoided naming this thing which "exudes from the corpse at such a viscosity as to pass through an open space of a handbreadth or more, but no less." I see no point in calling it the soul and to allege that the "uncleanness" of the corpse is the "soul" which is the "spirit" surviving after death and requiring a new locale. But Philo seems to have had just such a notion:

> Further too, those who enter a house in which anyone has died are ordered not to touch anything until they have bathed themselves and also washed the clothes which they were wearing. And all the vessels and articles of furniture, and anything else that happens to be inside, practically everything is held by him to be unclean. For a man's soul is a precious thing, and when it departs to seek another home, all that will be left behind is defiled, deprived as it is of the divine image. For it is the mind of man which has the form of God, being shaped in conformity with the ideal archetype, the Word that is above all.
> *Special Laws* 3:206-207 (Trans. F. H. Colson, p. 605)

It is only within the present supposition that we can understand how anyone will have asked about the "relationship" between a Tent and a utensil. Why in the world should that question have been troubling, if a tent is pretty much the same as a house, and a utensil is a pot? Surely the difference between a house and a pot is clear: You live in the one, excrete into the other. But if by Tent we mean, that which can contain the uncleanness exuded by a corpse, something a handbreadth in its breadth, depth, and height, then the difference between such a container and a pot or other utensil indeed is to be stated. It is not going to appear obvious. We are given two answers. One is that a Tent is large, a utensil is not. That satisfied Ushans, particularly Meir and Judah (M. Kel. 15:1, 18:1).

But Chapter Nine has given us another. A large object (here: a hive) which is whole and useful is indeed a utensil. If the same object is broken, it is no longer a utensil, therefore it can serve as a Tent. That obviously can have meant to no one that the object may serve as a house or a place of dwelling. The conception is quite different. It is this: when broken the object can contain corpse-uncleanness and will not let it exude. When whole and undamaged, it cannot do so. This conception, moreover, is already before us in the exegetical tradition. A Tent keeps back its uncleanness if it is merely covered, while a utensil has to be tightly sealed. So again we see that by Tent our Mishnah means something very concrete and specific, something to be defined. Yet it also means something quite abstract when measured against the given and established meaning of tent, or of house.

A utensil, whole and serviceable, compresses uncleanness; it does not scatter its affects against its own roof or cover, so to speak. That is why corpse-matter in a pot spurts upward or downward, but not to the sides, while corpse-matter in a Tent spreads upward against the cover of the Tent, will not pass through the roof and upward, cleaving perpendicularly. The stereotyped language, "breaks forth upward and donwward," vividly expresses the conception. What is the difference between the Tent, which diffuses the corpse-matter's uncleanness against the roof and prevents its passage beyond (or diffuses it so that it will not enter), and the utensil, which does not have that capacity? As we saw, one conception is that the difference is size. The utensil compresses the corpse-matter because it is a small object, and the corpse-matter gathers strength and bursts through the cover, unless it is tightly sealed. The Tent, as I said, diffuses that same power over a wider area, with the stated result, interposition or generalized contamination to the sides, as well as perpendicularly.

Yet the other conception—a Tent is a broken utensil—contains its own explanation. The utensil when whole cannot hold back the uncleanness. When broken, it can. This seems a strange paradox indeed. What is the meaning of the breakage? It is that the object no longer is susceptible to uncleanness, cannot be affected or acted upon by uncleanness. When the object is a utensil, it itself is subject to the uncleanness, and, as it were, it squeezes out the uncleanness within, causing it to spurt forth upward and downward. When it is not a utensil but a Tent, not subject to uncleanness, it contains that to which it is neutral and not susceptible. In a curious way, as ᶜAqiva claims, the object itself—utensil or Tent—thus plays an active role in the dispersion or containment of the uncleanness.

Philo might justly observe that the soul, having left its broken utensil, the corpse, now finds a domicile only in another broken utensil.

IV. Negaim Before 70

i. Definition of the Problem

As before (V, pp. 220-234), we now have to ask about the presuppositions of Yavnean rulings and their relationship to Scriptures, the Written Torah. Unlike our procedure in Kelim and Ohalot, we do not review the Scriptural materials to eliminate from our catalogue of principles and presuppositions those items which certainly derive from the written Torah. For if we did, we should have little left. Furthermore, the extant exegetical materials do contain items, the principles of which are logically prior to rules in Mishnah-Tosefta, e.g., the third week of quarantine for houses. To state the result at the outset, we shall now see that the development and articulation of the laws of Negaim in the Oral Torah depend wholly upon the laws of the Written Torah. When this has been fully spelled out, we shall ask about the purpose of the rabbis who stand behind our tractate.

Before proceeding, however, we had best call to mind the outline of our tractate as a whole (VI, pp. 2-18). There we observe the striking and exact parallel between the organization and the thematic structure of Mishnah Negaim and of Leviticus Chapters Thirteen and Fourteen. The only important change is in moving houses ahead of purification rites, that is, M. Chapters Twelve and Thirteen correspond to Lev. 14:33-53 and M. Chapter Fourteen covers the ground of Lev. 14:1-32. A second and even more basic correspondence between Mishnah and Scripture is in the topics of Mishnah itself: bright spots, boils and burnings, scalls, baldspots, garments, houses. To put it very simply, no primary theme or supposition of Mishnah seems to diverge from what is explicit in Scripture. This is remarkable, because the primary issues of Kelim, the uncleanness of domestic utensils, and of Ohalot, the Tent which is quantitatively and therefore qualitatively different from the tent of Num. 19:11-20, cannot be discovered in Scripture at all. Accordingly, even before we ask about the fundamental givens of Yavnean pericopae, we recognize that what is taken for granted in specific rulings reflects only part of what is common to Scripture and Mishnah.

ii. The Givens of the Yavnean Rules: Mishnah and Scripture

Items bearing two asterisks (**) are reliably assigned to Yavneh, those with one (*) are placed in Yavneh with a high degree of probability. Each item is characterized in the right-hand column in accord with its relationship to Scripture. At the end we shall summarize the several sorts of relationship between Mishnaic and Scriptural rules.

A. *The Role of the Priest*

*1. M. 3:1B-C: Anyone examines a plague-spot, but the priest announces the decision. The disappearance of symptoms *and* the priestly decision are both essential.   Lev. 13:3: Priest examines.

B. *Time of Inspection*

**1. M. 1:4D-E: We postpone the original inspection so that the seventh day does not coincide with the Sabbath, Hananiah. ᶜAqiva: We postpone the inspection from the seventh day, if need be.   Secondary issue.

C. *The Process of Inspection*

**1. M. 7:3-4, 4:7-10: Changes during the process of inspection, up to the priestly decision, are taken into account. Thereafter, the decision is final.   Secondary issue.

**2. M. 7:4-5: If a person removes tokens of uncleanness after certification, he can be purified.   Secondary issue.

D. *Susceptibility of Gentiles*

**1. M. 3:1, 11:1, 12:1: Gentiles are not susceptible to plagues.   Primary question, left open by Scripture.

E. *Doubt in Matters of Plagues*

**1. M. 4:11 + M. 5:4: Doubts about plagues are resolved in a lenient way.   New principle.

F. *Colors*

**1. M. 1:1: There are two shades of white, two shades of white, two shades of reddish-white. + Red, green in garments, houses.   Lev. 13:3, white
Lev. 13:19, red
+ SPHT = secondary shade for each, thus: two = four.

**2. M. 1:1, 3/T. 1:1: Colors join together. 3. T. 1:4: Scalls and quick raw flesh are not limited by color. Gold hair in scalls.   These are biblically founded.

*4. M. 7:2: If colors of a spot change, we have a new spot (ᶜAqiva). Eleazar b. ᶜAzariah: The old spot is clean.

Secondary issue.

G. Bright Spots

1. M. 1:5-6: Tokens of uncleanness in a bright spot
   a. White hair
   b. Boil around hair
   c. Raw flesh
   d. Square
   e. Hair encompassed
   f. Boil in raw flesh
   g. Spreading
   h. Primary sign
   i. Split bean (M. 6:1)

All but items d and i seem to restate Scriptural rules. The matter of color strikingly is absent.

**2. M. 4:7: If a token of uncleanness disappeared and reappeared, or if the spot contracted and spread, etc., ᶜAqiva says it is unclean (M. 7:2). That is, we take account of intervening changes. + M. 5:3: Residuary hair is unclean, for the same reason.

Secondary issue.

**3. M. 4:11: Bright spot must precede white hair.

Presumably based on exegesis, as is stated explicitly, e.g., M. 10:2.

**4. M. 8:1: Breaking forth: From unclean status—clean. From clean status, unclean. If tips reappear, status reverts. If quick flesh recurs, status reverts. If hair recurs, status does not revert. Joshua, M. 8:2, raises the issue of whether white hair is equivalent to quick flesh in this process, a secondary development.

Lev. 13:12-14: Since Lev. 13:4 speaks only of quick flesh, Joshua's thesis rests upon the exegesis of that item, claiming it applies to other tokens. T. 3:9 makes the exegetical issue explicit.

**5. M. 8:9: One unclean who is wholly white on whom reversion takes place is unclean, so Ishmael. Eleazar: clean.

Secondary issue (whatever it is!).

**6. SN 1:4A-D: An area not suitable to grow hair is still susceptible by reason of other tokens of uncleanness.

Secondary issue.

**7. M. 3:3
   Two weeks
   White hair
   Spreading
   Quick flesh

Lev. 13:3, 5; 6
Lev. 13:3
Lev. 13:5
Lev. 13:10

**8. M. 1:3A1-E
   a) What is unchanged at the end of a week is quarantined.
   b) After two weeks—clear.
   c) Certification

Lev. 13:2-3, 4-8

Lev. 13:4-8
Lev. 13:4-8, 9-11

**9. M. 4:7, 1:5-6, 6:1. The spot is a split bean, squared.

As above, these two definitions are important and primary.

H. *Boil and Burning*

**1.	M. 3:4	Boil	Burning
	Do not join together, spread from one to the other or to skin of the flesh (= bright spot)	Lev. 13:1, 21 Lev. 13:20 Lev. 13:22	25, 27 25 27
*2.	M. 9:1-3		
	Do not join together, spread from one to the other or to skin of the flesh (= bright spot).	Secondary issue.	

I. *Scalls*

**1. M. 3:5
    Two weeks   Lev. 13:30-3
    Golden hair   Lev. 13:30
    Spreading   Lev. 13:32
 *2. M. 10:1: Definition of thin.   Obviously secondary.
   3. M. 10:5A-C: How to shave around the scall.   Routine definition.

J. *Baldspots*

**1. M. 3:6
    Two weeks   Sifra proves.
    Quick flesh   Lev. 13:40-44.
    Spreading   Sifra proves.

K. *Clothing*

**1. M. 3:7
    Two weeks   Lev. 13:49, 51, 54
    Green, red   Lev. 13:49
    Spreading   Lev. 13:51
 *2. M. 11:5   Secondary issue.
    Symptoms of uncleanness disappear before inspection—Ishmael: launder anyhow. (T. has Simeon.)
**3. M. 11:7: Colored fabrics are not affected by plague.   This is new and important.
 *4. SN 16:13: Garments abroad are affected.   Secondary issue.
 *5. M. 11:1E-J: Fabrics which come from the ocean are exempt.   Routine.
 *6. SN 12:6: Tearing defined.   Obviously secondary.

L. *Houses*

**1. M. 3:8
    Three weeks   Sifra proves.
    Green, red   Lev. 14:37
    Spreading   Lev. 14:39
**2. M. 12:13: Houses susceptible to plagues defined   Secondary improvement.
**3. M. 13:6: House shading an unclean house.   This is a new development.

M. *Purification-Rites*

**2.	M. 14:7: Poor, rich offering	Lev. 14:10-21
*3.	M. 14:10A-K: If remainder of oil is not put on leper's head, etc.	Important principle, but secondary.
*4.	M. 14:13: Joshua's conundrum	—
*5.	SM 12:6: Definition of tearing.	Secondary improvement
*6.	SM I:4: No postponement of rite.	As above.
*7.	SM 2:7: If leper shaved on eighth day.	Refinement.
*8.	SM IV:4, 6:10: Offerings of poor and rich defined.	Secondary issues.
*9.	SM 2:7: Essential in the rite is what is done to the leper's body.	As above, No. 2.

Let us now categorize the several sorts of relationships between Scripture and Mishnah:

1. *Scripture is summarized*: F1, F3, G1a, b, c, e, f, g, h, G7, G8, H1, I1, J1, K1, L1.
2. *Mishnah defines details of Scriptural rules*: I3, K6, L2, M1, M2, M5.
3. *Mishnah raises secondary issues, generated by Scriptural rules*: B1, C1, 2, F2, 4, G2, 3, 4, 5, 6, 2, I2, K2, K4, K5, M3, M4, M6, M7, M8, M9.
4. *Mishnah's rule or its principle or particular problem is its own*: A1, D1, E1, G1d+i = G6, K3, L3.

This brief division of the materials shows three relationships between Scripture and Mishnah. First, Mishnah will simply summarize, restating in its own language, Scripture's rule. Second, Mishnah will either add some details to the Scriptural law or it will ask a second-order of questions generated by that law And, third, in a few items, Mishnah will either supply its own definition, not hinted at by Scripture, of a Scriptural item, e.g., the house which is susceptible to plagues, the size of the bright spot; or it will present a rule clearly based upon the themes and detailed laws of Scripture, yet not closely related to Scripture, as in the case of the role of the priest, the principle of doubts in respect to plagues, the status of colored fabrics, and the house which shades an unclean house. These items, to be sure, are interesting and important. But by themselves they hardly change the pronounced impression that Negaim contains much Scripture and little *halakhah*, as R. Papa says.

Thus far we have used Mishnah as our base, Scripture as our variable. The consequent impression is that Mishnah in its earliest stages of unfolding corresponds rather closely in themes, principles, and even detailed problems, to Scripture. Where Mishnah gives us more than definitions and second-order improvements of Scripture, it nonetheless carries forward the main lines of Scriptural law with little if any discernible conceptual innovation. This impression may be simply stated:

$$\frac{\text{Scripture}}{\text{Yavneh}} = \frac{\text{Yavneh}}{\text{Usha}}$$

That is to say, just as Ushan materials tend to build upon the rules and principles of Yavnean ones, with no discernible intervening layer of issues or problems, so Yavnean pericopae build upon the rules and principles of Scripture, with a remarkably thin intervening layer of issues, problems, or even exegeses, and this last primarily important in producing a few refinements or facts which themselves generate no important discussions. The results of exegesis clearly prior in conception to the earliest laws simply are taken for granted. The overall impression is that the laws of our tractate began when it was determined to spell out and clarify the Scriptural materials of Leviticus Chapters Thirteen and Fourteen, and that the Oral Torah, Negaim, is simply the result of an effort to fill in details or supply definitions necessary for a full comprehension of the Written Torah in the stated chapters.

Let us now test that impression by systematically comparing Scripture's conceptions to those of Mishnah, this time making use of the whole of the Mishnah-Tosefta. We shall present Scripture as the base and Mishnah as the variable and systematically compare the law of the one to the law of the other. This will require no speculation at all about how the Mishnaic authorities—Yavnean and Ushan alike—may be assumed to have read and understood or interpreted Scripture, because all we shall do is review the systematic account of Scripture-Mishnah relationships supplied by Sifra. We therefore do not need to ask about the "original" meaning of the laws of Leviticus, only about how the rabbis of the late first and second centuries read those laws and about the relationship between their conceptions of Negaim and Leviticus's rules.

iii. Scripture and Mishnah, Ṣaraʿat and Negaʿ

The impression formed from the consideration of the primary and fundamental conceptions of the Yavnean stratum is that there is no perceptible distance between Scripture and Mishnah. The Yavneans seem to take up exactly where Scripture leaves off, just as the Ushans take up where the Yavneans leave off. Indeed, the correspondences between Yavnean developments of Scriptural rules are fairly numerous and close, perhaps even closer, upon inspection, than those between Ushans and Yavneans. Accordingly, all that Mishnah-Tosefta Negaim seems to intend is to clarify or gloss the laws of Leviticus Thirteen and Fourteen.

Nothing could be further from the truth. I shall now demonstrate that what is new and significant in Mishnah-Tosefta Negaim is as striking, in its way, as what is new and significant in Mishnah-Tosefta Kelim and Ohalot. But there is an important difference. In the first two tractates, we can readily discern not only what is new, but also the significance of what is new. In Negaim we shall see what is new, but it will be difficult to determine the importance of what is new, of the work of the first-century authorities, down to the end of Yavnean times. Let us proceed, first of all, to show what is the fundamental and distinctive interest, the innovative conception, of Negaim.

In a single word, what is new in Negaim is the recognition of the *nega^c*—translated as "plague" throughout—as separate and distinct from the *ṣara^cat*—translated as "leprosy" throughout. The secret of our tractate is emblazoned in its title. Omitting reference to purification of *ṣara^cat*, M. Chapter Fourteen and T. Chapters Eight and Nine, we find reference to *ṣara^cat* in M. only in M. 13:11, (= T. 7:11) a leper who entered a house; T. 3:6, a leper who has been quarantined may circumcize himself and is free of the sacrifice; and T. 6:7, leprosy comes only because of arrogance. Accordingly, our tractate exhibits a strange disjuncture from Lev. 13-14, for those chapters treat *nega^c* and *ṣara^cat* as a single sort of ailment, *nega^c ṣara^cat* meaning spot of leprosy (RSV: *leprous disease*; LXX: *spot of leprosy*) and our tractate speaks only of one, treating the two as separate ailments. Indeed, T. 6:7 could not be clearer on this point, for it distinguishes between the origin of a *nega^c* and the origin of *ṣara^cat*, and then supplies a further view that the two different diseases have a single cause, arrogance.

We do not have to speculate about how the rabbis of the late first and second centuries read Scriptures, for Sifra supplies abundant information. Let us now survey Sifra's interpretation of Leviticus 13-14, with particular reference to the interpretation of *nega^c* and *ṣara^cat*, how each word is treated separately and in relationship to the other. We shall now see that in virtually no comment on the relevant Scriptures do the rabbis who stand behind Sifra-Mishnah-Tosefta ever regard the one as the same as the other, though they will argue that in important respects the one is equivalent to, or functions like, the other. That is a very different thing. In attending to Sifra's reading of Leviticus 13-14, we do not claim that the rabbis derive their viewpoints from Scripture, only that Sifra tells us how they do read Scripture. Accordingly, our purpose is to show that the failure of Mishnah-Tosefta Negaim to refer to *ṣaraʿat* except in connection with those matters in which Scripture itself refers only to *ṣaraʿat* and almost not at all to *negaʿ*—Lev. 14:1-32—is pointed and meaningful. What it proves, as I said, is that, to the rabbis, *negaʿ* is different from *ṣaraʿat*, even though the laws of the one are virtually identical, and spun out of the rules pertaining to, the laws of the other. The meaning of the difference does not concern us here. Our task is first of all to demonstrate the autonomous character of *negaʿ*.

My translation of the relevant Scriptures accords with the way I have translated Mishnah-Tosefta; except for preserving *negaʿ* as *negaʿ*, rather than calling it "plague," and *ṣaraʿat* as *ṣaraʿat*, not calling it "leprosy," I have assigned the same meanings to Scriptural words as are already given to the same words in Mishnah, Tosefta, and Sifra.

13:1 The Lord said to Moses and Aaron:		M. 7:1-2
13:2 When a man has on the skin of his flesh a swelling (SʾT), or an eruption (SPḤT) or a spot (BHRT), and it turns into *negaʿ ṣaraʿat*, and he shall be brought to Aaron the priest or to one of his sons the priests.	SN 1:1 Contrasts Lev. 13:2 to 13:38-9. Lev. 13:2 speaks of bright spots which are in unclean colors, yet which are clean, because their bearer is insusceptible.	

Interestingly, neither Sifra nor Mishnah, e.g., M. 1:1, ever treats SPḤT as an autonomous type of unclean spot, along with SʾT and BHRT. It is taken for granted by Sifra, moreover, that in Lev. 13:2 we speak of an unclean spot, and I assume the reason is the occurrence of *negaʿ ṣaraʿat*, These are, however, not differentiated from one another.

	SN 1:2-3 Spots which occur before Sinai are clean, and this cannot be proved logically. SN 1:4 A-C: A place which cannot produce white hair is susceptible if it can produce another token of uncleanness.	(M. 7: A1)

H, N-O:
SPHT means a secondary shade of white.
P:
Colors join together.
Q:
Skin is adjudged in accord with its appearance.
SN 1:5   M. 2:1

The obviously important point is the exclusion of SPHT as a distinctive type of uncleanness.

SN 1:6-7
A-C: Leper is pained.
E-K: (M. 6:1)
Nega⁽ ṣara⁽at proves that both are the size of a split bean.

The main point of SN 1:6-7 is that we prove the leprosy-sign must be equivalent to the plague in size, a split bean. This proof takes for granted that the one is different from the other, but they can be shown to exhibit the same requirements. The given here is the size of the ṣara⁽at, which then is applied to the nega⁽. This is the most common exegesis of ṣara⁽at.

13:3 And the priest shall examine the nega⁽ on the skin of the flesh, and if the hair in the nega⁽ has turned to white, and the color of the nega⁽ is deeper than the skin of the flesh, it is nega⁽ ṣara⁽at. And the priest will see it and declare it unclean.	SN 1:8-10: *Re* priests.	M. 3:K, 2:5
	SN 2:1	
	The priest's eyes must be on the nega⁽, all at once. Yosé b. R. Judah: There must be room for spreading.	(M. 6:7) M. 2:1F T. 2:12 M. 6:8K-L
	SN 2:2A = B Hair = two.	
	SN 2:2C-E Hair must be inside plague-sign	T. 2:2A
	SN 2:2F-H Nega⁽ must turn hair white.	M. 4:11
	SN 2:3	M. 4:4A-G T. 2:2B
	SN 2:4 White hair excludes golden hair, not a token of uncleanness in a bright spot.	
	SN 2:5 Colors of plagues.	(M. 1:1, 3)

	SN 2:6-7, 8A-B Links Lev. 13:3 to 13:11, to prove they do not shut up one already certified unclean.	M. 3:1F
	SN 2:8C-D-2:9 Negaᶜ ṣaraᶜat and he will see it—all at once.	M. 8:6
	SN 2:10 He will declare him unclean.	M. 7:4-4, T. 3:4B

Interestingly, this entire group makes no reference to *negaᶜ ṣaraᶜat* as a set. In fact, *negaᶜ* is never subjected to exegesis, even when it is cited with *ṣaraᶜat*, as at SN 2:8C-D—2:9. What is interesting to Sifra? The priest's sight, skin of the flesh, hair, turning the hair white by the *negaᶜ*, color of hair, colors of plagues, not judging what already has been judged, and so on. I am inclined to think the disinterest in *negaᶜ ṣaraᶜat* is because the use of the two together already has been explained: what applies to the one applies to the other. Therefore we are not going to distinguish among other laws applicable to the matter. All rules apply to each sort of uncleanness.

13:4 But if the spot (BHRT) is white in the skin of his body and its color is no deeper than the skin, and the hair in it has not turned white, the priest shall shut up the *negaᶜ* for seven days.	SN II:1-6 Swelling is white. The shade of white is snow, brighter than tetter (Lev. 13:38).	M. 1:1-2, 4, T. 1:1
	SN II:7-9 Hair must be wholly turned white by bright spot. Black hair does not diminish spot. Two quarantines.	M. 4:6, T. 2:3 (M. 4:4).

Here the bright spot (BHRT) is equated with the *negaᶜ*. This is a usage of *negaᶜ* familiar in M. Chapters Four through Eight.

13:5 And the priest shall examine him on the seventh day, and if in his eyes the *negaᶜ* has stood, and the *negaᶜ* has not spread in the skin, then the priest will shut him up seven days more.	SN 2*:1-3 Examination by day, by priest with good eyes, in average light.	M. 2:2
	SN 2*:4 If the spot changed and reverted to the original color, we ignore the change in the intervening period. The seventh day counts in both weeks. The same priest does the inspecting.	T. 1:15 (M. 4:7, 1:4, 3:8)

Again, *nega*ᶜ of Scripture and "bright spot" (BHRT) of Mishnah are identical.

13:6 And the priest shall examine him on the seventh day a second time. And lo, the *nega*ᶜ has grown dim, and the *nega*ᶜ has not spread on the flesh. And the priest shall declare it clean. It is an eruption (MSPḤT). And he will wash his clothes, and he is clean.	SN 2*:5-7 Dimming is relative. We do not take account of changes in the interval.	M. 4:7
	SN 2*:8 Lev. 13:5, 6 apply to man, not garment. SN 2*:9 It is clean even though colors did not change. SN 2*:10 Washing clothing diminishes uncleanness.	(M. 4:7) M. 5:2

The *nega*ᶜ of Scripture is the BHRT—bright spot—of M.

13:7 But if the eruption (MSPḤT) spreads in the flesh after it has been shown to the priest for its purification, then it shall be shown a second time to the priest. 13:8 And the priest shall see, and lo, the eruption has spread in the flesh. And the priest shall declare it unclean. It is *ṣara*ᶜ*at*.	SN 2*:11-12 Spreading is in any unclean color; we do not take account of changes in the interval. SN 2*:13 Priestly inspection. SN 2*:14-17 Spreading is in any unclean color. Lev. 13:8 proves this. (= Colors join together.)	(T. 1:1, 1 1:3A) M. 5:2

The force of *ṣara*ᶜ*at* is to prove that spreading is unclean only in a specified color-range. *It is leprosy* excludes tetter-spreading. Curiously, Sifra ignores the MSPḤT. It never enters M.-T.'s purvue either. Why not? Because MSPḤT is a sort of *ṣara*ᶜ*at*, not associated with the *nega*ᶜ, but something which makes its appearance *after* the *nega*ᶜ of Lev. 13:6 has been declared clean.

114   THE MISHNAH BEFORE 70

13:9 Nega^c ṣara^{c}at, when it will be on a man, and he shall be brought to the priest,

13:10 and the priest shall see, and behold, a white swelling is in the skin, and it has turned hair white, or quick raw flesh is in the swelling.

SN III:1
Swelling made unclean by quick flesh. Pursued because of association of Nega^c + Ṣara^{c}at: all colors which affect leprosy affect all forms of nega^c, including Ṣ⁾T.

SN III:2   (M. 8:2)
Recurrence of quick flesh means one who turns wholly white is unclean.

SN III:3-4, 5, 6   M. 5:3
Spot must turn hair white—   M. 4:10
vs. residuary hair.   M. 4:11

SN III:7
Quick flesh = two hairs in space.

SN III:8-11   M. 6:1
Ṣara^{c}at proves only one token   (1:56-I)
of uncleanness suffices. White hair and quick flesh must be inside swelling. Size: 36 hairs, squared.

This is particularly striking. Now *nega^c* is primary, *ṣara^{c}at* is understood to imply that various colors applicable to *ṣara^{c}at* apply to all sorts of *nega^{c}s*, just as above. In any case the two words are interpreted separately.

13:11 It is a chronic [old] ṣara^{c}at on the skin of his flesh. And the priest will declare him unclean. He will not quarantine him, because he is unclean.

SN 3:1
Ṣara^{c}at proves it must be the   (M. 6:1)
size of a split bean. Chronic means quick flesh need not be turned by spot.

SN 3:2
Chronic means quick flesh renders unclean if it appears after the spot appears, as above.

SN 3:3-4:
Re priestly inspection.

Again, the function of *ṣara^{c}at* is to link up traits assigned to the bright spot with other primary signs.

13:12 And if, breaking, the ṣara^{c}at will break forth on the skin, and the ṣara^{c}at will cover all the skin, the nega^c is from

SN 3:5-7   T. 3:11
Process is continuous, etc.   (M. 8:6)

SN 4:1
Ṣara^{c}at proves all colors apply,

his head to his feet; according to the entire vision of the eyes of the priest. 13:13 Then the priest will see, and behold, the *ṣara⁽at* has covered all his flesh, then he will declare the *nega⁽* clean. He has entirely turned white. He is clean.	excluding the tetter. SN 4:2 "All flesh" defined, excluding feet, head. SN 4:3	(M. 8:5, 6:8) M. 2:4, T. 1:8, M. 2:3.
	SN 4:4 *Ṣara⁽at* proves breaking forth is in all appropriate colors. SN 4:6 Breaking forth takes place at any point in the inspection process. SN 4:7	M. 8:1
13:14 And on the day on which appears on him living flesh, he will be unclean.	SN 5:1 Size of recurrence.	T. 3:7-8
	SN 5:2 SN 5:3 SN 5:4-5	M. 3:2 M. 8:5 M. 8:2,
13:15 And the priest will see the living flesh and declare him unclean. The living flesh is unclean. It is *ṣara⁽at*. 13:16 Or when the living flesh will return and will turn white, and he will come to the priest, 13:17 And the priest will see him, and lo, the *nega⁽* has turned white. And the priest will declare the *nega⁽* clean. It is clean.	SN 5:6 = 4:6 SN 5:7 *Ṣara⁽at* proves SN 5:6 = 4:6. SN 6:1 SN 6:2 Tetter color included. SN 6:3 = SN 4:6, 5:6 SN 6:4	T. 5:9 M. 8:4 M. 8:1

As before, *ṣara⁽at* serves in this group to link the several colors applying to other forms of the *nega⁽* to this particular one. *Ṣara⁽at* is thus extrinsic, *nega⁽* intrinsic, to the meaning of the passage.

13:18 And the flesh, when there will be on it, on its skin, a boil, and it is healed, 13:19 and there will be, in the place of the boil, a white swelling (SʾT) or a reddish-white bright spot (BHRT), and it will be shown to the priest. 13:20 And the priest shall see, and behold its color is deeper than the skin, and its hair has turned white, and the priest shall	SN 6:5-7 Festering boil is clean, etc. SN IV:1-2 Boil forms a scab over the rising. SN IV:3 *Nega⁽ ṣara⁽at* proves what applies to a bright spot applies to a rising.	(M. 6:8, 9:2) 7:1, 9:3

declare it unclean. It is a *nega^c sara^cat*. On the boil has it broken forth.	SN IV:4 Color SN IV:8 SN IV:5	M. 5:4
13:21 And if the priest will see it, and behold, there is no white hair in it, and it is not deeper than the skin, and it is dim, and the priest shall quarantine it for seven days.	Priest sees all at once.	(M. 6:7)
13:22 And if it will surely spread on the skin, and the priest shall declare it unclean. It is a *nega^c*.	SN IV:6-7 Spreading.	M. 5:2
13:23 And if the bright spot remains in one place and has not spread, it is the scar of the boil. And the priest shall declare it clean.	SN IV:4, 9 Spreading under it, not on to skin of flesh.	M. 9:1-2, 5:5

The force of *sara^cat* once again is to link *nega^c* to other forms of uncleanness, in this case, the rising.

13:24 Or flesh, when there will be on its skin a burning of fire, and raw flesh of the burning becomes a bright reddish-white or white spot,	SN 7:1-2 Boil and burning to not join together. SN 7:3 Festering—clean. SN 7:4 SN 7:5 = SN IV:3 SN 7:6 = SN IV:5 SN 7:7 = SN IV:4 SN 7:8 SN 7:9	M. 9:2 T. 3:13 M. 9:1
13:25 and the priest shall see it, and behold, the hair in the bright spot has turned white, and its color is deeper than the skin, it is *sara^cat*. In the burning has it spread. And the priest shall declare it unclean. It is *nega^c sara^cat*.	*Sara^cat* in Lev. 13:25, 27 proves: 1) split bean, 2) rising = bright spot, 3) burning = boil.	
13:26 And if the priest shall see it, and behold, there is no white hair in the bright spot, and it is not deeper than the skin, and it has grown dim, then the priest will quarantine it for seven days.		
13:27 And the priest shall see it on the seventh day: if it has surely spread on the skin, the priest shall declare it unclean. It is a *nega^c sara^cat*.		
13:28 And if it remains in its place, the bright spot has not spread in the skin, and it is		

dim, it is a swelling (S∍T) of the burn, and the priest shall declare it clean. It is the scar of the burn.

The interesting item is SN 7:9, which interprets the appearance of *ṣaraᶜat* in the way which by now has become routine: it is meant to link traits of various specific sorts of uncleanness. Does this mean that all are a form of *ṣaraᶜat*? Or does it mean that the connection is formal, the appearance of a word in common among all groups? It is difficult to say for sure. What is beyond doubt, however, is that *negaᶜ* and *ṣaraᶜat* are systematically interpreted as separate and distinct words, each with its own meaning or function. For our purposes, what is decisive is that *ṣaraᶜat* is not the same thing as *negaᶜ*.

13:29 And a man or a woman, when there will be on him a *negaᶜ* on the head or on the beard.	SN V:1 Scall inside of scall.	
13:30 And the priest shall see the *negaᶜ*, and lo, its color is deeper than the skin, and in it is thin golden hair, then the priest shall declare it unclean. It is a scall. It is *ṣaraᶜat* of the head or of the beard.	SN V:2-3 *Ṣaraᶜat* of the head *or* of the beard means they do not join together. SN V:4: Colors must be natural. SN V:5-6 SN V:7-9 Golden hair alone affects the scall. Golden hair does not affect bright spots.	M. 10:9 M. 10:1
13:31 And when the priest shall see the *negaᶜ* of the scall, and lo, its color is not deeper than the skin of the flesh, but black hair is not in it, then the priest shall quarantine the *negaᶜ* of the scall seven days.	SN 8:1-4 *Negaᶜ* means the gold hair must be turned gold by scall, just as in case of bright spot. 8:4 Just as scall does not spread inward, so *negaᶜ* does not (*vs.* Meir, M. 6:2-4). SN 8:5-6 Black hair affords protection, SN 8:7-8 SN 8:9 Black hair affords protection.	 M. 10:3 T. 4.1 M. 10:6-7
13:32 And the priest shall see the *negaᶜ* on the seventh day, and behold, the scall has not spread, and there was no golden hair in it, and the color of the scall is not deeper than the skin, 13:33 and he will shave himself. But the scall he will not shave,	SN 9:1-2 Day SN 9:3 Color SN 9:4-7	 T. 4:1B

and the priest will quarantine the scall seven days, a second time.		
13:34 And the priest will examine the scall on the seventh day, and lo, the scall has not spread on the skin of the flesh, and its color is not deeper than the flesh, and the priest shall declare it clean, and he will wash his clothes, and he will be clean.	SN 9:8 (2*:10)	
13:35 And if the scall will surely spread on the skin after his purification,	SN 9:9-12	M. 10:5
13:36 and the priest shall see, and behold the scall has spread on the skin. The priest shall not seek for golden hair. He is unclean.	SN 9:11-13 Golden hair without spreading is unclean.	M. 3:1
13:37 But if in his eyes the scall has stood unchanged, and black hair has grown up in it, the scall is healed. It is clean, and the priest shall declare it clean.	SN 9:14-15 SN 9:16 Symptoms must disappear *and* priest must say so.	M. 10:8 T 1:16

There is no effort to prove white hair affects the scall; the opposite is proved. The absence of ṣara‛at would seem to me to stand behind the insistence of Sifra that white hair is not unclean in a scall. For where we *do* have ṣara‛at, the opposite is proved. This seems to me virtually certain, because Simeon, SN 8:1, wants to interpret *nega‛* = bright spot (BHRT) for exactly the opposite purpose, to show that the traits required in the bright spot *are* required in the scall. Accordingly, the linking is through ṣara‛at, but only when the word occurs. Its presence would have served Simeon's argument. SN 8:4 accepts Simeon's reasoning, but for a different purpose.

13:38 And a man or a woman when there will on the skin of their flesh spots, white spots, 13:39 and the priest shall see, and behold, on the skin of their flesh are dim white spots, it is a tetter. It has broken forth on the skin. It is clean.	SN 16:1 Tetter is clean, but a bright spot which goes out of it is unclean.

The importance of the tetter to M.-T. is in establishing the shade of white which is not a symptom of uncleanness. What is brighter-white than the tetter is unclean.

13:40 And a man, when his head will grow bald, he is bald (QRH). He is clean.	SN 10:2-3, 5-6 Relationship of head and beard. ṢRW^c, Lev. 13:44, proves the law of 13:40 applies to man, woman, or child.	M. 10:9
13:41 And if from the forehead and his head he will become bald, he is bald on the forehead (GBH). He is clean.	SN 10:7	T. 4:9
13:42 And if there will be on the bald head or the bald forehead reddish white, nega^c ṣara^cat is breaking forth on his bald head or on his bald forehead.	SN 10:8 = SN 10:2-6 SN 11:1 Nega^c ṣara^cat: Nega^c teaches that a variegation is a token of uncleanness. Ṣara^cat shows quick flesh is a token of uncleanness. But, SN 11:2 adds, white hair is not.	M. 10:10
13:43 And the priest will see it, and behold, the swelling (Ś^ɔT) of the nega^c is reddish-white on his bald head or bald forehead, it is like the color of ṣara^cat of the skin of the flesh,	SN 11:3-5 Rising made unclean by variegation. SN 11:6V Ṣara^cat = split bean. SN 11:7-8 As above.	
13:44 he is a leprous man (^ɔYŠ ṢRW^c). He is unclean. The priest will declare him unclean. On his head is his nega^c.	SN 12:1 Leprous = includes woman and child. SN 12:2-4 Role of priest.	

As before, the use of ṣara^cat is to show that what applies to one sort of uncleanness applies to others. In this case ṣara^cat shows that the quick flesh applies to the baldspots and that baldspots can appear on a woman and a child as much as on a man. Ṣara^cat as quick flesh in particular recurs below.

13:45 The leprous person (ṢRW^c) on whom is the nega^c—his clothing will be torn, and his hair of his head will hang loose, and he will cover up his upper lip, and 'Unclean, unclean' will he cry out.	SN 12:5 Leper includes high priest. SN 12:6 Tearing clothes. SN 12:7-9 The same rule as applies to lepers applies to others afflicted with plagues, others who are unclean.	
13:46 All the days during which the nega^c is on him, he will be unclean. He is unclean. Solitary shall he sit, outside the camp is his dwelling.	SN 12:10-11	M. 7:4-5 T. 3:5
	SN 12:12-13 = 12:7-9 How do I know that the same	

rule applies to one afflicted with
plague?
SN 12:14   M. 13:7
   Garments also have to be sent
out.

The striking assumption (SN 12:7-9, 12:12-13) is that the leper and the person afflicted with plague are quite distinct from one another. But this is not proved by Lev. 13:45A = ṢRWᶜ/NGᶜ, presumably because it did not require proof. The *opposite* is what has to be proved: while distinct, they *are* subject to the same rule.

13:47 The garment, when there will be on it *negaᶜ ṣaraᶜat*—on a garment of wool or on a garment of linen,	SN 13:1-2 Mixtures of materials.	T. 5:5 (M. 12:2, 11:7)
	SN 13:3-4 Garments are susceptible only when undyed.	M. 11:3 T. 5:3
	SN 13:5-7 Susceptibility of warp, woof.	M. 11:8
13:48 in the warp or in the woof of linen or of wool, or on a skin, or on anything made of skin,	SN 13:8-12 What comes from the ocean is not susceptible.	M. 11:1 (M. 11:11)
	SN 14:1 Hides, dyed and not.	M. 11:3
13:49 and the *negaᶜ* will be greenish or reddish, on the garment or on the skin, or on the warp or on the woof, or on anything made of hide, it is *negaᶜ ṣaraᶜat*. And he will show it to the priest.	SN 14:2 Colors defined, join together.	(M. 11:4)
	SN 14:3 Size of cloth.	M. 11:10
	SN 14:4-6 *Ṣaraᶜat* = split bean.	
13:50 And the priest will see the *negaᶜ*, and he will quarantine the *negaᶜ* for seven days.	SN 14:7-8 Daytime.	
13:51 And he will see the *negaᶜ* on the seventh day. If the *negaᶜ* has spread on the garment, on the warp or on the woof, or on the hide, or on anything made of hide, *ṣaraᶜat* curses the *negaᶜ*. It is unclean.	SN 14:9-10 NGᶜ of Lev. 13:51 means it must be a split bean.	M. 11:7
	SN 14:11 Do not use leprous garment.	
	SN 15:1-3 NGᶜ = That which is suitable to receive the spot.	M. 11:10
13:52 And he will burn the garment, the warp or the woof of wool or of linen or any object of hide on which the *negaᶜ* will be, because it is a cursing *ṣaraᶜat*. In fire will it be burned.		

In the present group, both *ṣaraᶜat* and *negaᶜ* are called to show that the spot is the size of a split bean. The two are regarded as separate from one another, though analogous. On this set, see below, p. 248.

13:53 And if the priest will see, and lo, the *nega*ᶜ has not spread on the garment, on the warp or on the woof or on any object of leather,	SN 15:4 Thus is what is unchanged.	
13:54 then the priest will command, and they will wash that on which is the *nega*ᶜ, and he will shut it up seven days, a second time.	SN 15:5 We do not wash the spot only. SN 15:6 Seventh day.	
	SN 15:7 Changing, etc.	M. 11:5
13:55 And the priest will see after the *nega*ᶜ is washed, and lo, the *nega*ᶜ has not changed color (lit.: "turned its eye"), and the *nega*ᶜ has not spread, it is unclean. In fire will you burn it, it is diminished (PḤTT), whether on its front or on its back [RSV: whether the leprous spot (PḤTT) is on the back or on the front].	SN 15:8 PḤTT means diminution or that the spot is embedded in the body of the fabric. SN 15:9 Back, front.	M. 11:11
13:56 And if the priest will see, and lo, the *nega*ᶜ has grown dim after it has been washed, and he will tear it from the garment, from the hide, or from the warp or from the woof.	SN 15:10 *Nega*ᶜ means the spot dims to the second shade, so relatively. SN 16:1-2 Tearing. SN 16:3 Just as *nega*ᶜ means relative dimming to the second shade here, so elsewhere the meaning is the same.	
13:57 And if it will appear again on the garment, on the warp or on the woof or on any object of leather, it is breaking forth. In fire will you burn that on which is the *nega*ᶜ.	SN 16,4, 5, 6 Patch SN 16:7-9	M. 11:1 M. 11:7
13:58 And the garment, the warp or the woof, or any object of hide which you will wash, and the *nega*ᶜ will go away from them, then it will be washed a second time, and it is clean.	SN 16:10-11 Washing.	
13:59 This is the Torah of *nega*ᶜ *ṣara*ᶜ*at* of the garment of wool or of linen or of the warp or of the woof or of any leather object, for its cleanness or for its uncleanness.	SN 16:12 Garment compared to scall, etc. SN 16:13 Garment susceptible abroad.	

Once again, *nega*ᶜ functions as does *ṣara*ᶜ*at*, to establish an analogy between a rule applying to one case and one applying to another.

Negaᶜ in both instances means that in each case we do not require dimming to an absolutely clean color, that is, the fifth shade of white, but accept dimming relative to the former brightness. This is curious, because *ṣaraᶜat* is used earlier to show that all the unclean colors apply. Accordingly *negaᶜ* and *ṣaraᶜat* are carefully distinguished from one another, yet function in identical ways and for the same exegetical purposes, a result which is already familiar.

14:1 And the Lord spoke to Moses saying,	SM I:1-2 All lepers bring this sacrifice.

14:2 This is the Torah of the *meṣoraᶜ*: on the day of his purification, then he will be brought to the priest.	SM I:3
	    By day/priest's role.
	SM I:4
	    Rite not postponed.
	SM I:5
	    Leper-priest.

14:3 And the priest will go out of the camp, and the priest will see, and lo, *negaᶜ haṣaraᶜat* is healed from the *ṣaruᶜa*.
14:4 And the priest will command, and one will purchase for him who is to be purified...
	SM I:6-8
	    Healed: plague has left.
	    Plague: white hair is gone.
	    Leprosy: quick flesh.
	    From the leper: Applies rite to him over whom leprosy has broken forth.

Now Sifra's *negaᶜ* applies to white hair, *ṣaraᶜat* to quick flesh—a strange revision in the established sense of the words. Since *negaᶜ* next occurs at Lev. 14:32 and does not occur in Sifra's treatment of the intervening verses (except at SM 2:4), we skip directly to the end of the pericope.

14:32 This is the Torah of him on whom is *negaᶜ ṣaraᶜat*, who cannot afford the offerings for his cleansing.	SM IV:16: Status of wife.	M. 14:12, 14:11, etc.

Here both *negaᶜ* and *ṣaraᶜat* are ignored. What is odd is that no one has bothered to prove the rite for *negaᶜ* is the same as that for *ṣaraᶜat*. SM I:1-2 has occasion to refer to this matter and does not do so. On the other hand, the text commonly reads, "he who is to be purified" without specifying whether it is from *negaᶜ* or from *ṣaraᶜat*, thus assimilating the two in a single, undifferentiated rite. Sifra's disregard of the question of a separate purification-rite for *negaᶜ* is easily understood. Mishnah-Tosefta know no separate rite, nor do they ever assume that any detail of the rite for the one differs from that for the other. What is the result of being afflicted with a *negaᶜ*? It is that one is unclean. This is the same for one afflicted with ṣaraʿat. Once one is unclean through a *negaʿ*, he falls into the general category of people unclean by reason of this inclusive genre of afflictions, exactly the same category as one afflicted with *ṣaraʿat*, as I said. Accordingly, once one falls into the category of uncleanness, he is part of a homogeneous group to which a single set of rules apply: rules which lift a person up from that status to the status of cleanness. The rules of the *negaʿ* concern how one *falls*, by stages, from the category of cleanness to that of uncleanness. These stages and the phenomena which signify them are carefully differentiated. But the two extreme stages—cleanness, uncleanness—are themselves not differentiated. To use a homely analogy, we may say that, en route from cleanness down to uncleanness, there are several elevators, and each one stops at many floors. But en route from uncleanness to cleanness, there is only one elevator. Everyone must use it.

14:33 And the Lord spoke to Moses and to Aaron saying,
14:34 When you will come to the land of Canaan, which I am giving to you as a possession, and I shall put *negaʿ ṣaraʿat* on a house of your possession,

SM V:1-3
When houses are susceptible.
SM V:4
Negaʿ is good news, Judah.
Simeon: *Negaʿ* must be natural.
SM V:5
Jerusalem exempt.
SM V:6
Gentiles' homes not susceptible.

14:35 then the one who owns the house shall come and tell the priest, saying Something like a *negaʿ* has appeared to me in the house.

SM V:6-11
(1) Plagues come because of gossip.
(2) Plagues come because of arrogance.
II Chron. 26:19: *Ṣaraʿat*; 26:20: *ṣaraʿat*, because the Lord afflicted him with plague (NGʿW). The two are seen as separate but equivalent, and both are caused by arrogance.

ʿUzziah's arrogance, in II Chron. 26:19, brings leprosy upon him. But the story (II Chron. 26:20) also refers to his being smitten with *negaʿ*. Accordingly, plagues too come because of arrogance, just as does leprosy. The two clearly are differentiated as to their origination, the *negaʿ*, in gossip and/or arrogance, *ṣaraʿat*, in arrogance. Once again, the exegetical task is not to differentiate *negaʿ* from *ṣaraʿat*. That is assumed. The exegete has the opposite problem: to link the two and show what they have in common.

14:36 Then the priest will command, and they will empty the house before the priest comes to see the *negaᶜ*, so that whatever is in the house will not be unclean. And afterward the priest will come to see the house.	M V:12 Evil people are afflicted by plague. M V:13	M. 12:5 M. 13:9, 3:2
14:37 And he will examine the *negaᶜ*, and lo, the *negaᶜ* is on the walls of the house, spots (ŠQᶜRWRT) of green or red, and their color is deeper than the wall.	SM VI:1-4 *Negaᶜ* mentioned twice means the sign is to be two split beans. SM VI:5 Priestly examination and declaration. SM VI:6-8 Priestly examination.	M. 12:7 M. 12:6
14:38 Then the priest will go out of the house to the door of the house and quarantine the house for seven days.		
14:39 And the priest will return on the seventh day and see, and lo, the *negaᶜ* has spread on the walls of the house.	SM VI:9, 10 *Negaᶜ* in Lev. 14:39, 40 is a split bean SM VI:11 SM 4:1-3 Dismantling. SM 4:4 Discarding stones.	
14:40 And the priest shall command, and they shall dismantle the stones on which is the *negaᶜ* and throw them out of town in an unclean place.		

Once again, *negaᶜ* serves as does *saraᶜat*, to indicate the requisite size of the spot.

14:41 And he shall cause the inside of the house to be scraped round about, and they shall pour out the dirt which they scraped outside the city in an unclean place.	SM 4:5 Scraping. SM 4:6-10	M. 12:6
14:42 And they shall take other stones and put them in place of the stones, and other dirt will he take and plaster the house.		
14:43 And if the *negaᶜ* returns and breaks forth in the house after he has dismantled the stones and after scraping the house and after plastering,	SM VII:1-2 *Negaᶜ* = two split beans. SM VII:3-4 Color of spreading.	M. 12:7
14:44 then the priest shall come and see, and lo, the *negaᶜ* has spread in the house. It is a cursing *saraᶜat* in the house. It is unclean.	SM VII:5-6 Chronic *saraᶜat* in Lev. 14:44 and Lev. 13:51 means recurrence without spreading is a sign of uncleanness. SM VII:7-10 Third week of quarantine.	

	SM VII:11 Cursing *ṣaraʿat* in Lev. 13:49 and 14:44 links houses to clothing and shows we have a third week of quarantine. SM VII:13	(M. 13:4)

Now *ṣaraʿat* serves as does *negaʿ*, joining two unrelated laws to demonstrate the same rule applies to both. What is curious is that *negaʿ* is equivalently available for the present purpose. Accordingly, *negaʿ* is understood as intrinsic to the passage, *ṣaraʿat* as extrinsic, therefore available for a secondary purpose, the primary meaning of the passage being established by *negaʿ*.

14:45 And he shall demolish the house, its stones and its wood and all the dirt of the house, and take [them] outside the city to an unclean place.	SM 5:1-3	M. 12:2
14:46 And he that comes into the house during the entire time of quarantine will be unclean until evening.	SM 5:4-8, 9 SM 5:10-13	M. 13:9 M. 13:10
14:47 He that lies in the house will wash his clothing, and he who eats in the house will wash his clothing.		
14:48 And if the priest will come and see, and lo, the *negaʿ* has not spread in the house after plastering the house, then the priest shall declare the house clean, because the *negaʿ* has been healed.		
14:49 And he shall take, to purify the house, two birds, and cedar wood, and crimson, stuff, and hyssop.	SM VII:12	M. 13:1
14:50 And he shall slaughter one bird over a clay utensil, over living water.		
14:51 And he shall take the cedar wood and hyssop and crimson stuff and the living bird and dip them in the blood of the slaughtered bird and in living water and sprinkle over the house seven times.	SM 5:14	M. 14:1
14:52 And he shall purify the house with the blood of the bird and with living water and with the living bird and with cedar		

wood and with hyssop and with crimson stuff.		
14:53 And he will send forth the living bird outside the town, toward the field, and he will atone for the house and it will be clean.	SM 5.15 Why do we repeat purification at Lev. 14:53, *re* house, and Lev. 14:20, *re* leper? Because leper requires sacrifice, house does not, etc.	
14:54 This is the Torah for every *negaᶜ haṣaraᶜat*, and for a scall, 4:55 and for *ṣaraᶜat* of the garment and of the house, 14:57 to teach on the day of uncleanness and on the day of the cleanness. This is the Torah of the *ṣaraᶜat*.	SM 5:16 One should not examine plagues who is not an expert, until his master will teach him.	T. 1:1

In many ways SM 5:15-16 are the most satisfactory, for in both cases we clearly distinguish *negaᶜ* from *ṣaraᶜat*. SM 5:15 speaks about the house afflicted by plague as distinguished from the leper, observing that each requires a different sort of purification. Yet this is not decisive, since the main point is differences in the rite of purification, not in the traits of the two diseases. SM 5:16 by contrast is pointed in its reference to *plagues*; Sifra (= T. 1:1-2) omits reference to *ṣaraᶜat*, which is explicit in Lev. Lev. 14:54-7, and stresses the *negaᶜ*, to which Lev. 14:57 does not refer at all, a very strange shift, comprehensible only within the distinction established here.

iv. Negaim: The Rabbinical Disease

What difference does it make that *negaᶜ* and *ṣaraᶜat* are separate and autonomous, if also correlated and parallel, diseases? It seems to me the best way to find the answer is to reconsider the earlier of the two strata of the laws of Negaim. At what points do we discern a significant difference between the pronounced characteristics and tendencies of the biblical law of *negaᶜ ṣaraᶜat* and the Mishnaic law of the *negaᶜ*? In which laws do we seem to take a position or perspective self-evidently different from that of Scripture, so that the difference not only is evident but also produces important consequences? To state the answer in advance, the main differences between biblical *negaᶜ ṣaraᶜat* and Mishnaic *negaᶜ* are these: first, the two indeed are separate diseases; second, the latter is subject to the examination and determination of the expert, who is the sage, not only at the specified times of examination, but at all times. It follows that the *negaᶜ* is, functionally, the quintessentially rabbinic disease. The Mishnaic laws of Negaim in retrospect represent an effort to rabbinize—that is, redefine so as to subject to rabbinical authority—the biblical rules of *nega^c șara^cat*, distinguishing *nega^c* from *șara^cat* so as to supply to the former a distinctive set of requirements and to make room, as Scripture self-evidently does not and cannot, for an authority who is not a priest. It is ^cAqiva who accomplished the rabbinization of the *nega^c*, although the distinction itself, between *nega^c* and *șara^cat*, may not originate with him. That simple result, resting heavily, and perhaps placing even disproportionate weight, upon our exegesis of M. 4:7-10, 5:3, 5:4, 1:4-6, and 8:10, is the best I can offer.

1. M. 1:1, Colors of plagues are four. The antecedent materials give many more than four colors, which ^cAqiva attests. Sifra is clear that it knows four and identifies the four applicable to plagues with those applicable to leprosy. T. 1:1 makes it clear that the 'joining together' or interchangeability of the colors is one primary point important for ^cAqiva.

^cAqiva's further point, that one who is not an expert in them and in their names should not examine plagues, is central to our tractate. It is to be joined, as we have observed, to M. 3:1, the role of the priest is formal, not substantive, since the priest is told by the "expert," the sage, what he is to say. Accordingly, with ^cAqiva we enter the situation in which plagues are regarded as subject to the sages' rule. T. 1:2 then speaks of a *priest* who is not an expert in plagues and says he should not make examinations of plagues—without reference to leprosy at all!—unless he becomes an expert. This is still more pointed than the version of T. 1:1, which refers to anyone who is not expert, and is the version which Sifra selects.

2. M. 1:2, the reddish mixtures. The four Yavnean colors are two whites, two pinks.

3. M. 1:3, Four colors join together to clear, shut up, certify.

4. M. 1:4, Hananiah: Decisive are the seventh day and the priest's inspection on that day. ^cAqiva: At any time do they examine. If the seventh day coincides with the Sabbath, the next inspection is postponed. Hananiah's saying is phrased in terms of plagues. Clearly, ^cAqiva is the innovator, since Scripture leaves no doubt that the leprosy is inspected by the priest and on the seventh day. Accordingly, it would seem that ^cAqiva wishes to distinguish plagues from leprosy. Hananiah sees no difference between the one and the other, applying the Scriptural rule of leprosy to the inspection of plagues. M. 1:5-6 illustrate Hananiah's viewpoint, as does M. 8:10.

5. M. 3:3-8 follow the Scriptural agendum, as noted. "Skin of the flesh" is the Scriptural language, while M. generally prefers BHRT.

6. M. 4:7-10, ^cAqiva's position is what is significant. He is clear that we take account of changes which occur in a bright spot between one inspection and the next. This is congruent with, and flows from,

or generates, his position in No. 4. The expert is going to be available between inspections. Scripture is clear that the inspection is on the seventh day, and the priest does the inspection. So for ʿAqiva the *negaʿ* is different. True, he concedes, the priest his place. But the priest's position is less important than the one who is available to see the spot during the intervening week, "the expert in them and their names."

ʿAqiva seems to build upon the distinction between *negaʿ* and *saraʿat* and to see in that distinction important differences between them. The former, in particular, is in the hands of the expert, the sage. If we take account of changes which affect the primary sign between inspections, then we are not going to concur with M. 1:5-6 and 8:10, as stated, and to ʿAqiva the matter of the seventh-day-inspection by the priest is decidedly subordinated, again a formality preserved without regard to its meaning. The whole discussion, self-evidently, concerns plagues. We do not know what ʿAqiva will have held about leprosy. We may take for granted we do know Hananiah's position.

7. M. 4:11, Joshua seems to me to attest to Yavneh the view that the bright spot must precede the white hair, and the principle that, in matters of plagues, when we are in doubt, we issue a lenient ruling. We do not know the situation in respect to leprosy.

8. M. 5:1, Doubt concerning plagues is resolved in a lenient way; the dubious situation is regarded as clean. The illustrative case, curiously, assumes that we do *not* know what has happened in the intervening week. There may or may not have been a change. But no one has seen the spot and knows for sure whether we have the same or a new one. Accordingly, the principle of leniency is illustrated by a case which ʿAqiva should adjudge in his own way.

8. M. 5:3, ʿAqiva's position on residuary hair conforms to his principle that we take account of changes in the interval between inspections. It further rejects the principle of leniency in cases of doubt, because we are not sure whether we have the same spot, or whether the same spot has changed all the hair. Yet ʿAqiva has no doubt that the hair is a token of uncleanness. Of greater interest, ʿAqiva and ʿAqavya clearly stand against the established tradition; that is the point of the narrative. M. 5:4 places ʿAqiva in a similarly strict position about doubt in the case of two men. Here again, the authority who insists only experts should rule on palgues also insists that experts should know their business. There can be reason for the expert not to know the condition of two men, for he may not have seen both of them. But he most certainly can and should subject one man to continuous inspection; therefore there is no justification for a ruling of leniency.

10. M. 6:1, the requisite space of the bright spot is a Cilician split bean, squared. Sifra takes for granted that the occurrence of the word *saraʿat* carries the same implication. Quick flesh, it is assumed, is the size of a lentil, that is, one ninth the size of the bright spot. Sifra identifies *saraʿat* with the quick flesh. Accordingly, the matter of

measurements is exceedingly confused. But I do not see that much depends upon the confusion. All pertinent pericopae distinguish *nega^c* and *sara^{c}at*.

11. M. 7:2, if the color of a spot changed, Eleazar b. ^{c}Azariah says the spot is clean. ^{c}Aqiva says it is examined afresh. This accords with ^{c}Aqiva's position in M. 4:7-10 and places Eleazar b. ^{c}Azariah in agreement with Hananiah Prefect of the Priests.

12. M. 7:4-5, if one removes the tokens of uncleanness before he is certified unclean or during the quarantine, he is clean. This is ^{c}Aqiva's view. In it, he limits his position on the matter of taking account of intervening changes. Yet, from a different angle, he is entirely consistent, for we *do*, after all, take account of what happens between inspections: the signs have (forcibly) been made to disappear, so the man is clean. We do not burden the man with the presumed uncleanness which would have been confirmed at the next inspection. If a person has been certified unclean, Eliezer notes, he still is unclean, but can become clean under specified conditions. ^{c}Aqiva will concur with Eliezer's principle that the person certified unclean who removes the tokens of uncleanness is indeed still unclean. That is where he begins his inquiry. Interestingly, the question before Eliezer and ^{c}Aqiva does not make explicit reference to *nega^c* at all. On the contrary, the matter centers on quarantine and certification, without allusion to whether we speak of leprosy or of plague. But M. 7:5 has Eliezer refer to another *plague*. Sages demand breaking forth, and this can mean they have in mind either leprosy or plague. Eliezer's materials therefore conform to the established theme of the tractate, and the saying attributed to sages does not explicitly conform. Similarly Joshua and Gamaliel, to whom ^{c}Aqiva addresses his question, do not make clear whether they speak of plagues or leprosy or whether there is any difference.

13. M. 8:1, breaking forth, makes no reference to either plague or leprosy. All that we have is the reversal of the implications of the rule of Lev. 13:12-14. M. 8:2-3, Joshua says that the recurrence of white hair is equivalent to the recurrence of quick flesh. Here again we are not told whether we speak of plague or leprosy; but M. 8:2A speaks of a bright spot, and in the context of our tractate, this must mean we have *nega^c*, not *sara^{c}at*. Here is a good instance of extending Scripture's reference to *sara^{c}at* to the *nega^c*. Lev. 13:12, 13 refer to both, but Lev. 13:15 refers to the reversion of *sara^{c}at* through the living flesh. Why then should Joshua have imagined that the white hair should be equivalent? Perhaps because he wishes to say that in breaking forth and reversion as applied to the *nega^c*, we *do* take account of the white hair as much as of the quick flesh, though in the breaking forth in the case of *sara^{c}at*, we take account of recurrence only of the quick flesh. T. 3:9 assigns the view that Scripture speaks only of quick flesh, not white hair, specifically to ^{c}Aqiva. How then has ^{c}Aqiva interpreted the matter? To him, breaking forth with reference to *sara^{c}at* and with reference to *nega^c* means the same thing. The rule of the latter conforms to that of the former. Joshua wishes to

come at it from the tokens of uncleanness affecting the bright spot —white hair, quick flesh—and to treat the *nega^c* as essentially different from the *sara^{c}at*. Yet ^{c}Aqiva's position in this instance is not the whole story, as I observed above, pp. 199-200.

14. M. 8:9 seems to carry forward Joshua's interest in comparing modes and tokens of uncleanness.

15. M. 9:1-2 distinguish the boil from the burning. Why not, since Scripture treats them in separated contexts, not as a single item? Then who regards them as a single item? Those who come before the time of Eliezer, who attests these rules. They clearly understand M. 9:1-2's boil and burning as *nega^c*s different from the boil and burning of Scripture's *sara^{c}at*. T. 13:3 is clear that the two are "one sign" *but* do not join together.

16. T. 5:3's saying of Simeon in ^{c}Aqiva's behalf that all garments, colored or not, are insusceptible to plagues is a mystery to me. To be sure, ^{c}Aqiva must understand Scripture to speak, in regard to garments, only of *sara^{c}at*; then the matter of plagues in his view simply never arises in connection with clothing, colored or not. On what basis? Sifra gives not a single hint as to how ^{c}Aqiva will have read Lev. 13:47ff. That is not surprising, since no one later on agreed with ^{c}Aqiva.

One possible view is that Lev. 13:47 speaks of *nega^c sara^{c}at*, which here (but not in Lev. 13:3) ^{c}Aqiva will have understood to mean, *a nega^c unclean only because of sara^{c}at*, so too Lev. 13:49. The garment's *nega^c* is quarantined (Lev. 13:50)—but not declared unclean. If the *nega^c* spread, Lev. 13:51, then it falls into the category of "chronic leprosy." In my (idiosyncratic) translation: *sara^{c}at curses the nega^c*! It follows that the garment is unclean because of *sara^{c}at*, not because of *nega^c*. There is no ʾT, so no broadening of the category, *sara^{c}at*. It this strange exegesis is what ^{c}Aqiva had in mind when reading Lev. 13:47-52, why did he not interpret the bright spot in the same way? Clearly, the distinguishing issue is the use of *cursing sara^{c}at*. Where in Lev. 13:14 do we find it? Lev. 13:51, 52, in reference to garments, and Lev. 14:44, with reference to houses. Yet houses *are* susceptible to plagues. Why? Following the former mode of reading the relevant Scriptures, we see that Lev. 14:44 says a *nega^c* has spread in the house. So the house seems to be susceptible to the *nega^c*. Then comes the *cursing sara^{c}at*. The house is susceptible to that too. But, unlike Lev. 13:52-3, we do not then find that the *sara^{c}at* has cursed the *nega^c*. The *nega^c* is unclean on its own, and the *sara^{c}at* on its own.

To review: Lev. 13:51 says, "The *sara^{c}at* curses the *nega^c*. It is unclean." What is unclean? The *sara^{c}at*—not *nega^c*. Lev. 13:52, the *nega^c* is unclean because "it is a cursing *sara^{c}at*"—the same point. Accordingly, the *nega^c* on a garment is never itself declared unclean. That all of this is totally unfounded and pure conjecture hardly needs to be specified. It is the only way in which I can suggest how ^{c}Aqiva will have distinguished between garments, which are not susceptible to uncleanness through plagues, colored or not, and houses, which are susceptible to uncleanness through plagues, colored or not.

In any event ᶜAqiva cannot have held garments are not susceptible to uncleanness through leprosy. He surely distinguished between plagues and leprosy. Accordingly, if he did not distinguish the rules about houses from those about garments in this way, then according to Simeon's rule in his name, he certainly did distinguish them in some other way.

17. M. 11:7, Eliezer's discussion of colored and white fabrics, takes for granted the colored are insusceptible. But the distinction between plagues and leprosy does not occur. On the other hand, Scripture knows no such distinction as to colored and undyed fabrics in regard to garments. If Eliezer does know that distinction, it cannot have anything to do with Scriptural rules on leprosy, and, it follows, he has to have assumed plagues are different from leprosy, and rules given in Scripture about the former do not necessarily apply to the latter.

18. M. 12:3, how many stones in a house must be affected for plague to be present?

19. M. 13:6, Eleazar b. ᶜAzariah and Eleazar (Hisma?) on the uncleanness of the house afflicted with plague. The obvious supposition of both parties is that the house afflicted with plague is different from a house afflicted with leprosy, for the latter should be regarded as unclean in the way a corpse is unclean, on the basis of Num. 12:12. Eleazar b. ᶜAzariah does not think the house afflicted by plague is similarly unclean; its outer surface is not virulent. This is speculative.

This catalogue makes it clear that we have to proceed with two successive questions. First, at what point is the distinction between *negaᶜ* and *saraᶜat* clear? Second, when, and in the thought of which authorities, does that distinction produce a major difference?

To the first question, the answer seems to be that *negaᶜ* is understood as a separate ailment, different from *saraᶜat*, by Joshua, possibly also by Eliezer. *Negaᶜ* most certainly is understood by ᶜAqiva as distinct from *saraᶜat*.

The answer to the second question, self-evidently, is that ᶜAqiva does make a difference out of the distinction between *negaᶜ* and *saraᶜat*, a profound and important one. For in the thought of ᶜAqiva, *negaᶜ* is not only distinctive but is also, first, subject to the decision of the expert; and, second, subject to the continuous inspection of the expert; so that, third, what happens when the priest does not see the *negaᶜ* but when the expert (for who else knows them and their names?) is assumed to see the *negaᶜ* does matter. Within these three points virtually all of the particular and distinctive developments of our tractate—those involving more than a repetition of Lev. 13-14—are spun out. It follows that, whether or not the difference between *negaᶜ* and ṣaraʿat was recognized before ʿAqiva, it is ʿAqiva who took up the matter of the negaʿ and rephrased the law in such a way as to make it a particularly rabbinical concern. And, so far as I can see, the revision is in one fundamental way only, namely, the insistence upon the centrality of the "expert" or sage in the process of inspection, from which flow ʿAqiva's other rulings, and, it goes without saying, the developments of those rulings by the second century authorities who are supposed to have been his disciples.

v. Two Torahs—One Whole Torah

When we ask about the absolutely fundamental conception underlying, and generative of, the laws of utensils and Tents, we readily discern conceptions quite separate from those of the Written Torah. The datum of Kelim is that utensils outside the cult matter as to susceptibility or insusceptibility to uncleanness. That is not in Scripture. No rule of Kelim assumes otherwise. The datum of Ohalot is that a Tent is defined in terms of the standard measure, a handbreadth in the three dimensions, with a requisite opening as well. That too brings us into a situation unimagined by Scripture, to which a tent is a place in which people live. Both tractates, moreover, contain a fair amount of evidence that the fundamental conceptions had been reached before the destruction of the Second Temple, and that the significance and generative force of those data already had been appreciated.

Negaim presents a much different problem. Its datum is that the negaʿ is separate and distinct from ṣaraʿat, although, to be sure, once distinguished from one another, the two diseases are governed by parallel rules, those stated in Scripture concerning negaʿ ṣaraʿat. That simple datum—the autonomy of the negaʿ—carries with it no implications perceptible to me for the growth of the law of Negaim. On the contrary, so far as I can discern, it is a logical and heuristic dead-end. After we have agreed that the negaʿ is distinct from ṣaraʿat, we forthwith show that the distinction makes no difference whatever in the articulation of the laws of the negaʿ in particular. Even though the distinction may have been perceived before 70, I see no evidence whatever that it made a difference. And for most of the authorities represented by name, as well as for those unnamed masters who stand in the background of much of our tractate, I am unable to see that the distinction carried important implications after 70. ʿAqiva is the obvious exception.

Accordingly, we have to answer the question of the relationship of the Oral to the Written Torah, as portrayed by the laws of Negaim, from two viewpoints, both from that of ᶜAqiva, and from that of the people who accept the distinction between *negaᶜ* and *saraᶜat* but to whom the distinction makes no difference. To state the result at the outset, Negaim speaks of a social ailment. ᶜAqiva will add that the rabbi, in particular, is the physician of society.

Let us dwell first upon ideas in our tractate which will have been shared both by ᶜAqiva and his disciples as well as by everyone who agreed with Hananiah about the centrality of the role of the priest, the decisiveness of the priestly inspection on the seventh day, the inconsequentiality of changes which take place in the interval between inspections, and similar, controverted matters. To such people, that is, to all authorities before us, *negaᶜ* and *saraᶜat* are pretty much the same thing. Meanings found in the one apply to the other. One will not have had to agree with ᶜAqiva to be impressed by such meanings. From ᶜAqiva's perspective, then, there is a second order of meaning, not excluded by the first.

All parties will, first of all, have been impressed by Num. 12:1-15. Miriam speaks ill of Moses. Miriam is afflicted with leprosy. Aaron then says to Moses, "...Do not punish us because we have done foolishly and have sinned. Let her not be as one dead...." What is important is two assumptions, first, that leprosy is caused by sin, second, that the leper is like a corpse. To the second century rabbi, the message is clear. The leper, we know, is unclean. Lev. 14:46-7 has told us that a person who enters a house shut up on account of leprosy is unclean until evening, which means that the leprous house, shading its own unclean stones, spreads the uncleanness through the process of overshadowing, just as the tent over the corpse spreads the uncleanness through the process of overshadowing. Accordingly, the story about Miriam and the law about the afflicted house clearly imply that the uncleanness generated by the corpse and the uncleanness generated by *negaᶜ saraᶜat* are comparable. For people who assumed *negaᶜ* is distinct from *saraᶜat* but wholly analogous to it in its effects, this will pose no difficulty. A simple process of reasoning will have shown that both *negaᶜ* and *saraᶜat* are diseases analogous to death:

saraᶜat = corpse-uncleanness
negaᶜ = *saraᶜat*
negaᶜ = corpse-uncleanness

Now what is the meaning of that analogy? We already have seen the efforts, possibly beginning with Eleazar b. ᶜAzariah and Eleazar Ḥisma but certainly characteristic of the leading Ushan authorities, Yosé, Meir, Judah, and Simeon, to decide whether the contamination effected by the *negaᶜ* is equivalent to, or less than, the contamination effected by the corpse. That discussion depends upon the biblical story. Interestingly, no one asks about the *saraᶜat* in this context, because the *saraᶜat* is no different, in its contaminating power, from *negaᶜ*. But, since the distinction between the one and the other is important to ᶜAqiva, his disciples will assume the one has one cause, the other another, and, agreeing that the *negaᶜ* is caused by gossip, they discuss whether *saraᶜat* is caused only by arrogance, as in the story about ᶜUzziah, or also by gossip, as in the story about Miriam. That discussion does not change the picture. In point of fact, the second century authorities all associate the uncleanness of leprosy and of plagues with social evils and specifically with those evils which drive a person out of society. This is part of a larger conception of uncleanness, which holds that sin causes the symptoms of uncleanness, and the result of uncleanness is to be driven outside of "the camp," which now is understood not as the cult, but the community.

Death removes a person from the cult and community of the living. *Negaᶜ* and *saraᶜat* similarly remove a person from the cult and community. The latter give a kind of foretaste of death. Just as the effects of death—corpse-uncleanness—pass through a square shape, so the effects of incipient death—the uncleanness of *negaᶜ saraᶜat*—pass through a square shape, indicating their presence in square shaped spots upon the skin. The order of nature is upset by death, the economy of nature has to be restored. The order of society is upset by *negaᶜ saraᶜat*, and the economy of society, its wholeness, has to be restored, either by the breaking forth of the unclean sign over the entire skin, which signifies that the abnormal is made normal, or the disappearance of the tokens of uncleanness entirely. The analogy between the one sort of dying and the other is supplied, however, by the Written Torah. What the sages of the Oral Torah contribute is the spelling out of the analogy. The relationship of the Written Torah, which speaks of the cult, and the Oral Torah, which speaks of the community, the world outside the cult, itself sacred and to be sanctified, is just as it is for Ohalot and Kelim. Let us now dwell on that matter.

Uncleanness is not a metaphor for, but a sign of, sin, and, despite both the Israelites' uncleanness and the sin thereby connoted, still "God is in their midst":

> [*The Lord said to Moses, Command the people of Israel that they put out of the camp every leper* ... *that they may not defile their camp*] *in the midst of which I dwell"* (Num. 5:1-3).
> Israel are beloved, for even though they are unclean, the Presence of God is among them, and so Scripture says, *"Who dwells with them in the midst of their uncleanness"* (Lev. 16:16) ... and Scripture says, *"That they may not defile their camp in the midst of which I dwell,"* and likewise, *"And they not defile the land in which you dwell, in the midst of which I dwell"* (Num. 35:34).
> R. Yosé the Galilean says, "Come and see how strong is the power of sin, for before they put forth their hands in transgression, there were not found among them people unclean through having a discharge and lepers, but after they put forth their hands in transgression, there were among them people unclean through having a discharge and lepers. So we learn that these three things happened on the same day."
> Sifré Num. Naso 2

Yosé and his contemporaries treat uncleanness differently from the prophets. To them it is not a metaphor for sin. Yosé does not claim that cleanness is somehow figurative of ethical purity. The presence of uncleanness in a concrete and this-worldly sense itself *signifies* the antecedent commission of sin. Impurity as a symptom here is connotative; it is inseparable from its consequence and indicative of the presence of sin. It may be claimed that, as in the *yaḥad* at the Dead Sea, the impurity is like sin, sin therefore causes impurity. But while the rabbis say impurity connotes the commission of sin, they do not then follow the *yaḥad* in saying that committing certain sins automatically imposes a period of impurity.[1] This is in the hands of Heaven. No rabbi ever declared a gossip to be impure with the same impurity as a leper for example. The variety and character of the rabbis' list of social evils yielding leprosy—gossiping, arrogance, and the rest—are routine and unexceptional. Such commonplace social vices will characterize any sort of society. What is striking is not the catalogue of sins, therefore, but the imputation of leprosy as the result of those sins. This extreme interpretation begins with nothing more than the biblical use of impurity as a metaphor for sin. The metaphor, however, is shattered. Instead of maintaining impurity is *like* gossip or fornication, or gossip or fornication is *like* impurity, the rabbis held gossip or fornication *produces* impurity.

What is noteworthy therefore is the extensive rabbinical use of the symbols of impurity in connection with social ills. Sermons against

---

[1] See *Idea of Purity*, pp. 50-58.

gossiping or selfishness or about God's love as in M. 12:6/T. 6:7 may readily be constructed without inclusion of the claim that it is the leper in particular who has gossiped or acted selfishly. The cultic metaphor, *unclean*, and its specification in terms of leprosy or bodily discharge seem curiously inappropriate or unnatural to the specific social vices against which the rabbis inveighed. They are used by the rabbis because the community of Israel now is regarded as the Temple. What kept people out of the sanctuary in olden times therefore is going even now to exclude them from the life of the community. The thrust of the rabbis' sermons is to remove from the community people guilty of gossiping or arrogance and the like; this very act of removal is offered by them as the *explanation* for their relating gossiping to leprosy, as we observed.

The rabbis' larger tendency to preserve, but to take over within the rabbinical system, the symbols of the Temple is herein illustrated. Just as it would ultimately be alleged that the rabbi is the new priest, study of Torah is the new cult, deeds of loving-kindness the new sacrifice, so it is maintained at the outset that the community formed on the basis of the rabbinic Torah is going to be protected from social uncleanness just as the old Temple was protected from cultic uncleanness. This I think accounts not only for the preservation, but for the considerable elaboration and extension, of the cultic symbols of uncleanness.

ᶜAqiva obviously will agree with the viewpoint of the sages as a group. But he now proposes to carry forward the implications of that viewpoint in a very concrete and distinctive way. His contribution is not to revise but to enrich the implications of *negaᶜ ṣaraᶜat* characteristic of the first and second century authorities as a group. His additional conception is the predominance, in the decision-making process, of the sage, who may or may not be a priest, but who must be an expert. This, as I said, does turn a distinction into a major difference and carries forward to its logical next stage the conception that the community is analogous to the Temple. If that is the case, then who is analogous to the priest, if not the sage? For the priest knew the rules of the cult of old, just as the rabbi knows the rules of the sanctuary of the interim, the community. Just as the priest took charge through his sacerdotal inheritance, so now the sage takes charge, qualified by his learning, acquired through discipleship (as is pointedly stated in SM 5:16). With the broadening of the realm of the sacred to encompass the community therefore comes the extension of the sanctity of the priesthood to all who qualify themselves to function as do priests.

Sanctity and holiness are conferred upon what people do, are attained or achieved through the way they work or function, do not inhere passively only, but are gained in *sanctifying* activity, learning of Torah. We recall in this connection ᶜAqiva's notion that the Tent plays an active role in the transmission of corpse-uncleanness. It does not merely overshadow the corpse-matter as an ᵓ*ohel*-Tent. It participates in the spreading of the effects of corpse-matter as *maᵓahil*, something which actively affects what it overshadows.¹ It combines separated sources of corpse-uncleanness into a single requisite quantity. It thus takes a vigorous part in the process of contamination. Here now is the opposite side to the coin. Sanctity and holiness are things not merely conferred or inherited but attained. That is to say, they are active forces which sympathetically *respond to* the deeds and circumstances of men, traits of pathos, things which may be drawn —teased—out, through Torah in particular. ᶜAqiva's conception of the centrality of the sage in the processes of the *nega*ᶜ bears self-evident implications for the political life of the holy community, which will be shaped by the sage rather than the priest. Since, however, the division of human affairs into the political and the sacerdotal is inconceivable, we cannot interpret ᶜAqiva's primary intention as political, on the one side, or as a byproduct of a hieromythic conception, on the other. Both aspects of the matter are secondary to a primary conception of the meaning of the destruction of the holy Temple for the supernatural life of the world. For it is the destruction of the Temple —the place on which the lines of order, social and cosmic, had converged—which is the definitive trait of the new age. Formerly, holiness had its place, was defined and organized in the cult, priest-

---

¹ In our studies of Ohalot (Part V, pp. 174ff., 242ff.), we stressed the two conceptions of Tent, the one formal, a Tent with sides, openings, and the like, and the other functional, a Tent as that which interposes against uncleanness. These two separate conceptions are preserved in the two names of the tractate for M., Ohalot and, for T., Ahilot; thus Mishnah speaks of Tents as tents, and Tosefta speaks of Tents as things which overshadow. Both sides are found at Usha, but the conception based upon function seems to me to be distinctive to Usha. It is difficult to locate it in Yavnean materials. Yet the stress upon definition in accord with function clearly may be justified by reference to principles in ᶜAqiva's corpus of rulings. As we have observed here, so in Ohalot the developments at Usha depend upon the diverse readings of Aqiva's rulings by his continuators. As I think is invariably the case, the rabbis of the Talmud are the best historians of their own tradition, for they told us long ago that "all of them [rulings of the Ushans] are with reference to [based upon] the rulings of R. ᶜAqiva."

hood, and holy calendar, centered upon the cult. Sacred time, sacred space, sacred rite and deed—all of them were well regulated, corresponding to the regulation of Heaven. Now what? How has Heaven responded to the cosmic calamity upon earth? How will Israel regain the order, the sense of what is right and proper in all dimensions of being, natural and supernatural, lost in late summer, 70? In speaking of the holy or the sacred, therefore, we address ourselves to the most profound, the most encompassing dimensions of the social and the cosmic order.

When we asked about the relationship of the Oral to the Written Torah in the matter of utensils and Tents, we could allege, before the fact, that the two Torahs stood for the sacred and the profane, respectively. Negaim self-evidently cannot be interpreted in the same way. It is only after the fact that the interpretation appropriate to the origins of Kelim and Ohalot becomes congruent to Negaim as well. I do not think anyone before ʿAqiva will have seen *ṣaraʿat* as the cultic disease subject to priests, *negaʿ* as the social disease, subject to sages, the one the sort of disease which excludes a person from the cult, the other the kind which excludes a person from the community. Nor is it wholly evident that ʿAqiva made any such distinction. His silence on *ṣaraʿat* proves nothing. Accordingly, we cannot say of Negaim what seemed obvious about Kelim and Ohalot, that the Oral Torah (now: Negaim) legislated for the realm of the secular, outside of the cult, as the Written Torah (Leviticus 13-14) spoke of the realm of the sacred, within the cult. Here the historical process, the unfolding of the laws, seems to begin only when the cult ends, with the work of making the distinction between *negaʿ* and *ṣaraʿat*, which may have been recognized before 70, into a significant difference. But that difference is ʿAqiva's alone. Hananiah the Prefect of the Priests did not concede the most primitive principles meant to carry the difference forward and develop it. We have good evidence that ʿAqiva's position, even into the second century, was conceived to be his alone. All parties agree about the reinterpretation of diseases formerly pertinent primarily to the cult and their application to the community. That tendency, fully articulated only in the second century materials, simply carries forward an established view of Oral Torah and, for *negaʿ ṣaraʿat*, spells out and applies its meaning.

What I think ʿAqiva contributes is a still further recognition of the difference between the age in which the Temple stood and the present age, in which it lies in ruins. It is he who, I think, draws out the deepest implications of the destruction, implications not alone or primarily about the visible and material world and its political structures, but about the invisible world of the sacred and profane, the clean and the unclean, and the affects of that unseen world, its visible reflection, upon this world. Before 70 sacred reality was divided by walls, so to speak, spatially, thus vertically, between Temple and world. The earlier tractates of Oral Torah begin in the intent to legislate about the sacred realities of the world outside the Temple walls.

ᶜAqiva now perceives a second dimension, a temporal line dividing sacred reality—a line which is horizontal—between the age of the Temple and the age of no Temple. The community, made holy, even before 70, by legislation about its sanctity, now enters a *time* in which it is all that endures as bearer and avatar of the sacred. How this is expressed in terms of holy things and purities is not our problem. But a strangely apt analogy is before us for the expression of this movement, in terms of secular things and impurities. It is that bright spot, which, ᶜAqiva holds, indeed has a "history" of uncleanness, a *temporal history*, determined by the sage, and which, Yosé wishes to add, exhibits even a spatial continuum as well.

What is disappointing in these results, as I said at the outset and hasten to repeat, is that they are *post facto*. That is, we could discern in the fundamental presuppositions of Kelim and Ohalot the conception of Oral Torah as pertinent to the secular world, Written Torah to the cult. But the earliest presupposition of Negaim is simply that *negaᶜ* differs from *ṣaraᶜat*. That means very little, until ᶜAqiva develops the particular traits of the *negaᶜ*. And we cannot securely assume that he will not have said the same of *ṣaraᶜat*. For the second century authorities who tell us that *negaᶜ* is caused by one social evil, *ṣaraᶜat* by another, furthermore, it hardly matters that the two are different ailments. Their theological ideas may be, and were, attached, to a variety of types of uncleanness, not solely to the two before us. That fact underlines the extrinsic character of what seems to me important in Negaim, by contrast to the historically and conceptually intrinsic character of what is important in Kelim and Ohalot. Not only so, but the details of the laws themselves in the first two tractates relate to that intrinsic character, while in the one before us, there is little interplay between the laws themselves and the conceptions underlying, or expressed by, the laws, except in the instance of ᶜAqiva.

All I can propose in defense of these meagre results is the importance of that exception. If, as I think it is clear, Negaim, after all, really is the work of ʿAqiva and his Ushan continuators, then our results conform to our data. To repeat our slightly ludicrous characterization: Negaim tells us about a rabbinical disease and ʿAqiva discovered it.

V. Parah Before 70

i. THE PRESUPPOSITIONS OF THE YAVNEAN STRATUM

All rules and disputes assigned to Yavnean authorities take for granted the following principles, which are not under dispute at Yavneh and which also are not alleged in Yavnean pericopae to have been invented at Yavneh:

1. The cow must not be used for labor.
2. A. The cow is not offered in the Temple, therefore is not subject to the Temple's rules.
Or B. The cow is not offered in the Temple, but (since it is called a *ḥaṭʾat*), it *is* subject to the Temple's rules.
3. A. The cow must be perfectly red by nature.
Or B. The cow may be perfected by human action.
4. Details of the rite worked out: Kindling fire, throwing in of hyssop, etc., garments of priest, flaying, collecting ashes, collecting blood. The issues—if any—seem to devolve upon analogies of the rite: Is it like that of the Day of Atonement? Of the leper? Is it comparable to the Temple at all?
5. The water must be unadulterated by dirt or other unsuitable materials and liquids.
6. All persons and objects involved in the rite must be free of all uncleanness. The cow is brought to the Mount of Olives in such wise that it never is exposed to uncleanness. A degree of purity even higher than applies to the Temple on the Day of Atonement is required.
7. Purification-water which is suitable and sufficient for sprinkling causes uncleanness when moved. Unfit water does not do so to one clean for the rite.
8. An act of labor not connected with the rite spoils the cow, the water, and all other aspects of the conduct of the rite.
9. All objects used for lying and sitting are unclean for the rite.
10. The jar of water must be in a clean place.

Among these data of the Yavnean pericopae, let us now eliminate two sorts, first, those which repeat the obvious sense of Scripture and the Scriptural origin of which may be taken for granted; and second, those which seem to reflect disputes fresh at Yavneh, and not disputes about the application of principles available to, and shared by, all parties. In the first category are No. 1; the supposition of No. 3, that the cow must be red; No. 5, which is commonsense; No. 7, which is explicitly stated in Scripture; and No. 10, also contained in Scripture. In the second category are Nos. 2 and 4 (which simply repeats the primary principle of No. 2), not to mention No. 10. What remain are the following:

>Nos. 6, 8, and 9: The strict rules of cleanness applied to all who participate in the rite and to all objects used in that connection.
>
>No. 8: An act of labor not connected with the rite spoils the water, not to mention the cow and other aspects of the conduct of the rite.

These two matters, rules of cleanness different from, and higher than, these applying even to Holy Things, on the one side, and the taboo against doing labor not connected with the rite of burning the cow, on the other, form the foundation for the Yavnean stratum. Do we find in the compilations of exegeses a claim that these principles, or detailed exemplifications thereof, begin in the exegesis of Scripture?

ii. Scriptural Foundations of Parah

Let us now rapidly review the exegeses relevant to the two fundamental principles of our tractate.

>1. *Standard of Purity Higher than that Applied to Holy Things*
>   (1. Sif. Num. 124J: The person who throws in hyssop renders clothing unclean. This is irrelevant.)
>   (2. Sif. Num. 124K: All who are involved in the rite contaminate clothing, as above.)
>   3. Sif. Num. 124M: cAqiva [or, Ishmael] says *clean* in Num. 19:9 means the person who gathers the ash must be clean from all uncleanness. (Nathan says the person is unclean for heave-offering and clean for the purification-rite.)
>   4. Sif. Num. 129A: As above, *clean* from all uncleanness, so cAqiva. The gloss intruding the *ṭevul yom* contradicts cAqiva's saying. Rabbi = Nathan at No. 3.

We may state very simply that there is not the slightest effort to provide a Scriptural basis for such rules as M. 10:1-6 and similarly strict requirements of purity. The sole issue is whether the person involved in the purification-rite must be clean of all uncleanness, as cAqiva is made to say (and as is surely the presupposition of all Yavnean pericopae on the subject), or whether he may, or must, be a *ṭevul yom*, as Nathan and (possibly) Rabbi say here (and as is the presupposition of Ushan pericopae in which the rite is done at a less stringent level of purity than is required for heave-offering). Accordingly, the attributions are in alignment with the legal materials in the respective strata, and while exegeses are supplied in support of what is attributed, these clearly cannot, and are not claimed to, derive from the period before 70.

   2. *Labor Spoils the Cow, etc.*

    1. Sif. Num. 123G: Yoke not used for actual labor also is prohibited. The prohibition of extraneous labor is not the issue; it is (obviously) taken for granted. Furthermore, the taboo against extraneous labor is not even raised. The question is the cow.

    2. Sif. Num. 123J: *And he will slaughter it*—teaches that an act of labor spoils the cow during slaughter.

    3. Sif. Num. 124A: *In his sight* means an act of labor spoils the cow when it is being burned. The issue is as stated, again it is taken for granted that the extraneous act of labor spoils the rite—the slaughter.

    4. Sif. Num. 124B: *In his sight* is assumed to mean an extraneous act of labor is prohibited.

    5. Sif. Num. 124P: *Keeping... for the water* means that an act of labor renders water unclean—until it is mixed with ashes.

    6. SZ to 19:2, H 300 ls. 5-13: *In his sight* is understood as above, No. 3. HQH extends this rule to the water and ashes.

    7. SZ to 19:5: As above, No. 6. The reference is to the cow.

    8. SZ to 19:6: The rule is stated without an exegesis.

The situation is somewhat different from the foregoing. We do have an exegesis—*in his sight* means that *an act of labor spoils the cow*, which may be prior to all specifications of the rule. That is, *the act of labor spoils*—to which are added *the cow, the water*, and all other aspects of the rite until the water is mixed with ash. Now it is possible that the taboo against labor originated in such an exegesis. It may have been generated by the explicit Scriptural specification that the cow must not have done labor at all. Someone may then have come to the conception that just as the cow must not have been used for labor ("an act of labor spoils the cow"), so that which is going to be mixed with the cow's ashes, the water, likewise must not be subjected to an act of labor. But that is not the exegetical statement before us, and we cannot make much progress in specifying what is in the mind of the exegete behind the treatment of *in his sight*.

Since that is the case, we know only that, before 70, it was clear that an act of labor is not to be done in connection with the water unless the action has something to do with the drawing of the water. The case(s) referred to Yavneh surely represent very considerable developments in antecedent law, involving as they do so minor a matter as returning a rope used in connection with the rite. Accordingly, the prohibition against an act of labor by 70 surely had been highly developed to include relatively trivial gestures.

We cannot know the origins of the taboo, and we surely do not rule out the possibility that they lie in the reading of *in his sight—an act of labor spoils*.... On the other hand, the connection between *sight/oversight* and *labor* is surely not ineluctable. It is the Ushans, in particular, who tend to link *sight/oversight* to guardianship and thence to uncleanness and the complex of issues inhering in that matter. I tend to doubt that the law begins in an exegesis, but I cannot supply evidence or arguments to settle the matter. In any case, the underlying *meaning* of the law is yet to be worked out. We turn to that matter at part iv. First let us see whether what is important to Yavneans seems compelling to other Jews who deal with the red cow, whether Scripture tells to Josephus, Philo, Samaritans, Christians, Targumists, Essenes, what it tells to the authorities before 70 who stand behind the rabbis thereafter.

iii. Other Approaches to the Rite of the Red Cow

We shall now rapidly survey references to the red cow in other Jewish literature of ancient times.

1. *The Collections in Apocrypha and Pseudepigrapha*

   Bibliography

   R. H. Charles, ed., *The Apocrypha and Pseudepigrapha of the Old Testament* (Oxford, 1913, I-II).

In the vast corpus assembled by Charles, representing various periods, groups, and viewpoints, I find not a single reference relevant to the red cow, even to purification by the water and ashes.

2. *The Dead Sea Library*

   Bibliography

   John Bowman, "Did the Qumran Sect Burn the Red Heifer," *Revue de Qumran* 1957, 1:73-84.
   Frank Moore Cross, Jr., *The Ancient Library of Qumran* (N.Y., 1961).
   A. Dupont-Sommer, *The Essene Writings from Qumran*. Translated by G. Vermes (N.Y. and Cleveland, 1967).
   Chaim Rabin, *The Zadokite Documents* (Oxford, 1958).
   James A. Sanders, "The Dead Sea Scrolls. A Quarter Century of Study," *The Biblical Archaeologist* 1973, 36: 110-148.
   G. Vermes, *The Dead Sea Scrolls in English* (Harmondsworth, 1970).

I am unable to find any reference to the rite of the red cow in the Dead Sea library. Bowman points out that the community did require sprinkling with water for purification (Rule for the Community 3:9,

Bowman, p. 82) and argues that the Qumran sect prepared the ashes of the red heifer: "...we have no evidence of an altar at Qumran; but as the Red Heifer was not a sacrifice, what was to prevent them burning the Red Heifer without the Camp, all the more so as they were engaged in upholding proper standards of Levitical purity and showing that the Jerusalem varieties were invalid?"

3. *Philo*

Bibliography

F. H. Colson and G. H. Whitaker, trans., *Philo* (Cambridge and London, 1949), Vol. V, pp. 409-411: *On Dreams* I, 207-215. Vol. VII, pp. 251-257: *The Special Laws* I, 261-272.

Erwin R. Goodenough, *By Light, Light. The Mystic Gospel of Hellenistic Judaism* (New Haven, 1935).

——, *The Jurisprudence of the Jewish Courts in Egypt. Legal Administration by the Jews under the Early Roman Empire as Described by Philo Judaeus* (New Haven, 1929).

Harry Austryn Wolfson, *Philo. Foundations of Religious Philosophy in Judaism, Christianity, and Islam* (Cambridge, 1948) I-II.

Philo's one lengthy discussion of the red cow, *The Special Laws* I (49-50), 261-272 (trans. Colson and Whitaker, pp. 251, 3, 5, 7), is as follows:

> The following regulation also shows a far-sighted wisdom which should be noted. In almost all other cases men used unmixed water for the sprinkling. By most people it is taken from the sea, by others from the rivers, and by others it is drawn in ewers from the wells. But Moses first provided ashes, the remnants of the sacred fire, obtained in a manner which will be explained shortly. Some of these, he says, are to be taken and thrown into a vessel and afterwards have water poured upon them. Then the priests are to dip branches of hyssop in the mixture and sprinkle with it those who are being purged.
>
> The reason for this may be aptly stated as follows. Moses would have those who come to serve Him that is first know themselves and of what substance these selves are made. For how should he who has no knowledge of himself be able to apprehend the power of God which is above all and transcends all? Now the substance of which our body consists is earth and water, and of this he reminds us in the rite of purging. For he holds that the most profitable form of purification is just this, that a man should know himself and the nature of the elements of which he is composed, ashes and water, so little worthy of esteem. For if he recognizes this, he will straightway turn away from the insidious enemy, self-conceit, and abasing his pride become well-pleasing to God and claim the aid of His gracious power Who hates arrogance. For that is a good text which tells us that he

who sets his hand to words and deeds of pride "provokes" not only men, but also "God," the author of equality and all that is most excellent. So then, whilst they are being thus sprinkled, deeply moved and roused as they are, they can almost hear the voice of the elements themselves, earth and water, say plainly to them, "We are the substance of which your body consists; we it is whom nature blended and with divine craftsmanship made into the shape of human form. Out of us you were framed when you came into being and into us you will be resolved again when you have to die. For nothing is so made as to disappear into non-existence. Whence it came in the beginning, thither will it return in the end."

I must now also fulfill my promise to describe the special qualities of these ashes. They are not merely the ashes of wood consumed by fire but also of a living creature well-suited to a rite of purification such as this. He orders a red heifer which has never been yoked and without blemish to be taken outside the city and there slaughtered. Then the high priest is to take of the blood and sprinkle it seven times over everything in front of the sanctuary, then burn it wholly to ashes with the skin and flesh and blood and the belly filled with its ordure. When the flame is dying down, he is to cast right into the middle these three things, cedar wood and hyssop and scarlet wool. Then if it is quite extinguished, a clean man is to collect the ashes and deposit them outside the city in a clean place. What these things symbolically indicate has been described in full elsewhere where we have expounded the allegory. So we see that they who mean to resort to the temple to take part in sacrifice must needs have their bodies made clean and bright, and before their bodies their souls. For the soul is queen and mistress, superior to the body in every way because a diviner nature has been allotted to it. The mind is cleansed by wisdom and the truths of wisdom's teaching which guides its steps to the contemplation of the universe and all that is therein, and by the sacred company of the other virtues and by the practice of them shown in noble and highly praiseworthy actions. He, then, who is adorned with these may come with boldness to the sanctuary as his true home, the best of all mansions, there to present himself as victim.

Philo's promised explanation of symbolism of cedar wood, hyssop, and scarlet wool is not found elsewhere in his writings. The interpretation of the ashes and water has no counterpart in our tractate. The "special qualities" of the ashes simply are the Scriptural requirements. I doubt that ᶜAqiva and Ishmael will have agreed that the cedar wood, hyssop, and scarlet woool are thrown in when the flame is dying down; they are clear that the items are tossed into the cow while it is still discernible, not after it has been turned to ashes. Simeon holds that it makes no difference whether the ash is put on the water or the water on the ash; Philo wants the water poured on the ash, which is contrary to the opinion of sages *vis à vis* Simeon. But these are minor details, bearing no importance in Philo's narrative.

In fact, there are no important points of contact between the laws and underlying concepts of Mishnah-Tosefta and the interests of Philo's account of the same rite. What is important to Philo is also distinctive to him, a philosophy wholly alien to the sages of our tractate.

4. *Josephus*

Bibliography

Against Apion. In *Josephus. With an English Translation* by H. St. J. Thackeray (Cambridge and London, 1956). Vol. I. i, 199; ii, 198-203.

Jewish Antiquities Book III. In *Josephus*, etc. (Cambridge and London, 1957). Vol. IV. iii, 258-273.

Josephus refers to "purifications for various occasions, after a funeral, after child-birth, after conjugal union, and many others" (*Apion* ii, 198). Likewise in the later *Antiquities* (iii, 258), he refers to purification "with the waters of perennial springs," and tells us that "those who have paid the last rites to the dead, after the same number of days [a week] may rejoin their fellows..." (iii, 262). So far as I know, he does not refer to the burning of the red cow or even to the use of the ash of the cow mixed with water for purification.

5. *Targumim*

Bibliography

Dominique Barthelemy, *Les Devanciers d'Aquila* (Leiden, 1963).

A. Berliner, *Targum Onkelos. Herausgegen und Erläutert* (Berlin, 1884). I.

J. W. Etheridge, *The Targums of Onkelos and Jonathan ben Uzziel on the Pentateuch. With the Fragments of the Jerusalem Targum. From the Chaldee* (1862. Reprint: N.Y., 1968).

Alejandro Díez Macho, *El Targum. Introducción a las traducciones aramaicas de la Biblia* (Barcelona, 1972).

——, *Neophyti 1. Targum Palestinense MS de la Biblioteca Vaticana. Tomo IV. Números. Edición principe, introducción, y versión castellana* (Madrid, 1974). English: Martin McNamara.

Moses Ginsburger, *Das Fragmententhargum. (Thargum jeruschalmi zum Pentateuch)* (Berlin, 1899).

——, *Pseudo-Jonathan. (Thargum Jonathan ben Usiël zum Pentateuch). Nach der Londoner Handschrift (Brit. Mus. add. 27031)* (Berlin, 1903).

R. Le Déaut, *Introduction à la littérature targumique* (Rome, 1966) Vol. I.

Martin McNamara, *Targum and Testament. Aramaic Paraphrases of the Hebrew Bible: A Light on the New Testament* (Shannon, 1972).

David Rieder. *Pseudo-Jonathan. Targum Jonathan ben Uziel on the Pentateuch. Copied from the London MS. (British Museum add. 27031)* (Jerusalem, 1974).

Alexander Sperber, *The Bible in Aramaic. Based on Old Manuscripts and Printed Texts. Volume I. The Pentateuch According to Targum Onkelos* (Leiden, 1959).

Geza Vermes, *Scripture and Tradition in Judaism. Haggadic Studies.* (Leiden, 1973: Second, Revised Edition).

The Targums on Num. 19:1-10, 17, and 18 are now compared. I have copied the translations of McNamara for Neophyti and of Etheridge for Onkelos and Jonathan b. Uzziel ("Palestinian"), and compared the latter's translations with the superior texts of Berliner and Sperber, Ginsburger and Rieder, for Onkelos and Jonathan b. Uzziel, respectively. Our present purpose is simply to seek evidence for the way in which the relevant verses were understood before 70. The results are wholly negative. It suffices to observe that, as everyone knows, the Targum attributed to Jonathan looks like a kind of commentary to, or exegetical summary of, Mishnah-Tosefta. Ginsburger (Notes, pp. 262-3) cites the relevant passages in Mishnah and Sifré. Neither Onkelos nor Neophyti hints at an equivalent knowledge of, or interest in, issues important to Mishnah-Tosefta and Sifré. However these latter Targums are dated, they bear no relationship whatever to our tractate.

Onkelos	*Jonathan*	*Neophyti 1*
(Etheridge, pp. 294-5)	(Etheridge, pp. 402-3)	(Diez Macho-McNamara, p. 570-1)
1. And the Lord spoke with Mosheh and to Aharon saying,	1. And the Lord spoke with Moshe and Aharon, saying,	1. And the Lord spoke with Moses and with Aaron saying,
2. This is the decree of the law which the Lord hath commanded, saying, Speak to the sons of Israel that they bring to thee a red heifer, [whole] unblemished, with no spot on her, and upon which no yoke hath been put.	2. This is the decree, the publication of the law, which the Lord hath commanded, saying, Speak to the sons of Israel, that they bring to thee, from the separation of the fold, a red heifer, two years old, [Rieder: whole, on which is no blemish], on which no male has come, nor the burden of any work been imposed, neither hurt by the thong nor grieved by the goad or prick, nor collar or any like yoke.	2. This is the degree of the law which the Lord commanded saying, Speak with the children of Israel, and they shall take and bring to you a red cow, perfect, in which there is no blemish, upon which the servitude of a yoke has not come.

PARAH BEFORE 70   151

Onkelos

3. And you shall give her unto Eleazar the priest, that he may bring her without the camp, and (one) shall slaughter her before him.

4. And Elazar the priest shall take (some) of her blood with his finger, and sprinkle of her blood against the face of the tabernacle of ordinance seven times.

5. And one shall burn the heifer before his eyes; her skin, and her flesh, and her blood, with her food (ʾWK-LH) shall he burn.

6. And the priest shall take cedar wood, and hyssop, and scarlet, and cast it into the midst of the burning of the heifer.

Jonathan

3. And thou shalt give her unto Eleazar, the prefect of the priests, who shall lead her alone without the camp, and set round about her a railing of the branches of fig trees;
and another priest shall slay her
with the two signs before him,
after the manner of other animals,
and examine her by the eighteen signs of being *taref*.

4. And Elazar, in his priestly dress, shall take of her blood with the finger of his right hand,
without (first) containing it in a vessel,
and shall sprinkle the border of fig branches,
and afterwards from the midst of a vessel on one side towards the tabernacle of ordinance,
with one dipping, seven times (shall he sprinkle).

5. And they shall bring her out from the midst of the railing,
and another priest, while Elazar looketh on, shall burn the heifer, her skin, flesh, and blood with her dung shall he burn.

6. And another priest shall take a piece of cedar wood and hyssop
and wool whose color hath been changed to scarlet,
and throw them into the midst of the burning of the heifer;
and he shall enlarge the burning, that the ashes may be increased.

Neophyti 1

3. And you shall give her to Eleazar the priest, and he shall take her outside the camp and sacrifice her before him.

4. And Eleazar the priest shall take some of her blood with his finger and sprinkle some of her blood seven times (shall he sprinkle).

5. And he shall burn the cow before him; her skin and her flesh and her blood with her excrements shall be burned.

6. And the priest shall take cedar wood and hyssop and precious crimson materials, and he shall throw and cast them into the midst of the burning of the cow.

Onkelos

7. And the priest shall wash his clothes and bathe his flesh in water and afterwards come into the camp, but the priest shall be unclean until the evening.

8. And he who burneth her shall wash his clothes with water, and bathe his flesh in water, and be unclean until evening.

9. And a man who is clean shall gather up the ashes of the heifer, and lay them up without the camp in a clean place, and it shall be for the congregation of the children of Israel to keep, for the sprinkling with water. It is (a purification) for sin.

10. And he who gathereth up the ashes of the heifer shall wash his raiment, and be unclean until the evening. And it shall be for the children of Israel and for the strangers who dwell among you a statute forever.

17. And for the unclean person they shall take of the ashes of the burnt sin-offering and put spring water (MY MBW^c) upon it in a vessel.

Jonathan

7. And the priest who slew the heifer shall wash his dress in forty se$^{\jmath}$ahs of water, and afterwards he may go into the camp; but the priest shall be unclean until the evening.

8. And the priest who was employed in the burning shall wash his dress in forty se$^{\jmath}$ahs of water;
and his flesh in forty se$^{\jmath}$ahs, and before his ablution he shall be unclean until the evening.

9. And a man, a priest, who is clean, shall gather up the ashes of the heifer
in an earthenware receptacle, its opening covered round about with clay;
and shall divide the ashes into three portions,
of which one shall be placed within the wall (of Jerusalem), another in the Mount of Olives, and the third portion be in the custody of the Levites;
and it shall be for the congregation of Israel for the Water of Sprinkling; it is the heifer (immolated) for the remission of sins.

10. And the priest who gathered up the ashes of the heifer shall wash his clothes, and before his ablution be unclean until the evening. And this shall be for the cleansing of the children of Israel, a statute forever.

17. And for him who is unclean they shall take of the ashes of the burnt sin-offering and put spring water upon them in an earthen vessel.

Neophyti 1

7. And the priest shall wash his clothes and bathe his body in water and afterwards he shall come into the camp; and the priest shall be unclean and removed from holy things until evening.

8. And he who burns her shall wash his clothes in water and shall bathe his body in water and shall be unclean until evening.

9. And a man who is clean shall gather up the ashes of the cow and deposit them outside the camp in a clean place; and the congregation of the children of Israel shall have them for the ritual use of the waters of asperation. She is a sin-offering.

10. And he who has gathered the ashes of the cow shall wash his clothes and shall be unclean until evening. And this shall be a perpetual statute for the children of Israel and for the sojourners who sojourn among you.

17. For the unclean person they shall take some of the ashes of the burning of the cow, and from an earthen vessel they throw on them pure waters from a fountain.

Onkelos	Jonathan	Neophyti 1
18. And a man who is clean shall take hyssop and dip it in the water and sprinkle upon the tent and upon every vessel...	18. And let a man, a priest, who is clean, take three branches of hyssop bound together and dip them in the water at the time of receiving the uncleanness, and sprinkle the tent and all its utensils...	18. And a pure man shall take hyssop and dip it in water and asperse it upon the tent, and upon all its utensils...

What is particularly interesting in Targum Jonathan is his attention, at 19:2, to anything which is like a yoke, echoing the discussions of why the yoke is specified. I know no basis in Mishnah-Tosefta, Sifré Numbers and Sifré Zutta, for his specification, 19:3, that the cow is surrounded by a railing or the branches of fig trees, or, 19:4, that the sprinkling of the blood is first upon the border of fig branches. This detail is unknown to the legal compilations we have examined. Num. 19:4 insists that there be one dipping for the seven sprinklings, which is surprising. The stress on receiving the blood by hand, not with a utensil, settles a dispute. Judah will have been pleased with 19:6, the adding of more wood to produce abundant ashes, but not with 19:18, which has three branches of hyssop bound together but not three buds on each branch. In all, the one amazing detail is the fence of fig branches and the sprinkling on that fence. For the later history of the exegesis of Scripture in the light of the Oral Torah, the present materials are interesting.

Earlier we observed that, if any exegesis in Sifré Numbers and Sifré Zutta should go back to the period before 70, it is *in his eyes*.... We observe that none of the Targums is interested in the issue either of extraneous labor or of the degree of uncleanness or cleanness required for the rite. These considerations, fundamental to our tractate, influence the treatment of Scripture in no passage of the three Targums before us. It is curious that Targum Jonathan, which cites Mishnah explicitly, does not see need to pay attention to the issue of extraneous labor, for instance, in reference to the water, let alone to the ashes. I find this puzzling.

6. *The Christian Community in the First Century*

A. *Hebrews*

Bibliography

Alexander Balmain Bruce, *The Epistle to the Hebrews. The First Apology for Christianity. An Exegetical Study* (N.Y., 1899).

F. F. Bruce, *The Epistle to the Hebrews. The English Text with Introduction, Exposition, and Notes* (Grand Rapids, 1964).
——, "Recent Contributions to the Understanding of Hebrews," *Expository Times*, October 1968-September, 1969, 80: 26-264.
George Wesley Buchanan, "The Present State of Scholarship on Hebrews," in J. Neusner, ed., *Christianity, Judaism, and Other Greco-Roman Cults. Studies for Morton Smith at Sixty* (Leiden, 1975) I, pp. 299-330.
——, *To the Hebrews. Translation, Comment, and Conclusions* (Garden City, 1972).
Samuel T. Lowrie, *An Explanation of the Epistle to the Hebrews* (N.Y., 1884).
Hugh Montefiore, *A Commentary on the Epistle to the Hebrews* (N.Y., 1964).
Alexander Nairne, *The Epistle of Priesthood. Studies in the Epistle to the Hebrews* (Edinburgh, 1913).
Theodore H. Robinson, *The Epistle to the Hebrews* (N.Y., 1933).
C. Spicq, *L'épitre aux Hébreux* (Paris, 1952) I-II.
Ronald Williamson, *Philo and the Epistle to the Hebrews* (Leiden, 1970).
Hans Windisch, *Der Hebräerbrief* (Tübingen, 1931).

The pertinent passage of Hebrews is as follows:

9:13-14: For if the sprinkling of defiled persons with the blood of goats and bulls and with the ashes of a heifer sanctifies for the purification of the flesh, how much more shall the blood of Christ, who through the eternal Spirit offered himself without blemish to God, purify your conscience from dead works to serve the living God.

This is the sole allusion in the New Testament to the red cow. The reference, Hebrews 13:11-12, to burning a sacrifice outside the sanctuary introduces Lev. 16:27; the author of Hebrews does not confuse the sin-offering (*ḥaṭʾat*) of the Day of Atonement with the purification-offering (*ḥaṭʾat*) of the red cow.

B. *Epistle of Barnabas*

G. Allon, "Halakhah in the Epistle of Barnabas," *Tarbiṣ* 1939-1940, 11:23-38 (Hebrew).
F. F. Bruce, *The Epistle to the Hebrews*, p. 203, n. 88.
Robert A. Kraft, *The Epistle of Barnabas: Its Quotations and their Sources* (Unpublished Ph.D. thesis, Harvard University, 1961). [Not used.]
S. Lowy, "The Confutation of Judaism in the Epistle of Barnabas," *Journal of Jewish Studies* 1960, 11:1-33.
Alexander Roberts and James Donaldson, eds., *The Ante-Nicene Fathers*. (Repr. Grand Rapids of ed. Edinburgh, 1885) I, pp. 133-149. Translation cited: p. 142.

The Epistle of Barnabas contains an interesting interpretation of the rite of the burning of the red cow (Chapter Eight: The Red Heifer a Type of Christ):

> Now what do you suppose this to be a type of, that a command was given to Israel, that men of the greatest wickedness should offer a heifer and slay and burn it, and that then boys should take the ashes and put these into vessels and bind round a stick of purple wool along with hyssop, and that thus the boys should sprinkle the people, one by one, in order that they might be purified from their sins?
>
> Consider how he speaks to you with simplicity.
>
> The calf is Jesus: the sinful men offering it are those who led him to the slaughter. But now the men are no longer guilty, are no longer regarded as sinners. And the boys that sprinkle are those that have proclaimed to us the remission of sins and purification of heart. To these he gave authority to preach the Gospel, being twelve in number, corresponding to the twelve tribes of Israel.
>
> But why are there three boys that sprinkle? To correspond to Abraham and Isaac and Jacob, because these were great with God.
>
> And why was the wool [placed] upon the wood? Because by wood Jesus holds his kingdom, so that [through the cross] those believing on him shall live for ever.
>
> But why was hyssop joined with wool? Because in his kingdom the days will be evil and polluted in which we shall be saved, [and] because he who suffers in body is cured through the cleansing efficacy of hyssop.
>
> And on this account the things which stand thus are clear to us, but obscure to them, because they did not hear the voice of the Lord.

The reference to the boys of course recalls M. 3:2-3. But the boys' role in that set is to gather the ashes (collected from former times, etc.), not to sprinkle the ashes on the people. M.-T. knows nothing of *three* boys. The requirement that the people be sprinkled one by one will not have astonished the authority behind M. 12:2. I take it the "sinful men" are supposed to be the unclean ones who slaughter the cow; they are known to be unclean because, having participated in the rite, they have to wash their clothing. But this is probably far-fetched. The note (p. 142, n. 3) says that the reference, literally, is to "men in whom sins are perfect."

7. *Samaritans*

Bibliography

Ze'ev Ben Ḥayyim, ʿIvrit veʾAramit Nusaḥ Shomron (Jerusalem, 1957-1967), I, II, III, i, ii.

John Bowman, "Did the Qumran Sect Burn the Red Heifer?" *Revue de Qumran* 1958, I: 73-84.

———, *Samaritanische Probleme. Studien zum Verhältnis von Samaritanertum, Judentum, and Urchristentum. Franz Delitzsch-Vorlesungen, 1959* (Stuttgart, 1967).

Moses Gaster, *Samaritan Oral Law and Ancient Traditions* (London, 1932.) [Not used.]

Abraham S. Halkin, "Samaritan Polemics against the Jews," *Proceedings of the American Academy for Jewish Research* 1935-1936, 7: 13-59.

Hans Gerhard Kippenberg, *Garizim und Synagoge* (Berlin, 1971).

John Macdonald, *The Theology of the Samaritans* (London, 1964).

James Alan Montgomery, *The Samaritans* (Philadelphia, 1907).

James D. Purvis, *The Samaritan Pentateuch and the Origin of the Samaritan Sect* (Cambridge, 1968).

Until late medieval times the Samaritans used ashes of the red cow in connection with the waters of impurity (Macdonald, p. 267). Bowman cites Gaster (Bowman, p. 78, Gaster, pp. 195f.) to this effect, the last such rite having taken place in 1348. An eleventh-century Samaritan writer attacks Judaism "on the latter's neglect of the use of the water for impurity and the consequent breakdown of the observance of the full Biblical laws of Purification" (Bowman, p. 79). The Samaritans continued to burn the red cow because they had a priesthood.

8. Conclusion

Our purpose is to see whether the suppositions underlying the earliest cases of Yavneh are shared by, or even known to, other Jewish literature. The answer is wholly negative. Indeed, what is surprising is that only groups demonstrably in close touch either with Pharisees before 70, the Christians, or with the rabbis of Mishnaic times, the author(s) of Targum Jonathan, to begin with even display an interest in the rite of the heifer. The Targumist could, of course, not have missed the topic, given his task; but he made some effort to include rabbinic exegeses and laws in his Targum. The author of Hebrews refers to the rite of the cow in passing and makes no serious effort to exploit its symbolism. The Letter of Barnabas, by contrast, took an interest in the matter, as part of his larger polemic. Obviously, the two basic Yavnean conceptions of the rite which go back to the period before 70 bear no relationship to and do not derive from groups represented by the extant writings just now surveyed. I see nothing whatever in common among the references to Numbers 19:1-20. In all cases, the rite is accommodated to a larger philosophical or theological hermeneutic or apologetic. That, it is clear, also is the case with the Pharisaic legacy to the Yavneans. For the Pharisees, the laws on the rite in various ways state that cleanness and holiness, are not restricted to the Temple. The laws on the rite of the cow constitute simply one more, and rather elaborate, way of saying so.

iv. RITUAL WITHOUT MYTH: THE MEANING OF THE LAWS OF PARAH

In order to investigate, or at least speculate about, the meaning of the legal conceptions fundamental to our tractate which do originate before 70, we have now to stand back from the concrete data before us and seek perspective on their nature and structure. At the same time, in the present section, we review pericopae already abundantly familiar from our discussions in Part IX. Let us begin, then, with some fairly obvious facts about Mishnaic law as a whole.

While some religions, Christianity and Islam for example, are rich not only in law but also in theological writings, and others in myth, still others make their statements about the nature of being and the realm of the sacred primarily through law. In the case of early rabbinic Judaism we have a considerable corpus of laws which prescribe the way things are done but make no effort to interpret what is done. These constitute ritual entirely lacking in mythic, let alone theological, explanation. Accordingly, the processes and modes of thought of earlier Rabbinic Judaism turn out to be wholly encapsulated in descriptions of ritual. Yet much of the law contained in Mishnah in fact was not practiced; indeed, the earlier rabbis scarcely claim that it was. Further, the laws about ritual cleanness or purity, so far as they had to be kept so that a person could enter the Temple, bore no more concrete relevance to everyday life than did the cultic laws, and only a small part of the Jewish population of Palestine was expected to keep those laws outside of the cult. Accordingly, we have before us the paradox presented by most serious effort to create a corpus of laws to describe a ritual life which did not exist. The processes of making those laws themselves constituted the rabbis'—and their predecessors'—mode of thinking about the same issues investigated, in other circumstances, through rigorous theological thought, on the one side, or profound mythic speculation, on the other. *So far as the laws describe a ritual, the ritual itself is myth,* in two senses.

First, the ritual is myth in the sense that it was not real, was not carried out.

Second, while lacking mythic articulation, the ritual expresses important ideas and points of view on the structure of reality.

What is lacking, specifically, is not myth, but articulated and explicit articulation of myth. The law contains myth in that it encompasses cognitive content. The law does not explicitly articulate the content in a particular form of abstract discourse, but leaves its content embedded in ritual. What people are supposed to do, without a stage of articulation of the meaning of what they do, itself expresses what they think. The explanation of the ritual, the drawing out of that explanation of some sort of major cognitive statement, is skipped. The world therefore is mapped out through gesture. The boundaries of reality are laid forth through norms on how the boundaries of reality are laid forth.

Accordingly, we deal with laws made by people who never saw or performed the ritual described by those laws. It is through thinking about the laws that they shape and express their ideas, their judgments upon transcendent issues of sacred and profane, clean and unclean. It follows that thinking about the details of the law turns out to constitute reflection on the nature of being and the meaning of the sacred. The form—the ritual—lacking myth is wholly integrated to the content, the mythic substructure. The structure of the ritual is its meaning. We turn to the particular ritual in hand, the burning of the red cow for the preparation of ashes, to be mixed with water and sprinkled upon a person who has become unclean through contact with a corpse.

Let us first consider once again the way in which the priestly author of Numbers 19:1-10 describes the rite, the things he considers important to say about it:

> Tell the people of Israel to bring you a red cow without defect, in which there is no blemish, and upon which a yoke has never come. And you shall give her to Eleazar the priest, and she shall be taken outside the camp and slaughtered before him. And Eleazar the priest shall take some of her blood with his finger and sprinkle some of her blood toward the front of the tent of meeting seven times. And the heifer shall be burned in his sight; her skin, her flesh, and her blood, with her dung, shall be burned; and the priest shall take cedarwood and hyssop and scarlet stuff and cast them into the midst of the burning of the heifer. Then the priest shall wash his clothes and bathe his body in water, and afterwards he shall come into the camp, and the priest shall be unclean until evening. He who burns the heifer shall wash his clothes in water and bathe his body in water and shall be unclean until evening. And a man who is clean shall gather up the ashes of the heifer and deposit them outside the camp in a clean place; and they shall be kept for the congregation of the

people of Israel for the water for impurity, and for the removal of sin. And he who gathers the ashes of the heifer shall wash his clothes and be unclean until evening (Num. 19:1-10a).

How is the ash used? Num. 19:17 states:

> For the unclean they shall take some ashes of the burnt sin-offering and running water shall be added in a vessel; then a clean person shall take hyssop and dip it in the water and sprinkle it upon the tent... (in which someone has died, etc.).

Let us now ask, what to the biblical writer are the important traits of the rite of the burning of the cow and the mixing of its ashes into water?

The priestly author stresses, first of all, that the rite takes place outside of the camp, which is to say, in an unclean place. He repeatedly tells us that anyone involved in the rite is made unclean by his participation in the rite, thus, 19:7, the priest shall wash his clothes; Num. 19:8, the one who burns the heifer shall was his clothes; Num. 19:10, and he who gathers the ashes of the heifer shall wash his clothes and be unclean until evening. The priestly legislator therefore takes for granted that the rules of purity which govern rites in the Temple simply do not apply to the rite of burning the cow. Not only are the participants *not* in a state of cleanness, but they are in a state of uncleanness, being required to wash their clothes, remaining unclean until the evening, only then allowed back into the camp which is the Temple. Accordingly, the world outside the Temple cannot be clean. Only to the Temple do the cleanness taboos pertain. It follows that a rite performed outside of the Temple is by definition not subject to the Temple's rules and is not going to be clean.

What is interesting, when we turn to our tractate, is its distinctive agendum of issues and themes. As we have seen, the predominant concerns of Mishnah-Tosefta Parah, deriving from the period before 70, are two: first, the degree of cleanness required of those who participate in the rite and how these people become unclean; second, how the water used for the rite is to be drawn and protected, with special attention directed to not working between the drawing of the water and the mixing of the ashes referred to in Num. 19:17. The theoretical concerns of Mishnah-Tosefta Parah thus focus upon two important matters of no interest whatever to the priestly author of Numbers 19:1-10, because the priestly author assumes the rite produces uncleanness, is conducted outside of the realm of cleanness, and therefore does not involve the keeping of the Levitical rules of cleanness required for participation in the Temple cult. By contrast, Mishnah-Tosefta Parah is chiefly interested in that very matter. An important body of opinion in our tractate demands a degree of cleanness higher than that required for the Temple cult itself. Further, the whole matter of drawing water, protecting it, and mixing it with the ash, is virtually ignored by the priestly author, while it occupies much of our tractate and, even more than in quantity, the quality and theoretical sophistication of the laws on that topic form the apex of our tractate. Accordingly, the biblical writer on the rite of burning the red cow wishes to tell us that the rite takes place outside the camp, understood in Temple-times as outside the Temple. The rite is conducted in an unclean place. And it follows that people who are going to participate in the rite, slaughtering the cow, collecting its ashes, and the like, are not clean. The Mishnaic authorities stress exactly the opposite conception, that people who will participate in the rite must be clean, not unclean, as if they were in the Temple. And they add a further important point, that the water which is to be used for mixing with the ashes of the cow must be mixed with the ashes without an intervening act of labor, not connected with the rite.

At the outset I pointed to two facts. First, the authorities of the Mishnah describe a ritual which, in fact, they have never seen, and about which they claim to have few historical traditions. The ritual under description is, as I said, a myth in two senses. The first has just now been stated: it is something which is not part of observed reality. But the second remains to be spelled out. The laws of the ritual themselves contain important expressions about the nature of the sacred and the clean. I shall now attempt to illustrate how the articulation of the laws, through the standard legal disputes of the late first and second-century authorities, contains within itself statements about the most fundamental issues of reality, statements which, in describing the form of the ritual, also express the content of the ritual, its myth. These statements, it goes without saying, further carry forward the conceptions of the period before 70.

For the purpose of the present discussion, we have now to review familiar materials. The first dispute concerns which hand one uses for sprinkling the blood toward the door of the Holy of Holies; the second asks about how we raise the cow up to the top of the pyre of wood on which it is going to be burned; and the third deals with whether intending to do the wrong thing spoils what one actually does. The first is at M. 3:9:

> They bound it with a rope of bast and place it on the pile of wood, with its head southward and its face westward.
>
> The priest, standing at the east side, with his face turned toward the west, slaughtered it with his right (northern) hand and received the blood with his left (southern) hand.
>
> R. Judah says, "With his right hand did he receive the blood and he put it into his left hand, and he sprinkled with (the index finger of) his right hand."

Before analyzing the pericope, we call to mind the corresponding Toseftan supplement (T. 3:9):

> They bound it with a rope of bast and put it onto the wood pile.
> And some say, "It went up with a mechanical contraption."
> R. Eliezer b. Jacob says, "They made a causeway on which it ascended."
> Its head was to the south and its face to the west.

In the present set, therefore, are the first two of the issues mentioned earlier: which hand we use for sprinkling the blood, and how we raise the cow to the top of the pyre of wood.

Let us notice, first of all, the placing of the cow and the priest. The rite takes place on the Mount of Olives, that is, to the east and north of the Temple mount in Jerusalem. Accordingly, we set up a north-south-east-west grid. The cow is placed with its head to the south, pointing in the direction of the Temple Mount, slightly to the south of the Mount of Olives, and its face is west—that is, toward the Temple. The priest then is set east of the cow, so that he too will face the Temple. He faces west—toward the Temple. When he raises his hand to slaughter the cow, he reaches over from north and east to south and west, again, toward the Temple. We have, therefore, a clear effort to relate the location and slaughter of the red cow, which takes place outside the Temple, toward the Temple itself. In fact each gesture is meant to be a movement toward the Temple. Just as Scripture links the cow, outside the camp, to the camp, by having the blood sprinkled in the direction of the camp (a detail which Mishnah takes for granted), so that the sprinkling of the blood, which is the crucial and decisive action which effects the purpose of the rite—accomplishes atonement, or *kapparah*, in Mishnaic language—so all other details of the rite here are focused upon the Temple.

This brings us to Judah's opinion, which disagrees about slaughter with the left hand. As observed, we have set up a kind of mirror to the Temple, with the whole setting organized to face and correspond to the Holy Place. The priest in the Temple slaughtered with his right hand, and received the blood in his left. Likewise, the anonymous rule holds, the priest now does the same. In other words, our rite in all respects replicates what is done in the Temple setting: What is done there is done here. Judah, by contrast, wants the blood received with the right hand and slaughtered with the left. Why? Because we are not *in* the Temple itself. We are facing it. Thus if we want to replicate the cultic gestures, we have to do each thing in exactly the opposite direction. Just as, in a mirror, one's left is at the right, and the right is at the left, so here, we set up a mirror. Accordingly, he says, if in the Temple the priest receives the blood in his left hand, on the Mount of Olives and facing the Temple, he receives the blood in his right hand. All parties to the dispute, therefore, agree on this fundamental proposition, that the effort is to replicate the Temple's cult in every possible regard.

This brings us to the dispute about how we get the beast up to the top of wood pile. The anonymous rule, shared by Mishnah and Tosefta, is that we bind the sacrificial cow and somehow drag it up to the top. But in the Temple the sacrifices were not bound; they would be spoiled if they were bound. Accordingly, Eliezer b. Jacob, a contemporary of Judah, imposes the same rule. He says that there was a causeway constructed from the ground to the top of the woodpile on which the cow will be slaughtered and burned, and the cow walks up on its own. Self-evidently, both parties cannot be right, and the issue is not what really was done in "historical" times—let us say, seventy-five years earlier. As in the dispute between Judah and the anonymous narrator, the issue is precisely how we shall do the rite, on the Mount of Olives, so as to conform to the requirements of the rite on the Temple Mount itself.

To state matters in general terms, it is taken for granted by all parties to the present pericope that the rite of the cow is done in the profane world, outside the cult, *as if* it were done in the sacred world constituted by the Temple itself.

How is the contrary viewpoint expressed? The simplest statement is in Mishnah Parah 2:3B-D:

> B. The harlot's hire and the price of a dog—it is unfit.

That is to say, if the red cow is purchased with funds deriving from money spent to purchase the services of a prostitute or to buy a dog, the cow is unfit for the rite. The pericope continues:

C. R. Eliezer declares fit,

D. since it is said, *You will not bring the harlot's hire and the price of a dog to the house of the Lord your God* (Deut. 23:18). But this (cow) does not come to the house (of the Lord, namely, the Temple).

The issue could not be drawn more clearly than does the glossator (D). Eliezer holds that since the burning of the cow takes place outside of the Temple, the Temple's rules as to the acquisition of the cow simply do not apply.

A more subtle question appears at M. 4:1 and M. 4:3. The first item, M. 4:1, is as follows:

> The cow of purification which one slaughtered not for its own name (meaning, not as a cow of purification, but for some other offering), or the blood of which one received and sprinkled not for its own name, etc., is unfit.
> R. Eliezer (Eleazar) declares fit.

What is at issue? In the sanctuary, we have correctly to designate the *purpose* of a sacrifice. Eleazar holds that this is not a rite subject to the rule of the Temple cult. The rule continues,

> And if this was done by a priest whose hands and feet were not washed, it is unfit.
> R. Eliezer declares fit.

Priests in the Temple of course had to be properly washed. Since the rite is not in the Temple, Eliezer says that the priest need not even be washed. In this connection, Tosefta supplies:

> If one whose hands and feet were not washed burned it, it is unsuitable.
> And R. Eleazar b. R. Simeon declares fit,
> as it is said, *When they come to the Tent of Meeting, they will wash in water and not die* (Ex. 30:20)—lo, the washing of the hands applies only inside (the Temple, and not on the Mount of Olives).

The issue is fully articulated, and the glosses in both the matter of the harlot's hire and the matter of washing spell out the implications. The law which describes the ritual—the *structure* of the ritual itself—also expresses the *meaning* of the ritual. The form imposed upon the ritual fully and completely states the content of the ritual. If now we ask, What is this content? we may readily answer: The ritual outside of the cult is done in a state of cleanness, as is the ritual done inside the cult.

The laws of the cult, furthermore, apply not only to the conduct of the slaughtering of the cow (the cases given here), but also to the preservation of purity by those who will participate in the slaughtering.

Mishnah presupposes what Scripture takes for granted is not possible, namely, that the rules of purity apply outside of the Temple, just as the rules of Temple slaughter apply outside of the Temple. And the reason is, of course, that the Mishnah derives, in part, from the Pharisees, whose fundamental conviction is that the cleanness-taboos of the Temple and its priesthood apply to the life of all Israel, outside of the Temple and not of priestly caste. When Israelites eat their meals in their homes, they must obey the cleanness-taboos as if they were priests at the table of God in the Temple. This larger conception is expressed in the acute laws before us.

Let us now proceed to a matter which is by no means self-evident, and which was not understood in the way in which I shall explain it even by the second century authorities. It concerns the issue of drawing the water. The rule, as we know, is that if I draw water for mixing with the ashes of the red cow, and, before actually accomplishing the mixture, I do an act of labor not related to the rite of the mixing of the ashes, I spoil the water. This is stated very succinctly, "An act of extraneous labor spoils the water." This conception is likely to originate before the destruction of the Second Temple in 70, because taken for granted at M. 7:6-7 is the principle, evidently deriving from Pharisaism before 70, that an act of extraneous labor done between the drawing of the water and the mixing of ashes and water spoils the drawn water.

The rule lies far beyond the imagination of the priestly writer of Numbers, because he tells us virtually nothing about the water into which the ashes are to be mixed. But that is of no consequence. As we observed earlier, what is interesting is the language which is used, *unfit*, not *unclean*. So the matter of the cleanness of the water—its protection against sources of contamination—is not at issue. Some other consideration has to be involved. The drawing of the water is treated as intrinsic to the rite. That is: I burn the cow. I go after water for mixing with the ashes of the cow. That journey—outside of the place in which the cow is burned—is assumed to be part of the larger rite.

Now this matter of extraneous labor is exceedingly puzzling. We have to ask, to begin with, for some sort of relevant analogy. Do we know about other rites in which we distinguish between acts of labor which are intrinsic and those which are not? And on what occasion is such a distinction made? The answer to these questions is obvious. We do distinguish between acts of labor required for the conduct of the sacrificial cult, and those which are not required for the conduct of the sacrificial cult; in particular we make that distinction *on the Sabbath*. On the Sabbath-day labor is prohibited. But the cult is continued. How? Labor intrinsic to the sacrifices required on the Sabbath is to be done, and that which is not connected with the sacrifice is not to be done.

When we introduce the issue of extraneous labor (and the issue extends to the burning of the cow itself, but I think this is secondary), what do we say about the character of the sanctity of the rite? Clearly, we take this position: The rite is conducted by analogy to the sacrifices which take place in the Temple, so that the place of the rite and all its participants must be clean, exactly as the place of the Temple and all the participants in the Temple sacrifices must be clean. So too with the matter of labor. When we impose the Temple's taboos, we state that the rite is to be conducted in *clean space*. When we introduce the issue of labor, we forthwith raise the question of *holy time*, the Sabbath. For it is solely to the Sabbath that the matter of labor or no labor, labor which is intrinsic or labor which is extrinsic, applies. When we impose the taboos applicable to the Temple on the Sabbath, we state that the rite is to be conducted in holy time—wherever it is done.

The cleanness-laws in the present instance create in the world outside of the cult a *place of cleanness* analogous to the cult. The Sabbath-laws in the present instance create in the world outside of the cult a *time of holiness* analogous to the locus of the cult. The ritual constructs a structure of clean cultic space and holy Sabbath time in the world to which, by the priestly definition, neither cleanness nor holiness (in the limited sense of the present discussion) apply. The laws, it is clear, do not contain explanations. The issues themselves are trivial, ritualistic; yet even the glossators at the outset introduced, into the consideration of legal descriptions of ritual, extra-legal conceptions of fundamental importance. Accordingly, the processes of thought which produce the rabbis' legal dicta about ritual matters also embody the rabbis' judgments about profound issues.

The final stage is to consider other sorts of sayings, in which the rabbis speak more openly and directly about matters we should regard as theological, not ritual, in character. These are general, not specific, theologico-mythic sayings which lack ritual altogether and treat questions of salvation, not the conduct of rite. They constitute a quite distinct mode of expression about the same questions answered by Mishnah through law. These theological sayings contrast, therefore, to the ones about ritual law, showing a separate way in which the authorities of the same period form and express their ideas.

The issue at hand, in particular, is the relationship between cleanness and holiness. We have already considered the matter in our interpretation of the ritual laws, showing that cleanness is distinct from holiness, and the two are related to and expressed by the laws about burning the red cow. Pinhas b. Ya'ir gives us a statement (M. Sot. 9:15, translated following MS Kaufman) which links the issues of cleanness and holiness to salvation:

> R. Pinhas b. Ya'ir says, "Attentiveness leads to (hygienic) cleanliness, cleanliness to (ritual) cleanness, cleanness to holiness, holiness to humility, humility to fear of sin, fear of sin to piety, and piety to the holy spirit, the holy spirit to the resurrection of the dead, and the resurrection of the dead to Elijah of blessed memory."

Pinhas therefore sees cleanness as a step in the ladder leading to holiness, thence to salvation: the resurrection of the dead and the coming of the Messiah. Maimonides, much later, introduces into the Messianic history the burning of the cow of purification. Referring to the saying that nine cows in all were burned from the time of Moses to the destruction of the Second Temple (M. 3:5), he states (*Red Heifer* 3:4):

> Now nine red heifers were prepared from the time this commandment was received until the Temple was destroyed the second time... and a tenth will King Messiah prepare—may he soon be revealed.

Maimonides thus wishes to link the matter of burning the red cow which produces water for ritual purification to the issue of the coming of the Messiah. Both sayings, those of Pinhas b. Ya'ir and Maimonides, show that it is entirely possible to speak directly and immediately, not through the language of ritual law, about fundamental questions. And when we do find such statements, we no longer are faced with ritual laws at all, but have theology: *myth without ritual*. Yet it seems to be clear that Pinhas b. Ya'ir and Maimonides saw in the issues of purity, in the very specific questions addressed by the rabbinic lawyers who provide the ritual law, matters of transcendent, even salvific, weight and meaning.

Let us now return to the issues raised at the outset and summarize the entire argument. It is now clear that the Mishnaic rabbis express their primary cognitive statements, their judgments upon large matters, through ritual law, not through myth or theology, neither of which is articulated at all. Indeed, we observe a curious disjuncture between ritual laws and theological sayings concerned with the *heilsgeschichtliche* meanings of the laws.

Since the ritual was not carried out by the authorities of the law, the purpose and meaning of legislation in respect to the ritual of burning the cow are self-evidently not to describe something which has been done, but to create—if only in theory—something which, if done, will establish limits and boundaries to sacred reality. The issue of the ritual is *cleanness* outside of the Temple, and, if I am right about the taboo connected with drawing the water, *holiness* outside of the Temple as well. The lines of structure, converging upon, and emanating from, the Temple, have now to be discerned in the world of the secular, the unclean, and the profane. Where better to discern, to lay out these lines of structure, than in connection with the ritual of sacrifice not done in the Temple but outside of it, in that very world of the secular, unclean, and profane. As I have stressed, the priestly author of Numbers cannot imagine that cleanness is a perquisite of the ritual. He says the exact opposite. The ritual produces contamination for those who participate. The second century rabbis who debated the details of the rite held that the rite is performed just as it would have been done in the Temple. Or, in the mind of Eleazar b. R. Simeon, the rite is performed in a way different from the way it would have been done in the Temple. The laws which describe the ritual therefore contain important judgments upon its meaning. With remarkably little eisegesis of those laws—virtually none not coming to us from the glossators themselves—we are able to see that their statements about law deal with metaphysical reality, revealing their effort to discern and to define the limits of both space and time.

The structure of the ritual contains its meaning. Form and content are wholly integrated. Indeed, we are unable to dissociate form from content. It follows that what is done in the ritual, the sprinkling with one hand or the other, the binding of the cow or the use of a causeway to bring it to the pyre, the purchase of cows with the wrong sort of money, the employment of unwashed priests, the exclusion of the issue of the wrong intention—all of these matters of rite and form alone contain whatever the rabbis will tell us about the meaning of the rite and its forms. The reason, as I have stressed, is that the rabbis before us think about transcendent issues primarily through rite and form. When, as I showed at the end, they choose another means of discourse and a different mode of thought entirely, matters of rite and form fall away. Theological and mythic considerations to which ritual is irrelevant take their place. Judah, Eleazar b. R. Simeon, Eliezer b. Jacob, and the others cited, however, refer to no myth, make use of neither mythic nor theological language, because they think about reality and speak about it through the norms of the law. Since, as I have stressed, the law concerns a ritual which these authorities have never seen and certainly would never perform, *the law itself constitutes its own myth*: (1), the fabulous myth of a ritual no one has ever done; and (2) the transcendent myth of the realm of the clean and the sacred constructed through ritual and taboo in the world of the unclean and the secular. The ritual *is* the myth. What people are told to do is what they are supposed to think. The gestures and taboos of the rite themselves express the meaning of the rite, without the mediation of myth.

VI. Tohorot Before 70

i. Introduction

The Yavnean materials on doubts and on the ʿam haʾareṣ are so sparse that it is difficult to determine what, if any, conceptions deriving from the period before 70 form the substratum of laws on those matters. It seems probable that a formula, *doubt about plagues/clean*, stands behind the exemplifications of doubts in Negaim (M. Neg. 4:11-5:1); I see no reason that a formula requiring specification and differentiation, such as *doubts about uncleannesses/clean/unclean* should not have come down from masters before 70. But if that is what did come down, and is what is clarified in the distinction between public and private domain, then it is not a prepossessing tradition. Like the Ushans' effort to figure out what to do with *doubts about liquids/clean +/— unclean*, the creative work on the matter is that of the exegetes of the inherited formula. And even such an obscure gnomic formula as the foregoing does not appear to have been received in connection with the ʿam haʾareṣ. Self-evidently, the certain heritage of the period before 70 is of a different order: the conception that people who keep clean must avoid contamination by people who do not. But that matter is inherent in the very structure of the law. The articulation of the matter in terms of assessing what the ʿam haʾareṣ will and will not likely do in one or another circumstance seems to begin, at the earliest, in later Yavnean circles; but most of the work is Ushan.

ii. Removes of Uncleanness, Levels of Sanctification

Self-evidently, with the cleanness of foods and liquids, Yavneans deal with conceptions of considerable sophistication. The major ideas are not merely generalities, as with the ʿam haʾareṣ,—he will or will not do so and so, multiplied in dozens of instances—but in conceptual density. One matter, minor to be sure, which, I take for granted, derives from the period before 70 is the conception that food must be of the bulk of an egg to impart uncleanness. A second, and one generative of the dynamic of Mishnah's laws, is the conception of removes of uncleanness, on the one hand, and the variations among unconsecrated food, heave-offering, and Holy Things, in respect to receiving or imparting uncleanness, on the other. This last aspect—receiving or imparting uncleanness—is under debate, therefore in process of development, at Yavneh. It is highly unlikely that any sort of antecedent tradition on the subject was available. This is the meaning of sayings attributed to Yoḥanan b. Zakkai by Joshua, to ʿAqiva, to Eleazar, and to Eliezer, in the several contexts. The sayings deal with most elementary questions, e.g., the capacity of unconsecrated food in various removes to impart uncleanness and the like.

Do the later rabbis attribute to authorities before 70 the conception of removes of uncleanness and the related matter of the affects *upon* unconsecrated food, heave-offering, and Holy Things, of food unclean at the several removes? A review of the materials assembled in *The Rabbinic Traditions about the Pharisees before 70* shows that not a single pericope attributed to named authorities before 70 or to the Houses makes significant reference to the issue of removes, whether or not in relationship to the differentiation of unconsecrated food, heave-offering, and Holy Things. Sifra's exegeses in which the concept of removes occurs are assigned to ʿAqiva, as at M. Sot. 5:2 (T. Sot. 5:13) (Shemini VII:12) and still later authorities (Ṣav. 9:2). This of course cannot prove that the twin-conceptions were not thought of before 70. But it does make it difficult to demonstrate that the notion was subjected to deep analysis in pre-Yavnean times.

The earliest attribution of materials on the theme of removes of uncleanness is to the Houses. At M. Shab. 1:4 (b. Shab. 13b) we are told, "These are [some] of the laws which they stated in the upper room of Ḥananiah b. Ḥezeqiah b. Gurion when they went up to visit him. They took a count, and the House of Shammai outnumbered the House of Hillel. Eighteen things did they decree on that very day." M. Shab. 1:5-8 then supplies a number of Houses' disputes on Sabbath-law. b. Shab. 13b, commenting on the superscription which refers to the eighteen measures, states:

> What are the eighteen thing[s]?
> DTNN:
> These render the heave-offering unfit:
> 1. he who eats food unclean in the first remove;
> 2. and he who eats food unclean in the second remove;
> 3. and he who drinks unclean liquids;
> 4. and he who enters to the extent of his head and the greater part of his body into drawn water;

5. and a clean person on whose head or the greater part of whose body three *logs* of drawn water fall;
6. and the scroll;
7. and the hands;
8. and the one who has immersed on the selfsame day and awaits sunset;
9. and foods and utensils which were made unclean by [unclean liquids].

Self-evidently, what we are told is decree No. 1 of the Houses is assigned to Joshua at M. Toh. 2:2, as Rabbah b. Bar Ḥanah points out at b. Shab. 14a. The anonymous discussion observes, moreover, that No. 3 makes the same point as Nos. 1-2. The other elements in the list are not of interest here. The main thing is that, if we take at face value the story that the Houses (how many can have been present?) held such a meeting at the sick bed of Ḥananiah, then this is the first point at which it is taken for granted that removes of uncleanness are to be taken into account, on the one side, and exhibit special relationships to heave-offering, in particular, on the other. b. Shab. 14b contains the further observation, also anonymous, that the uncleanness (No. 9) in respect to liquid is explicitly stated in Scripture, Lev. 22:7, *And all drink that may be drunk in every such vessel shall be unclean*: "We deal, therefore, with liquid contaminated by hands." It remains to observe that the Scriptural passages which refer to heave-offering do not tell us that heave-offering suffers greater susceptibility to uncleanness than unconsecrated food (Num. 18:8, 11-12, 25-32, Lev. 22:10-14, Deut. 12:6, Nehemiah 10:38-40 [following the catalogue of H. Albeck, *Seder Zeraʿim*, pp. 171-2]).

The impression that the issue of removes of uncleanness in relationship to foods at various levels of sanctification is first raised at Yavneh or shortly before 70 is confirmed by parallel discussions, attributed to Ḥanina (Ḥananiah) Prefect of the Priests, the Houses, and Eliezer and Joshua, on whether we distinguish uncleanness imparted by a Father and an Offspring of uncleanness. The theme is whether we distinguish uncleanness imparted by various sources of uncleanness, or whether we treat all unclean things as equally unclean, without regard to whether they were made unclean, for example, by a Father or an Offspring of uncleanness. Ḥanina Prefect of the Priests states, "The priests never refrained from burning flesh that had become unclean from an Offspring of uncleanness together with flesh that had become unclean from a Father of uncleanness, even though they thereby added uncleanness to uncleanness" (M. Pes. 1:6). Along the same lines, the Houses (M. Sheq. 8:6, M. M.S. 3:9, etc., *Rabbinic Traditions about the Pharisees* II, pp. 100ff., 113ff.) do not distinguish between uncleanness imparted by a Father and that imparted by an Offspring to second tithe. On the other hand T. Pisḥa 1:6 states:

> The House of Shammai say, They do not burn clean meat with unclean meat.
> And the House of Hillel permit.

The same dispute is assigned to Eliezer and Joshua. Clearly, in the present instances we find the view that whatever the source of uncleanness, once something is unclean, it is in the undifferentiated status of uncleanness and disposed of accordingly. (Simeon, T. 1:1, attests this view and imposes it upon M. 1:5-6.)

Food, on the other hand, is treated somewhat differently. We do take account of varying removes, on the one side, and varying levels of susceptibility or capacities to impart uncleanness, on the other. But, we recall, this differentiation takes place when we assess whether something is unclean. Once it is unclean, we treat it in accord with a common rule. Accordingly, a great deal of theoretical work seems to be underway, in particular in connection with food. Not much effort will be generated by Ḥanina's saying or that in T. Pisḥa. But once we ask the range of questions in the tractate before us, we shall self-evidently produce major legal conceptions.

It remains to observe that the underlying thesis of Eleazar, that that which is more susceptible to uncleanness—at a higher level of sanctification—also has the greater power of contamination is beautifully developed by Judah (M. Neg. 13:7-10, T. 7:9): "The power of that which is susceptible to uncleanness is greater to afford protection than is the power of that which is clean to afford protection. Israelites receive uncleanness and afford protection for clothing in the house afflicted with plague, and the gentile and the beast are insusceptible to uncleanness and do not afford protection for clothing in the house afflicted with plague." Eleazar will not have been displeased with this extension of his principle that that which is of a higher order of sanctification is capable of conveying uncleanness at a deeper remove than that which is of a lower order of sanctification. Judah turns the matter on its head: not only conveying uncleanness but also *affording protection from uncleanness*. Here is a good example of the conceptual and thematic progression of issues matched by attributions of primitive or logically prior conceptions to earlier authorities and contingent, logically posterior ones to later authorities.

The upshot is that the primary conceptions of the Yavnean stratum of law on removes of uncleanness and their relationship to the levels of sanctification of foods and liquids take shape in Yavneh itself. If we make the unlikely assumption that the story about Hananiah's upper room speaks of a real, historical event, something which actually happened as the story says it did, and the equally unlikely assumption that the garbled and contradictory lists of what "eighteen things" were decided supply the actual agendum of that meeting—if we conceded all this, then the earliest evidence on the matter comes from the time of the Houses at all events, not half a century before 70 at the outset. But those assumptions on the face of it are untenable. The nine things are not "eighteen"; the Amoraic authorities themselves do not agree on what eighteen things were decided. Whatever happened (if anything happened), the sources themselves scarcely are able to give us a clear account. More interesting: unless Joshua is taken to be a Shammaite, we have to take for granted that he, for one, knew nothing about that decision, coming to his position quite separately from the Houses.

We cannot ask ourselves to claim greater antiquity for laws than the tradents and (in the present instance) redactors (M. Shab. 1:4) claim in their behalf. If the laws are assigned to the Houses, no one even alleges that they go back before the Houses. Whether they belong to the time of the Houses is a question less decisively settled. But the probabilities are clear. Yavneh is the point of origin of the laws under discussion, just as, at the earliest, the remainder of the laws of the tractate originate after 70.

iii. Conclusion

When the Temple stood, cleanness and uncleanness bore concrete meanings and produced practical effects. They were 'real,' in the sense of producing concrete and material results; something which touched a Father of uncleanness was *unclean*, so could not be brought to the Temple, might have to be destroyed (as in the case of unclean heave-offering). A hundred years after the destruction, by contrast, cleanness and uncleanness are represented as relative to unseen and impalpable forces, to time and circumstance, individual will and private intention. The ordinary person is assumed to be unclean. At the time of the vintage he is assumed to be clean. Liquid makes things susceptible to uncleanness. But if it is placed on dry food without the approval of the owner, the food is not susceptible to uncleanness; a *Zab* may walk on the wet olives and they remain clean as before; one may take grapes or olives to the market and bring them back, without regard to liquid on them, and toss them into the vat, for they still are clean. Clearly, a major shift has taken place in the perception of the concreteness and vividness of uncleanness, a movement from a perception of something real and capable of presenting material danger, e.g., to the cult, or to the person who proposes to eat his food as if he were in the cult, to a perception of a status which is attained or imposed without regard to material, physical realities. One might say we have moved from the realm of the absolute and religious to the world of the relative, the speculative, and the philosophical.

Indeed, if we stand back from the details of the law and ask, What is it that the second century rabbis regarded (in general terms) as subject to their speculative inquiry, we should describe their agendum as follows: In respect to society, we want to know what people usually do, how various classes of society may be expected to behave. In respect to happenings in the natural world, the world of animals for example, we ask about what are the likely principles by which we may interpret events we do not know have taken place. In respect to material processes, we wish to speculate on the nature of mixtures. If I have a substance of one sort and it is joined to a substance of another, how do the traits of the one combine with the traits of another?

This generalized way of stating the problem of M. 1:5-9, for example, will not have surprised Alexander Aphrodisiensis who writes:

> Certain mixtures ... result in a total interpenetration of substances and their qualities, the original substances and qualities being preserved in this mixture; this he calls specifically *krasis* of the mixed components. It is characteristic of the mixed substances that they can again be separated, which is only possible if the components preserve their properties in the mixture ... This interpenetration of the components he assumes to happen in that the substances mixed together interpenetrate each other such that there is not a particle among them that does not contain a share of all the rest. If this were not the case, the result would not be *krasis* but juxtaposition. [1]

When we hold that a substance at the first remove and one at the second remove interpenetrate and are regarded as entirely unclean at the first remove, we say much the same thing. Can they now be sepa-

---

[1] S. Sambursky, *Physics of the Stoics* (London, 1959), p. 122.

rated? And if they are separated, what is the result? We know full well that our authorities raise precisely that issue, in terms of removes of uncleanness to be sure. The matter of connection is of the same order of theoretical interest. Uncleanness affecting all parts of materials after they have been connected affects them all when they are separated. But if something is made unclean, then connected to something else, that latter substance is unclean just as is the former all the time that it is connected to the former. But when it is separated, it is unclean in a lower remove, only by virtue of its contact with that which was originally contaminated. So now we have a mosaic-like mixture, in which each element in the whole preserves its own individuality. The set of pericopae turn out to be remarkably relevant to the Stoic theory of mixture, stated by S. Sambursky in the following terms:

> As far as classification is concerned, the Stoic theory is much clearer. It distinguished between three types of mixture. One of them, mingling or mechanical mixture, is identical with what Aristotle defines by 'composition' (as in the case of the mixture of barley and wheat), and it applies essentially to bodies of a granular structure where a mosaic-like mixture results, each particle of one component being surrounded by particles of the other. The other extreme is fusion, which leads to the creation of a new substance whereby the individual properties of each of the components are lost ... Between these two types lies a third case of 'mixture' proper (*krasis* for liquids, *mixis* for non-liquids), which, from the Stoic point of view, represents the most important category of blending. Here a complete interpenetration of all the components takes place, and any volume of the mixture, down to the smallest parts, is jointly occupied by all the components in the same proportion, each component preserving its own properties under any circumstances, irrespective of the ratio of its share in the mixture. The properties are preserved in all cases where, as opposed to the case of fusion, the components can be separated out by putting a sponge into the mixture... 2

Certainly an example of fusion is the contamination of liquids. Once unclean, they are unclean always at a single remove; the uncleanness affects the whole equally and profoundly. An example of mingling is connection which takes place after uncleanness has affected one part of what is connected. And an example of the middle sort of mixing is the blending of solids unclean in various removes, as I said. We recall, also, the issue of whether the presence of a single drop of spit which is unclean means all drops are unclean; whether blood and urine are

---

2 *ibid.*, pp. 14-15.

ever sufficiently diluted to be of no effect, and similar issues on the nature and meaning of mixtures, both of liquids and of solids.

That is not to suggest that among the second century Galilean rabbis were Stoic philosophers, importing into the Torah of Moses, in the guise of discussions on matters of cleanness and uncleanness, the grand issues of physics. It is only to point out a curious congruence between the arcane language and problems worked out by the rabbis and the clear and lucid interest in physics and other philosophical matters under discussion elsewhere. Speculation on social behavior, on certainties and commonalities in the movement of objects and substances, on the mixture and separation of foods and liquids—that speculation, translated into more general language, surely will have proved not without its point to people familiar with the philosophical issues of the contemporary Greco-Roman world. If philosophy in time became transmuted into religion, in the case of the earlier rabbis, the opposite also may be said: the religious world of cult and cleanness generated issues remarkably pertinent to the speculations of philosophers.

VII. Miqvaot Before 70

i. Miqvaot and Parah

The law of Miqvaot originates in the following fundamental conceptions:

> 1. Rain-water gathered together on the ground, in requisite volume, serves for the process of purification.
> 2. Rain-water which has been subjected to human agency, e.g., in its gathering, is unfit for the process of purification.
> (3. Diverse kinds of water bear diverse traits, but water does unite or intermingle. This is derivative of No. 1.)

To state matters simply, what is the subject of our tractate? *Miqva'ot—gatherings—in particular of rain-water by other than human agency* (of which the prohibition against utensils is a principal illustration). The gathering of rain-water is the *miqveh* under discussion. This gathering, or collection, of water, achieved without human agency, further bears the potential of effecting purification, just as spring water effects purification. To be sure, human agency is taken into account, as Sifra neatly states matters, in the digging of the cistern. In other words, what naturally must be done by man is done by man; but the rest is done by nature. Purification is the work of nature, a result of natural processes.

The law therefore might well be summarized in the statement, "Work [done by human agency] spoils the [rain] water," a statement entirely familiar from M. Par. 4:4: "Work [extrinsic to the rite of burning the cow] spoils the [spring] water." Indeed, as noted (Part X, p. 208), the fundamental and earliest supposition of M. Parah is that an act of labor is not to be done in connection with the water to be used for mixing with the ashes of the cow for purification unless the action has something to do with the drawing of the water and mixing of the ashes therewith. That conception was highly developed by 70, for the issues raised thereafter extended to relatively trivial gestures. The rules of the two tractates begin in a conception common to both and clearly taken for granted, in the case of Miqvaot, before the turn of the first century C.E.: the role of man in the process of purification is limited to actions or gestures secondary to, but necessary for, the working out of natural processes. These are digging the hole to which rain-water would naturally flow; bringing the spring water to the ash of the cow and mixing it therein, so that, the mixture having been accomplished, the water would take on its supernatural properties—conveying uncleanness when wrongfully or purposelessly used, effecting purification when properly employed. The two tractates spell out traits of water which effects purification, and, in ways pertinent to each, the diverse versions of the rule state exactly the same thing.

The relationship between the two tractates, moreover, is by no means limited to a general congruence in principle. On the contrary, there is a number of points of direct contact. Central to our tractate is the rule that the use of a utensil spoils water for the immersion-pool. Basic to the discussion of utensils in Parah is that water for the purification-rite must be collected in a utensil. What is required for the one therefore is prohibited for the other. M. Par. 5:5 specifies that broken utensils or broken parts of utensils cannot be used for the purification-rite (Part IX, pp. 85f.); our tractate knows that these same objects do not spoil water for the immersion-pool. M. 4:5 of course is shared at M. Par. 5:7. Interestingly, T. Par. 5:8 is very clear that water which flows in a water channel is not deemed drawn in a utensil, and our tractate accepts exactly that sort of water for the immersion-pool. In the matter of mingling or mixing water, M. Par. 5:8 tells us that with two troughs, in a single stone, if we mix water and ash in one of them, water in the second is not mixed. On the other hand, if they are perforated from one to the other through a hole the size of the spout of a waterskin, the mixing in one affects the water in the other. If water overflowed on top of them, even a film of water the thickness of a garlic peel, they are deemed mixed together (Part IX, p. 89)— a pericope which is wholly in accord with the conceptions of our tractate (Part XIII, pp. 151-153). M. Par. 5:9 has two troughs placed close to one another. Water in them is not deemed mixed. If, on the other hand, we so arrange them with plaster or gypsum that the water flows from one to another, the water between them is deemed mixed. These considerations again are familiar (Part XIII, pp. 131ff). In our discussion of M. Par. 6:4, we observed that a distinction is made between collecting water by something which is susceptible to uncleanness, which is unfit for the purification-rite, and collecting water by means of something which is not susceptible to uncleanness, in which case the water is fit for the purification-rite. We now know that that distinction, which seems to bear no clear relationship to any other rule of M. Parah, in fact is based upon Yosé's conception, M. 5:5, that one does not guide the flow of water for the immersion-pool by something which is susceptible to uncleanness (Part IX, pp. 99-100, Part XIII, pp. 120-124). It is no accident, therefore, that the reason adduced at b. Zev. 25b by Yohanan in the name of Yosé b. Abba should derive from Lev. 11:36, *"Nevertheless, a fountain or a cistern wherein is a gathering of water shall be clean*—its existence must be brought about in a state of cleanness." So the consideration—to those who hold it in the first place—concerns both M. Parah and M. Miqvaot, and for the same reason: each tells us an aspect of the attainment of purification from uncleanness by means of water of one sort or another, and the principle of Yosé applies without distinction to both tractates. Finally, M. Par. 6:5 is concerned that the flow of running or spring-water not be diverted into a cistern, in which the water will be prevented from continuing to bubble along, a point familiar at Part XIII, pp. 114-117. But M. Parah explains that the cistern is not deemed a utensil. Maimonides (*Red Heifer* 6:9) by contrast stresses that the water has not been taken in a vessel *from a spring*. These are points of clearcut and direct contact. The rules of the two tractates take into consideration a common principle, expressed in diverse ways. For Parah the use of the utensil is crucial, and so it is, in a negative way, for Miqvaot. The focus of our tractate and that of Parah are one and the same: the use of water for purification from uncleanness; the center of interest in each instance is cultic uncleanness. The reason the utensil spoils water for the immersion-pool is that the flow of the water into the pool is interrupted and no longer follows the course of nature. Rain-water must gather on its own, without human help. Spring water, by contrast, must be collected in a utensil for mixing in the ash. Its normal flow must be interrupted, because, in the preparation of the purification-water, human agency is required, specifically, in the preparation of the ash, then in the mixing of the ash in water. Since Scripture has given the human being a role in the preparation of the purifying mixture, that role is extended to the collection of the water. There is no role for human agency in the gathering of the rain-water, by contrast, and this water must do its work wholly by natural processes. In both cases, the utensil is the crux, the way to assure human intervention for the purification-rite and to prevent human intervention in the matter of the immersion-pool. As stated above (p. 1), uncleanness is the result of upsetting the wholeness, the economy, of nature. It derives, for example, from a corpse or a person who is like a corpse or a person who exudes various fluids. It is imparted to that which is susceptible by reason of its wholeness, completeness, normality, or to him or her who is susceptible by reason of his or her being Israelite. It is, then, removed through immersion in water in its natural state, deriving from the springs below or from the heavens above, unaffected by human agency. Just as it is water which inaugurates the susceptibility to uncleanness of dry foodstuffs, thus, so to speak, igniting the system, so it is water which effects the restoration to cleanness of persons or objects which, to begin with, constitute that natural system to which uncleanness and cleanness pertain.

ii. The Scriptural Foundations of Miqvaot

It would be pointless to catalogue all Scriptural references to water, for Miqvaot is uninterested in water as such, but only in the purificatory power of water under certain circumstances and for certain purposes. Accordingly, what is pertinent is the Scriptural conception of water within the process of purification for the cult. Since our tractate repeatedly refers to *miqveh* (immersion-pool), let us begin by noting the sole Scriptural references to *miqveh* or *miqveh mayyim*, the gathering of water: *And the waters that were gathered together he called seas* (Gen. 1:10). Sifra, moreover, has already alerted us to the importance of Lev. 11:36: *Nevertheless a spring or a cistern holding water (BWR MQWH MYM) will be clean.* On the surface, the comparison between the spring and any other gathering of water is invited by Lev. 11:36, which modifies BWR with MQWH MYM, a cistern, a gathering of water.

Let us now rapidly review the Targumim for the relevant verses. The sources are as follows: Onqelos: Alexander Sperber, *The Bible in Aramaic*, edited by Alexander Sperber. *I. The Pentateuch according to Targum Onkelos* (Leiden, 1959); A Berliner, *Targum Onkelos* (Berlin, 1884) I; J. W. Etheridge, *The Targums of Onkelos and Jonathan ben Uzziel on the Pentateuch. with Fragments of the Jerusalem Targum* (1862: Repr. N.Y., 1968); Jonathan: David Rieder, *Pseudo-Jonathan. Targum Jonathan ben Uzziel on the Pentateuch* (Jerusalem, 1974); M. Ginsburger, *Pseudo-Jonathan (Thargum Jonathan ben Usiel zum Pentateuch)* (Berlin, 1903); Neophyti: Alejandro Diez Macho, *Neophyti 1. I. Génesis* (Barcelona, 1968). *III Levítico* (Barcelona, 1971).

Genesis 1:10

Onqelos	Jonathan	Neophyti
And the place of the collection of **waters he called sea.**	And the place of the gathering of waters he called sea.	And the gathering place of the water he called seas.

Nothing in the treatment of Gen. 1:10 is of interest to our tractate. Certainly Yosé's comparison of the sea-water to smitten spring water, which purifies when in motion, but only in the volume of forty *seah*s, can have emerged from his interpretation of Scripture. But the Targums have no interest in the matter—because they know nothing of an immersion-pool consisting of forty *seah*s of still water which has been collected through natural processes. There is not a hint that such a category is in mind in the following.

Leviticus 11:36

Nevertheless a fountain or a pit, the place of a collection of waters... shall be clean.	But springs and pools, the place of the collection of *flowing waters* (MYYN NB'YN) shall be clean.	Only a spring or a cistern collecting water shall be clean.

The sole point of interest is Jonathan's view that the pool receives flowing waters, assuming that *place ... flowing waters* stands in apposition to pools only; or, excluding the use of rain-water entirely, he wants the pools to be comparable to springs. The former, like the latter, are formed by running or flowing water, along the lines, I suppose, of M. 1:1-3, 6, rain-drippings which have not ceased to flow. That is, the view that such still water is susceptible to uncleanness is understood here. More interesting: the main interest of our tractate, in prohibiting drawn water and permitting only water naturally collected in a cistern or pit, is not introduced into the Scripture by the Targums. The obvious point of Lev. 11:36, however, is simply to exclude from the effects of contamination by the creeping thing the specified collections of water: *a spring or a cistern holding water shall be clean, but whatever touches their carcass* [of the creeping thing] *shall be unclean.* In fact, the simple meaning of Scripture does not yield the notion of purification in an immersion-pool. That has to be imposed. Scripture is talking about something else entirely.

We shall now see that Scripture knows absolutely nothing of the immersion-pool, containing forty *seah*s of rain-water which has flowed naturally and not been gathered by human agency. It knows nothing of a special pool, subject to its own requirements, in which washing for the purpose of purification must take place. The Priestly Code does not imagine such a thing as an immersion-pool formed by rain-water which has collected and lies still in the ground. It knows only that when one is contaminated by sources of uncleanness, he or she is to wash in water, the location, character, and volume of which is simply not specified. The reason it is not specified is that in any event *the water does not accomplish the purification.* It removes the contamination. The setting of the sun completes the purification. All we learn is that, after certain forms of contamination, a person is supposed to wash in water and await sunset. But the water does not purify.

To be sure, appropriate proof-texts to indicate that water does purify are not lacking, particularly in prophetic literature. Ezekiel (36:25) supplies, "I will sprinkle clean water upon you, and you will be clean from all your uncleannesses, and from all your idols I will cleanse you." But Zechariah (13:1) knows only the purifying power of fountains and living waters, "On that day there shall be a fountain opened for the house of David and the inhabitants of Jerusalem to cleanse them from sin and uncleanness"; and, along the same lines, he says (14:8), "On that day living waters shall flow out from Jerusalem..." The prophets, however, speak of eschatological cleansing from the uncleanness of idolatry or other sins. The purification besought by the Pharisees was from the uncleanness described in Leviticus, which had to be removed so that the person might be purified and attain fitness for the cult. This sort of purification is in the here-and-now and for cultic purposes; it has nothing whatever to do with purification from sin, let alone baptism in an eschatological context.

iii. Blood, Spring-Water, and Still Water

Purification for cultic purposes is accomplished, so far as the priestly code is concerned, not by water but by blood, spring water, normally mixed with another substance, blood or cow-ash, and by sunset. Washing in water is routinely said to leave a person or object unclean until sunset, so sunset, not plain water, purifies. The definitive discussion on blood in purification of the cult is that of Baruch A. Levine:

> What was the specific purpose of such utilization of blood, conveyed by the verb *kippēr?* For his own protection, the High Priest had employed incense. For the protection of the worshippers, outside the tent, the blood libation had been offered. It seems to us an inescapable conclusion that the blood was placed on those areas and objects so as to

protect the deity and his immediate surroundings from the incursion of impurity which would penetrate the sanctuary through a route leading from the courtyard, outside the tent, through the entrance of the tent, past the altar of incense, and through the *pāroket*, opened to let the priest in, and into the very spot where the deity sat, astride the cherubim. These were figures made as part of the sculptured *kapporet*-lid of the ark.

What we observe here is the protection of a route or channel from contamination. This route was rendered particularly vulnerable by the entry of a human being, the High Priest, into the most sacred section of the sanctuary. This interpretation is suggested not only by the graphics of the purification rites prescribed in Leviticus, chapter 16. From other sources we learn that the placing of blood from expiatory sacrifices on a particular person or object may have as its clear purpose the protection of that person or object from contamination, or the elimination already existing.

According to Leviticus 14:14, the priest is instructed to dab blood from the ᵓāšām sacrifice on the person who had been afflicted with a skin ailment known as ṣāraᶜat. In connection with this rite, a bird was to be dispatched into the open field, to carry with it the feared disease. It is clear, in this case, that the sacrificial blood was used to immunize the afflicted person in a magical way, against the recurrence of the ailment. The same objective is observable in the dabbing of blood on the persons and vestments of Aaron and his sons during the rites of their installation as priests. Before assuming cultic duties which would necessitate their entry into sacred areas, they had to take precautions against contamination which would have resulted in the introduction of their own impurities into the sanctuary.

The same magical objective of "washing off" impurity was operative in the placing of blood on the doorposts and lintels of the Israelite houses in Egypt (Exodus 12:7, 13, 23). In the account, as we have it, the identities of Yahweh and the *mašḥit*, a destructive force, are somewhat muddled, but it is clear, nevertheless, that the *mašḥit* was conceived as a distinct force which, once unleased, was not controllable, even by Yahweh, himself!

Other prescriptions relevant to the placing of blood from expiatory sacrifices on various objects are also instructive. Thus, in Numbers 19:13 it is explicitly stated that one who had become impure as a result of contact with a dead, human body and had not subsequently purified himself in the proper manner had actually caused the contamination of the sanctuary, itself. The purification rites undertaken on behalf of one so contaminated included the sprinkling of blood from the red heifer on the surface of the Tent of Meeting, itself, preliminary to the preparation of a mixture of ashes and water to be used in subsequent rites (*ibid* 19:4). The purificatory rites of those impure as a result of contact with a dead, human body had a two-fold purpose: to purify the persons directly contaminated, and at the same time to protect the abode of the resident deity from contamination....

> Impurity was viewed as an external force which entered the person or attached itself to him. The primary purpose of expiation was, therefore, to rid one's self of this foreign force. The verbs employed in biblical literature to connote the elimination of sins, such as *māḥāh* "to wipe away, erase," *heᶜebir* "to cause to pass away," and, of course, *kippēr* "to wipe off, cleanse" convey this notion clearly.
>
> In our view, expiation addressed itself to the presence of impurity, the actualized form of evil forces operative in the human environment. This was the function of expiation as a phenomenon. It was not so much that Yahweh had to be appeased for the offenses committed. To the extent that this was the case, such mollification took the form of the sacrifice, itself. The accompanying expiation through blood, as distinct from the sacrificial gift, itself, became necessary because Yahweh demanded that the forces of impurity, unleashed by the offenses committed, be kept away from his immediate environment. There is a reason for Yahweh's wrath. It was not mere displeasure at being disobeyed. His wrath was a reaction based on a vital concern, as it were, for his own protection. The sacrificial blood is offered to the demonic forces who accept it in lieu of God's "life", to to speak, and depart, just as they accept it in lieu of human life in other cultic contexts. [1]

The Priestly Code knows three means of purification, one for general purposes, and two for special cases. The first is blood. Sacrificial blood is utilized for the purpose of purification, as the discussion of Levine has shown.

The two other substances, beside blood, which play a role in the purificatory process, are fire and living water or spring water. Fire occurs in the following:

> Num. 31:23-24: Everything that can stand the fire you shall pass through fire and it shall be clean. Nevertheless it shall also be purified with the water of impurity; and whatever cannot stand the fire you shall pass through the water. You must wash your clothes on the seventh day, and you shall be clean...

R. de Vaux (*Ancient Israel* [London, 1961] p. 461) observes, "Metal objects were first passed through fire before being washed."

When water is said to accomplish purification, it is always spring water (living water). The following are the pertinent verses:

> Lev. 14:5: And the priest shall command them to kill one of the birds in an earthen vessel over living water.... (+ Lev. 14:50). (The running water is mixed with the blood.)
>
> Lev. 15:13: And when he who has a discharge shall be cleansed of his discharge, he shall wash his clothes; and he shall bathe his body in running water, and he shall be clean.

---

[1] Baruch A. Levine, *In the Presence of the Lord* (Leiden, 1974), pp. 73-5, 77-8.

Num. 19:17: For the unclean they shall take some ashes of the burnt purification-offering, and running water shall be added in a vessel....

In the case of the purification of the *meṣoraʿ*, the living water is mixed with blood; in the case of the purification-water, the living water is mixed with the ashes, including the blood, of the cow. Living water by itself purifies the one who has had a discharge (for which Mishnah (M. 8:2-4) accepts drawn water [!].).

The Priestly Code presents various other references to washing, bathing, and laundering. Those which deal with the matter of attaining cleanness *from uncleanness in particular* specify, time and again, that once an object or person is washed, has been laundered, or has been put in water, the object or person remains unclean—until sunset. It is perfectly clear, therefore, that water is distinguished from spring water or living water and is not understood as a substance capable of purifying anything from uncleanness. Let us consider the pertinent verses.

Lev. 11:31-2: And anything upon which any of them [creeping things] falls when they are dead shall be unclean... it must be put into water, and it shall be unclean until evening; then it shall be clean.

The water here does not purify the object, which remains unclean after it has been washed. By contrast, living water does purify, as we saw above:

Lev. 15:13: And when he who has a discharge is cleansed of his discharge, then he shall count for himself seven clean days for his cleansing and wash his clothes and he shall bathe his body in running water and shall be clean.

The purification of the *Zab* in a spring (not in an immersion-pool) of course is taken for granted by our tractate. But a spring and an immersion-pool are quite different. *Miqvaot* does not claim that a *miqveh* and a spring serve the same purposes. And Leviticus is clear that the spring (running water) does purify; other water does not. The contrast is entirely clear. Further instances of the same fact are as follows:

Lev. 11:32: It [what is touched by a creeping thing] must be put in water and it shall be unclean until evening; then it shall be clean.
Lev. 11:40: He also who carries the carcass shall wash his clothes and be unclean until evening...
Lev. 14:8: And he who is to be cleansed shall wash his clothes and shave off all his hair and bathe himself in water and he shall be clean

(+ Lev. 14:9, 16, 24). (But he has already been sprinkled with blood.)

Lev. 15:5: And any one who touches his [the *Zab*'s] bed shall wash his clothes and bathe himself in water, and he shall be unclean until evening (+ Lev. 15:6, 7, 8, 10, 11, 12).

Lev. 15:16: And if a man has a discharge of semen, he shall bathe his whole body in water and be unclean until evening (+ Lev. 15:17, 18).

Lev. 15:21: And whoever touches her bed shall wash his clothes and bathe himself in water and be unclean until evening (+ Lev. 15:22, 23).

Lev. 15:27: And whoever touches these things shall be unclean and shall wash his clothes and bathe himself in water and be unclean until evening.

Lev. 16:28: And he who burns them shall wash his clothes and bathe his body and afterward he may come into the camp (+ Lev. 16:26). Compare Num. 19:7, 19.

Lev. 17:15: And every person that eats what dies of itself ... shall wash his clothes in water and be unclean until evening. Then he shall be clean.

Lev. 22:6-7: The person who touches any such shall be unclean until evening and shall not eat of the holy things unless he has bathed his body in water. When the sun is down, he shall be clean.

Num. 19:7: Then the priest shall wash his clothes and bathe his body in water and afterwards he shall come into the camp. And the priest shall be unclean until evening (+ Num. 19:8, 10).

Num. 19:19: And the clean person shall sprinkle upon the unclean... and he shall wash his clothes and bathe himself in water and at evening he shall be clean (+ Num. 19:21, 22).

Note also Deuteronomy's equivalent:

Deut. 23:11-12: If there is among you any man who is not clean... but when evening comes on, he shall bathe himself in water, and when the sun is down, he may come into the camp.

Once again we observe that the washing in water is not developed through definition of the nature of the 'gathering of water' which is required or involved. On the contrary, water is in no way subject to specification and delimitation, *since it does not, in any event, effect purification*. Sunset does. Our tractate, by contrast, simply takes for granted that when an unclean utensil is dipped in the water in the appropriate way, it loses its uncleanness and rises to the level of cleanness. The same is so of a human being who dips into the pool. Proof that immersion in a pool effects purification is the invention of the category of the *tevul yom*, one who has immersed and awaits sunset for the completion of purification, as specified in various Scriptural verses.

He is deemed *clean*, yet not wholly so. By contrast, Scripture is explicit that he is unclean until sunset. The contrary claim, in the later rabbinic law, is necessitated solely by the primary allegation in behalf of the immersion-pool.

iv. MISHNAH AND SCRIPTURE: THE IMMERSION-POOL AND THE SPRING

On the surface, therefore, it would appear that Mishnah's contribution is primarily to add some details to Scripture's conception of the role of water in the process of purification. Yet, we must ask, what, in the Priestly conception, accomplishes purification? It is not still water, but spring water or blood. The shift is that for the Priestly Code blood and living water, not still water, purify; for the Oral Torah, still water accomplishes purification, in the absence of blood for the cult or living water for persons. That is why—quite tangentially—water must be preserved in its natural state, like spring-water. And that is why—quite crucially—the analogy to the spring is so vital. For spring-water does purify, in the Scriptural view. Accordingly, the blood which accomplishes purification at the altar and the water which accomplishes purification in the immersion-pool act in analogous ways, and the living water, which flows like blood but which *is* water, like still water, forms the analogical nexus. (And this accounts for Yosé's view that the immersion-pool must be constructed of materials which are insusceptible to uncleanness.)

In point of fact, therefore, our tractate wholly lacks Scriptural foundations of any kind. Its most basic supposition—that immersion is to take place in an immersion-pool, in a *gathering* or collection of water—thus, *still* water, by contrast to flowing water, which Scripture does know—is wholly outside the imagination of the Priestly legislator. The Priestly Code, as we have seen, refers to washing in water, laundering in water, and bringing into water, but never speaks of the character of the water—drawn or flowing naturally, or of the traits of the water—still or flowing, or of the volume of the water—any amount at all, forty *seah*s, or whatever.

Yet that is not the whole story. Miqvaot knows the flowing spring. It takes for granted, that, because the stream is flowing, a specific volume of water will not be collected together in any one place. Mishnah thus sets up the *miqveh*, the immersion-pool of forty *seah*s, as a contrast: the spring flows, the immersion-pool is still. The spring may purify in any volume whatever, the immersion-pool requires the requisite volume. Yet since the spring derives from natural, not artificial, sources, and not by means of human agency, in this respect, the pool is exactly alike. Accordingly, the rules of Mishnah for the immersion-pool begin in the analogy between the spring and the pool (just as the redactor, coming at the end of the process of the formation of our tractate, has told us): the spring and pool are alike in that neither is subject to human agency; both accomplish purification through natural means: and they are different solely in the obvious fact that spring-water flows, and the 'gathering of water' which is the immersion-pool is still water. What seems to lie at the base, from the viewpoint of exegesis, is that the conception of the still pool which purifies has been attached to the Scriptures which speak merely of washing in water. Yet the essential trait of the still pool, so far as the Hillelites are concerned, is exactly the opposite of that of the spring: its water is still, it is not flowing. Accordingly, at the basis of the capacity of the immersion-pool to effect purification is the notion that spring-water, deriving from the earth, and immersion-pool-water, deriving from heaven, are equivalent in their purificatory power, so long as they are preserved in their equivalent, natural, form. So long as rain water is unaffected by human agency, it is equivalent to spring water, flowing naturally. But just as rain water is spoiled when it is drawn, so spring water is spoiled when it is collected in a utensil, which water, indeed, diminishes in its puissance as it is allowed to cease its flow and dammed up in a pool. The position of the Shammaites, that immersion may take place in a rain-stream, certainly rests upon the original analogy between spring water and rain water. The Hillelites, as I said, underline the limits of the analogy: rain water purifies when it is not flowing, but does not purify when it is flowing—for it *is like* spring water, but it *is not* spring water.

To summarize: The main point of the Priestly Code is that *for cultic purposes* purification is attained through the application of blood, or through immersion in living water, or through sunset. But for purification our tractate speaks only of immersion in the appropriate pool, or, self-evidently, a flowing stream. The Pharisees accept immersion in a pool of water, the natural properties of which have not been affected by human agency. Since the purpose of immersion is the attainment of cultic purity, they take a position quite outside that imagined in Scripture. The obvious reason is that the Pharisees are priests and laymen outside of the Temple engaged in the pretense that they attain the purity characteristic of the cult. Lacking a sacrificial service, therefore without access to blood, they maintain that water would serve. They add, however, that even rain-water, not only spring-water, purifies, because the two are deemed analogous.

What evidently happened, probably in the first century B.C., before the time of the later pairs and the Houses, therefore, is that a mode of purification was created, in addition to the available means specified in Scripture, blood-rites for the cult, living water for people specified in Scripture. How to attain cleanness for the table? In that other sort of water, rain-water, lying still upon the ground, and unaffected by human agency.[1] (To be sure, in time it would be taken for granted that the immersion-pool served the cult as much as the table.)

To return to our starting point, the comparison of Parah and Miqvaot. In Parah we create a place for a sacrifice outside of the Temple, a place of cleanness and holiness. In Miqvaot we call into being a means of attaining cleanness outside of the Temple, a kind of water not used for the Temple described in the Priestly Code. Spring water (which serves as well) is different from rain water. The one is exceptional, the other ordinary, the one flows with force, the other stands still, the one (our tractate says) cleans in any amount, the other serves the body or the utensil only in the volume of forty *seah*s. The spring water, which can purify for the cult and for the table alike, therefore has traits quite distinct from the sort of water which serves for the table. That is as it should be, for the difference between the altar of the Temple and the table of the home, both to be clean, to be sure, is not to be obscured.

What is the fundamental achievement of our tractate? The Oral Torah provides a mode of purification different from that specified in the Written Torah for the Temple, but analogous to that suitable for the Temple. Still water serves for the table, living water cleans the *Zab*, and, when mixed with blood or ashes, the leper and the person unclean by reason of touching a corpse. All those other things cleaned

---

[1] We have already stressed (p. 1) that the use of water for purification, specifically in connection with eating, is not limited to Pharisees and need not derive, to begin with, from the Pharisaic group or be seen as distinctively a Pharisaic notion. Josephus explicitly links purification through bathing in water and eating as a characteristic trait of Essenism, interestingly omitting reference to a similar practice among the Pharisees. Accordingly, in contrasting the conceptions of the two Torahs, Written and Oral, I do not mean to suggest that there is a linear development from the one to the other or that nothing happened in Jewish religion between the completion of the Priestly Code and the beginning of the Oral Torah in the suppositions just now specified. The contrast derives from literary history and is meant to produce a comparison for phenomenological, not for historical purposes, just as is the case at Part III, pp. 381-384, and Part V, pp. 251-256.

by the setting of the sun, the passage of time, in the Oral Torah are cleaned in the still water, gathered in the ground, in the rains which know no time, but only the eternal seasons. In an age in which men and women immersed themselves in spring-fed lakes and rushing rivers, in moving water washing away their sins in preparation for the end of days, the Pharisees observed the passing of the seasons, which go onward through time, immersing in the still, collected water which falls from heaven. They bathe not in running water, in the anticipation of the end of days and for the sake of eschatological purity, but in still water, to attain the cleanness appropriate to the eternal Temple and the perpetual sacrifice. They remove the uncleanness defined by the Written Torah for the holy altar, because of the conviction of the Oral Torah that the hearth and home, table and bed, going onward through ages without end, also must be and can be cleaned, in particular, through the rain: the living water from heaven, falling in its perpetual seasons, trickling down the hills and naturally gathering in ponds, ditches, and caverns, for time immemorial. As sun sets, bringing purification for the Temple, so rain falls, bringing purification for the table.

VIII. Niddah Before 70

i. INTRODUCTION

A strikingly large proportion of the rules is attributed to authorities before 70 and generates an appropriately sizable proportion of the rules assigned to those afterward. Accordingly, Niddah before 70 appears to encompass a fair measure of the tractate's fundamental structure of themes. In our earlier inquiries, asking about the law before 70 raised the question of the tractate's primary and basic conception, that is, the conception prior to developments exhibited by, or contained within the presuppositions of, pericopae assigned to authorities after 70. Self-evidently, in Niddah this is not the case. It would be better to ask about Niddah before the turn of the first century A.D., that is, the time of Shammai and Hillel. But for the sake of continuity with the thematic organization of the preceding parts of the study, I have preserved what is here a title which is slightly misleading. But that is not entirely the case.

The question before us is this: At what point in the period before 70 do the fundamental and generative conceptions of our tractate appear? Upon what foundation do they stand? From what source do they derive? The answer, to be given at the outset, is that our Mishnah tractate begins in Scripture itself and contains no conception of fundamental and generative importance which Scripture itself does not reveal or logically require and invite. The distinction between menstrual- and *Zibah*- days is clearly made in the appropriate passage, Lev. 15:25. The fact that the former is for seven days is explicit in Scripture. The eleven days assigned to the latter are not; it is the sole matter in our tractate which both is taken for granted and is not clearly assigned to an authority after the fathers, Shammai and Hillel. But it is a datum of the tractate, everywhere assumed as such, but no where more than part of the background of facts subjected to the creative work of the legislators. It does not contribute any more—or any less—to the tractate than the fact that menstrual blood is unclean. I assume that the eleven days assigned to the *Zibah*-period derive from the period before the fathers, though I cannot demonstrate that that is the case. But I perceive in the sequence of seven menstrual and eleven *Zibah*-days no profound conceptions, no formative and generative notions basic to the tractate's intellectual unfolding. That unfolding proceeds along quite distinctive lines, already familiar to us in the traits of mind of Yavneans and Ushans.

ii. Scripture and Mishnah: Oral Torah as the Completion of the Written Torah

Since the Priestly Code presents the menstrual taboo, in all its peculiarity, as something to be kept by everyone, not only by people intending to go to the Temple, its law by definition accords with the Pharisaic conception of cleanness. Pharisaism maintained that people outside of the Temple should eat their food as if they were priests in the Temple. Those laws which begin in that assumption by definition are sectarian. Then Niddah's theme and problems by definition are not. Lev. 15:31 makes that point clear. Accordingly, we have an excellent occasion to see how a Mishnah-tractate develops laws beginning in Scripture and conceived to apply to all of the people. We shall now see that the progression indeed begins in Scripture, not in a conception alien to or wholly separate from Scripture, and proceeds, upon virtually no intervening layer of exegesis or mediating conceptions, directly from Scripture to the materials attributed to the Houses before 70, thence to Yavneh, and finally to Usha.

Accordingly, before us is a dramatic instance of the way in which, from the turn of the first century A.D., Pharisaic and later Rabbinic law in a distinctive way spun out commonly accepted rules. To provide striking visual evidence of that fact, we shall consider the matter through tables, each beginning in the pertinent Scriptural rule, given for emphasis in bold-face type, then proceeding to list all materials of the period before 70, with their Yavnean and Ushan developments, followed by materials new to Yavneh, with *their* Ushan developments, and, at the end, rules without clear precedent before Ushan times. It should not be thought that all rules stand in the same relationship to Scripture. In order to show, within each stratum, which rules serve to gloss Scripture, the pertinent, dependent materials are given in italics. Expansion of Scriptural themes and new rules based upon problems generated by these expansions is printed in regular type. New rules, not clearly based upon, or generated by, Scripture then are given at the end in bold-face type. In this way we shall see very clearly how the law unfolds and show, beyond any doubt, that Niddah conforms to the hithertofore unproved theory that the function of Oral Torah is to fill in gaps left by the Written Torah or otherwise to carry forward the task of interpretation and application of the Written Torah.

To simplify the following tables, reference is made only to the basic entries at Chapter Sixteen, parts ii and iii, along with the topic under discussion. The elaboration and development of the several entries and their topics need not detain us, since the primary purpose is to show at what points the thematic and logical development of the tractate is generated by direct encounter with the Scriptural rules, which are simply given definition and detail; at what points it is secondary to Scripture, but generated by Scripture's concerns; and at what points it is entirely independent of Scripture, based upon conceptions or problems distinct from those supplied by the Written Torah.

A. *The Menstrual Period. 1. Menstrual Blood is Unclean*

Lev. 15:19: **When a woman has a discharge of blood which is her regular discharge from her body, she shall be in her impurity for seven days.**

Before 70	Yavneh	Usha
1. ii.A.1: *Colors of blood which are unclean:* red shades. Brown, yellow are disputed.		1. ii.C.1: *Colors of blood which are unclean.*
		ii.C.4: Yellow blood: is it a blood at all?
		iii.C.5: *Blood of uterus is unclean, of wound is clean.*
	iii.B.6: Bloodstain attributed to wound, clean. 'Aqiva: Bloodstains are adjudicated in a lenient way.	iii.C.6: Bloodstain may be unclean. It is +/— *not* treated more strictly than blood. Woman may be *Zibah* by reason of bloodstain. + Various other applications to bloodstain of rules applying to unclean blood. Attributing bloodstain to uterine blood. + iii.D.1.
2. ii.A.2.A: Status of blood of a gentile woman [= unclean as a *Zabah*], of a woman		2. ii.C.5: Status of Samaritans, Sadduceans They are not gentiles, but also not entirely

Before 70	Yavneh	Usha
with ṣara'at: Unclean or clean.		Israelites. +iii.C.6: Bloodstains of Samaritans.
3. iii.A.1: Does the menstrual uncleanness begin only when blood is discovered, or do we suppose it was present prior to discovery? Examination is required, using test-rags, in this connection. A fixed period means contamination begins only when the fixed period begins, and not retroactively. iii.A.2: Use of test-rags.	3. iii.B.1: Women who do not regularly have a flow impart uncleanness only when they perceive flow. *Vs.* women who have a regular period do so. iii.B.2: Regular examinations, test-rags.	3. iii.C.1: Minors are assumed to be clean and are not examined. iii.C.2: Fixed period established through three occurrences of same phenomenon followed by flow of blood. iii.C.3, 4 glosses of iii.B.1.
4. [iii.A.5: Woman who sees blood on eleventh day, immerses in the evening, then has intercourse, etc. This issue belongs to *Zabim*.]	4. iii.B.5: She who sees blood at twilight is in disarray—may be Zabah, may be menstruant.	4. —
5. ii.A.5: Status of woman who die during their menstrual period (or: of all women after death) in relationship to vaginal excretions. Is this blood now unclean as menstrual blood or merely as an excretion from a corpse? (If former, in any amount, if latter, quarter-*log* in liquid volume).	5. —	5. ii.C.3: Status of blood which exudes from a female corpse. ii.C.7: Zab, Zabah, menstruant, woman after childbirth, meṣora' who died impart uncleanness when carried until flesh has decayed. [Thereafter, they impart uncleanness like all other corpses.]
6. iii.A.3: Status of hymeneal blood of a girl who has not reached puberty, who has reached puberty but has had no flow, and who has had a flow.	6. —	6. iii.C.3, 5: Distinguishing hymeneal from menstrual blood.
7. —	7. —	7. ii.C.8: **Blood of menstruant and flesh of a corpse impart uncleanness wet or dry. Zab's flux etc.**

Before 70	Yavneh	Usha
		does so only when wet, not when dry.
8. —	8. —	8. ii.C.6: **Infants are subject to uncleanness of menstruation, Zab.**
9. —	9. —	9. ii.C.9: **Women are unclean when blood is in vagina, but men only when flux or semen is emitted.**

B. *The Menstrual Period. 2. Things Touched by the Menstruant Are Unclean*

Lev. 15:19b: ...she shall be in her impurity for seven days, and whoever touches her shall be unclean until the evening ... **Lev. 15:24:** And if any man lies with her, and her impurity is on him, he shall be unclean seven days ...

Before 70	Yavneh	Usha
1. —	1. iii.B.3: *Woman imparts uncleanness to one who has intercourse with her* (= Lev. 15:24).	1. ii.C.9: *Man and woman are equivalent vis à vis contamination.* See iii.C.6.

C. *The Zibah-Period Distinct from the Menstrual Period of Seven Days*

Lev. 15:25: If a woman has a discharge of blood for many days, not at the time of her impurity, or if she has a discharge beyond the time of her impurity, all the days of the discharge she shall continue in uncleanness; as in the days of her impurity, she shall be unclean.

Before 70	Yavneh	Usha	Unattributed
1. ii.A.2.C: Blood of woman who has given birth while a *Zabah* is unclean like that of a *Zabah*.	1. —	1. —	1. —
2. —	2. —	2. —	2. ii.E.3: *Blood in menstrual days has no bearing on Zibah.*
3. —	3. iii.B.4: *Zab* or *Zabah* who did not exa-		3. [iii.C.8: See Chart E, Usha No. 1]

D. The Woman after Childbirth

Lev. 12:2: **If a woman conceives and bears a male child, then she shall be unclean seven days; as at the time of her menstruation she shall be unclean.**

Before 70	Yavneh	Usha
(cont.) mine selves on intervening days assumed clean on those days, so Eliezer. 'Aqiva: Unclean.		
1. ii.A.4: *Blood of a woman in labor not during Zibah-days is unclean as menstrual blood.* This simply attributes to the blood before delivery the same status as blood after delivery: It is unclean as menstrual blood.	1. ii.B.1: *Woman in hard labor during the Zibah-days who gives birth after labor, without respite, is unclean as a menstruant, not as a Zibah.* Scripture is made to say: As at the time of menstruation—not as a Zabah.	1. ii. C.2: *How Long is hard labor?*
2. ii.E.1: *Woman after childbirth contaminates through intercourse (= like menstruant).*	2. —	2. —
3. —	3. ii.B.3: She who produces an abortion which was not formed —Joshua: It is a valid birth. Sages: It is not a valid birth. This is a secondary issue. The child invokes the rules of childbirth—what about the abortion?	3. ii.C.11-15: (11) Status of a shapeless object. Meir applies Joshua's principle. (12) Sages concur with Yavneh's sages. Meir: An abortion whose sex and status are unknown imposes rules of male, female birth and of menstruation. (= ii.C.7.) (13) Abortion like sandal or placenta treated as above, Meir. (14) Placenta imposes rules of corpse-uncleanness, so Meir. (15) Still-born child imparts uncleanness of childbirth to mother = ii.B.3. + ii.D.1. + iii.C.7: Uncleanness of childbirth —male or female?—of

Before 70	Yavneh	Usha
		tumtom, androgyne, and abortion of unknown sex.
4. —	4. (M. Bekh. 2:9: Ṭarfon and ʿAqiva.)	4. ii.C.10: Blood of Caesarean delivery is +/— *not* equivalent to blood of normal childbirth. This is clearly a secondary development.

E. *The Woman after Childbirth. The Days of Purifying*

Lev. 12:4: **Then she shall continue for thirty-three days in the blood of her purifying; she shall not touch any hallowed thing nor come into the sanctuary until the days of her purifying are completed.**

Lev. 12:5: **But if she bears a female child, then she shall be unclean two weeks, as in her menstruation, and she shall continue in the blood of her purifying for sixty-six days.**

Before 70	Yavneh	Usha
1. ii.A.2.B: *Blood of a woman who has not immersed after childbirth—importance of immersion after seven/fourteen unclean days.* + iii.A.4: It imparts uncleanness wet +/— dry.	1. ii.B.2: Status of hard labor during the eighty days of purifying. Secondary issue, combining days of purifying with labor.	1. ii.C.8: A woman who does not mark the distinction between unclean and clean days is assumed to be unclean, so Judah. [Parallel to iii.B.4, Chart C, No. 3.]
2. ii.A.3: Status of woman in clean days after childbirth: *ṭevul yom*? Secondary issue, ii.A.6: Does she have to immerse after the days of purifying, or is the immersion after the unclean days sufficient?	2. —	2. —
3. ii.B.4: *Male completed on forty-first, female on eighty-first — Ishmael explains the different intervals assigned to the two sexes.*	3. —	3. —

Of the items before us, A. 7, 8, 9, C. 3, D. 3, 4, do not clearly begin in Scripture or among the Houses. The point of A. 7 is to contrast the *Zab*'s flux with the blood of the menstruant. A. 8 is new and interesting. A. 9 is Simeon's own viewpoint. C. 3 is the secondary sort of problem popular at Yavneh and Usha. We have seen the same sort of issue in connection with M. Miq. 2:1-2, for one example; it is commonplace in Tohorot. The problem of determining, without concrete evidence, the matter of status is something of keen interest to the lawyers after 70, and especially, after 140. D. 3's issue raises a question Scripture leaves open, about the status not only of the stillborn child but also of the unformed abortion. D. 4 likewise is a logical question left open by Scripture.

These exceptional matters leave no significant doubt as to the history of the laws of our tractate. They begin in Scripture and rise in necessarily sequential and logical stages therefrom. Accordingly, the laws of our tractate clearly begin at the point at which someone determined to undertake a careful reading of Scripture on the matter of Niddah and draw practical consequences from the results of that reading. The earliest assigned rules belong to Shammai and Hillel, and the Houses, coming later, then Yavneans and Ushans still later clearly work out the implications of the rule of Hillel, in particular. Accordingly, whether or not the historical fathers, Shammai and Hillel, said what is attributed to them, the fact is that the laws assigned to them do originate earlier than, and in striking and concrete ways stand behind, the laws attributed to their successors, later in the first century and even after 70.

The interest in the laws of Niddah seems to come, therefore, at that point at which Pharisaism begins its history as a table-fellowship sect and so undertakes the specification of the rules of cleanness important in the life of such a sect.[1] Whether that takes place at the beginning of the first century or shortly before that time, or whether it was much earlier, we do not know. We have only the evidence in our hands, however, and this evidence does point to the beginning of the process. The tractate claims not much greater antiquity for its laws than the turn of the first century A.D., and I do not think we may profitably claim more than do our sources.

iii. Sectarian Views of Menstrual Uncleanness

The laws of Niddah contained in Mishnah-Tosefta in the main derive from a careful, if creative, reading of Scripture. The develop-

---

[1] *Rabbinic Traditions about the Pharisees before 70.* III, pp. 304-306.

ment of these laws, after 70, is to be attributed to the rabbinical group. Mishnah is clear, in any case, that its authorities do not perceive the Samaritans to keep the laws as they prescribe and are not certain about the practice of Sadducees (which is not surprising, since there were not many Sadducees to consult in the mid-second century). But are the results of that careful reading of Scripture, to which we attribute the origin of the bulk of the laws of Niddah, distinctive to the Pharisaic forerunners of the rabbis after 70? Even at their origins, do the laws of our tractate reflect a particular and sectarian beginning? We cannot definitively answer that question. We find nothing in the careful reading of Scripture which presupposes rules both distinctive to and absolutely characteristic of what is essential to Pharisaism. Nothing in the Written Torah itself limits the observance of menstrual and related taboos to the sanctuary, even though Lev. 15:31 implies just that. Accordingly, the development of the law revealed in the earliest strata of Niddah need not be the work of Pharisees. In the examination of the earlier tractates of our Order, we have asked about the relationship between Written and Oral Torah. We find, in each case, that Mishnah, which is to say, Oral Torah, bears at best an antiphonal, but really, no relationship whatsoever to the Written Torah. Its primary and generative conception of the law time and again begins in notions wholly alien to, even at variance with, the givens of the Written Torah. In the present tractate, by contrast, we do not discover a single central conception of Mishnah which stands apart from, let alone at variance with, the Written Torah. Mishnah serves, as we have seen essentially to fill out areas opened, but left undefined, by Scripture.

At the same time, we observe that the laws of menstrual and related uncleanness in the Written Torah take for granted precisely the central affirmation of Pharisaism, which is that cleanness is important outside the cult. While, as I said, Scripture's subscription, Lev. 15:31, proposes that even these laws be kept to keep the sanctuary clean, the detailed laws themselves bear no such implications. Accordingly, the identity of viewpoint between Pharisaism and the conception of menstrual uncleanness and its pertinence in Scripture provides no stimulus for the revision of Scripture along lines important within the Pharisaic perspective. Indeed, we have no reason to suppose the careful reading of Scripture constituted by Mishnah begins, in the first place, within the Pharisaic sect at all, even though the secondary developments and later expansions of the law obviously are wholly congruent with other developments and expansions undertaken by the rabbis after 70 and stand entirely within the trends and modes of thought characteristic of Yavneans and Ushans.

We must now ask whether other sects in fact reached the same conclusions through close attention to the Scriptural rules on menstruation and the woman after childbirth.

1. *Targumim*

Let us now rapidly review the Targumim for the relevant verses. The sources are as follows:

Onqelos: Alexander Sperber. *The Bible in Aramaic*, edited by Alexander Sperber. *I. The Pentateuch according to Targum Onkelos* (Leiden, 1959); A Berliner, *Targum Onkelos* (Berlin, 1964), I; J. W. Etheridge, *The Targums of Onkelos and Jonathan ben Uzziel on the Pentateuch, with Fragments of the Jerusalem Targum* (1862: Repr. N.Y., 1968); Jonathan: David Rieder, *Pseudo-Jonathan. Targum Jonathan ben Uzziel on the Pentateuch* (Jerusalem, 1974); M. Ginsburger, *Pseudo-Jonathan (Thargum Jonathan ben Usiel zum Pentateuch)* (Berlin, 1903); Neophyti: Alejandro Diez Macho, *Neophyti 1. III Levitico* (Barcelona, 1971).

Onqelos	*Jonathan*	*Neophyti*
Lev. 12:2b	*Lev. 12:2b*	*Lev. 12:2b*
A woman, when she has conceived and borne a male child, shall be unclean seven days; according to the days for the removal of her uncleanness she shall be unclean.	When a woman has conceived and borne a male child, she shall be unclean seven days, as the days of the removal of her uncleanness shall she be unclean.	If a woman conceives and bears a male son, she shall be unclean seven days; as (in) the days of the removal of her menstrual flow she shall be unclean.
Lev. 12:4	*Lev. 12:4*	*Lev. 12:4*
And she shall con inue thirty-three days in the purification of blood. No holy thing shall she touch, nor may she come into the sanctuary, until the days of her purification be completed.	And thirty-three *continuous* (RṢYPYN) days she shall have for the purification of the whole blood; but (BRM) she must not touch holy things nor come into the sanctuary until the days of her purification are completed.	And for thirty-three days she shall continue waiting by the blood of purification. She shall not touch anything holy nor shall she enter the sanctuary until the time the days of her purification are completed.
Lev. 12:5	*Lev. 12:5*	*Lev. 12:5*
But if she bear a female	And if she has borne a	And if she bears a fe-

Onqelos	Jonathan	Neophyti
child, she shall be unclean fourteen days, according to the law of her separation; and sixty-six days she will remain for the purification of the blood.	daughter, she shall be unclean fourteen *continuous* days according to her separation; *and on the fifteenth she shall be released* [M. 4:3E-G]; but sixty-six continuous days shall she have for the purification of the blood.	male daughter she shall be unclean for fourteen days, according to the removal of her menstrual flow; and for sixty-six days she shall continue waiting by the blood of purification.
Lev. 15:19 If a woman has a flux of blood in her flesh, seven days shall be for her separation, and whoever touches her shall be unclean until evening.	*Lev. 15:19* And if a woman has an issue of blood, *red or dark, yellow as saffron, or water of clay, or as red wine mixed with two parts of water* [M. 2:6-7], she has an uncleanness of blood in her flesh; she shall dwell apart seven days; any one who touches her shall be unclean until evening.	*Lev. 15:19* And when a woman has a flux of blood—her flux being in her body—seven days she shall be in the removal of her menstrual flow, and any one who touches her shall be unclean until evening.
Lev. 15:25 And if a woman has a flux of blood many days beyond the time of her separation, or when it flows after the days of her separation, all the days of the issue of her uncleanness shall be as the days of her separation; she shall be unclean.	*Lev. 15:25* But a woman who has a flux of blood *three days* beyond the time of her separation, or when it flows after the days of her separation, all the days of her flux shall she be unclean.	*Lev. 15:25* And when a woman has a flux for many days, outside the time of her flow, all the days of the flux she shall be unclean; as in the days of her menstrual flow she shall be unclean.

The Onqelos' and Neophyti Targums indicate no point of clearcut contact with the law of our tractate. Jonathan introduces M. 2:6-7 into Lev. 15:19, as given in italics; he agrees with the House of Hillel and with 'Aqavya. He also seems to allude to the fact that the woman after childbirth must immerse at the end of the unclean days. M. 4:3E-G takes this rule for granted. Otherwise I see no indication that the rules of Mishnah, or the principles taken for granted by Mishnah, are before the Targumists. Jonathan shows us what might have been, but was not, done.

2. The Dead Sea Library

Bibliography

Matthew Black, *The Scrolls and Christian Origins* (N.Y., 1961).

J. Carmignac and P. Guilbert, *Les Textes de Qumran. Traduits et annotés* (Paris, I: 1961; II: 1963).

A. Dupont-Sommer, *The Essene Writings from Qumran*. Translation by G. Vermes (N.Y. and Cleveland, 1967).

Bertil Gärtner, *The Temple and the Community in Qumran and the New Testament* (Cambridge, 1965).

Chaim Rabin, *Qumran Studies* (Oxford, 1957).

Chaim Rabin, *The Zadokite Documents* (Oxford, 1958).

H. H. Rowley, *The Zadokite Fragments and the Dead Sea Scrolls* (Oxford, 1955).

Geza Vermes, "The Impact of the Dead Sea Scrolls on Jewish Studies during the Last Twenty-Five Years," *Journal of Jewish Studies* XXVI, 1-2, 1975, pp. 1-14.

Geza Vermes, *The Dead Sea Scrolls in English* (Harmondsworth, 1970).

Naphtali Wieder, *The Judean Scrolls and Karaism* (London, 1962).

The one important allusion to menstrual uncleanness in the library of Qumran is the claim in the Damascus Covenant (CD 5:6-7, Rabin, p. 18) that the priests of Jerusalem do not observe the law of Lev. 15:25:

> Also they convey uncleanness to the sanctuary, inasmuch as they do not keep separate according to the Law but lie with her that sees the blood of her flux ...

Along these same lines, at CD 12:2 (Rabin, p. 58), it is enjoined not to have sexual relations in Jerusalem:

> Let no man lie with a woman in the city of the sanctuary so as to convey uncleanness to the city of the sanctuary with their impurity (BNDTM).

Rabin, p. 59, N. 2, sees the reference as applying to the *Zab*.[1] On

---

[1] Professor Lawrence Schiffman, New York University, kindly supplies the following comment: As to CDC 5:6-7, cf. Ps. Sol. 8:13 (Rabin), Rabin's point is that this is *zabah*, not *niddah*, those who do not count the "seven clean days." In the case of 12:2, the word niddah is *probably* a general term for impurity, as it is in DSD 3:4, 9, and in numerous *Hodayot* passages. There are *Hodayot* texts in which the "original" or better, classical meaning of the word seems to underly the poetic imagery. DST 1:22 (1:22, *sod ha-ʿerwah u-meqor ha-niddah, kur ha-ʿawon*, are all descriptions or names for the female sexual organs) and a similar phrase in 12:25. In other words, there is not a single published passage in which *niddah* is halakhically used to describe menstrual impurity. Note that CDC 10:10-13 discusses the legal aspects of water purification and the theological or religious aspects are taken up in DSD 3:4-12.

the other hand, Dupont-Sommer comments (p. 154, n. 4), "The city of the Sanctuary is Jerusalem. According to Lev. 15:18, a man and a woman who have had intercourse must wash themselves, and are in a state of impurity until the evening. The present ordinance forbids all sexual relations in Jerusalem in order not to defile the Holy City. Observe that according to Jubilees (50:8) it is similarly forbidden to have intercourse on the Sabbath in order not to defile the holy day."

3. *Philo*

Bibliography

F. H. Colson and G. H. Whitaker, trans., *Philo* (Cambridge and London, 1949-1952) I-X.

The index by J. W. Earp to *Philo* contains no allusion to Lev. 12:1-8. On Lev. 15:18, we find the following (*Special Laws* 3:63, Colson, 7:515):

> So careful is the law to provide against the introduction of violent changes in the institution of marriage that a husband and wife who have intercourse in accordance with the legitimate usages of married life are not allowed, when they leave their bed, to touch anything until they have made their ablutions and purged themselves with water.

This has nothing to do with menstrual uncleanness.

4. *Josephus*

Bibliography

H. St. J. Thackeray, Ralph Marcus, Allen Wikgren, and L. H. Feldman, *Josephus* (Cambridge, 1956-1965) I-IX.

Josephus's marrying-Essenes (*War* 2:161) marry only after the woman has "by three periods of purification given proof of fecundity." This seems to have no relevance to the equivalent importance of three periods of Niddah, which establish a regular period. In context, the present passage speaks of a concern to make sure that the woman has a period and so can give birth. At *Antiquities* 3:261, he notes that women "when beset by their natural secretions, he [Moses] secluded until the seventh day, after which they were permitted, as now pure, to return to society." He further alludes to Lev. 12:1-8 (*Antiquities* 3:269), without doing more than summarizing the biblical passage.

5. *The Collections in Apocrypha and Pseudepigrapha*

Bibliography

R. H. Charles, ed., *The Apocrypha and Pseudepigrapha of the Old Testament* (Oxford, 1913, I-II).

It is clear that one accusation made by a sect against its enemy will be that the enemy practices fornication or violates the menstrual taboo and pollutes the holy place thereby. We noted that CD takes exactly that view of the Jerusalem priesthood. Similarly, Black (*Scrolls and Christian Origins*, pp. 31-2) summarizes equivalent accusations of the Sadducees in Testament of Levi. The Psalms of Solomon 8:13 accuses the priests as follows:

> They trode the altar of the Lord, (coming straight) from all manner of uncleanness;
> And with menstrual blood they defiled the sacrifice, as (though these were) common flesh.

II Maccabees 6:4 accuses the heathen of having sexual relations in the Temple. So too the Epistle of Jeremy (29) accuses the priests of allowing unclean women to touch the holy things:

> The menstruous woman and the woman in childbed touch their sacrifices . . .

Jubilees Chapter Three explains the difference between uncleanness and cleanness for the male and female child (3:8-14):

> In the first week was Adam created, and the rib—his wife; in the second week He showed her unto him; and for this reason the commandment was given to keep in their defilement for a male seven days and for a female twice seven days. And after Adam had completed forty days in the land where he had been created, we brought him into the garden of Eden to till and keep it, but his wife they brought in on the eightieth day, and after this she entered into the garden of Eden. And for this reason the commandment is written on the heavenly tablets in regard to her that gives birth: "If she bears a male, she shall remain in her uncleanness seven days according to the first week of days and thirty-three days shall she remain in the blood of her purifying, and she shall not touch any hallowed thing, nor enter into the sanctuary until she accomplishes these days which are enjoined in the case of a male child. But in the case of a female child she shall remain in her uncleanness two weeks of days, according to the first two weeks, and sixty-six days in the blood of her purification, and they will be in all eighty days." And when she had completed these eighty days we brought her into the garden of Eden, for it is holier than all the earth besides, and every tree that is planted in it is holy.

> Therefore there was ordained regarding her who bears a male or a female child the statute of those days that she should touch no hallowed thing, nor enter into the sanctuary until these days for the male or female child are accomplished...

As noted, Jubilees 50.8 prohibits sexual relations on the Sabbath as a desecration. None of these allusions suggests much interest in the exegesis of the pertinent verses such as is accomplished in Mishnah-Tosefta.

6. *New Testament*

Among Jesus' instant healings is the cure of a *Zabah* (Mt. 9:20-22, Mk. 5:25-34, Lk. 8:43-48). There are no other references to the uncleanness of the menstruant, the *Zabah*, or the woman after childbirth.

7. *Conclusion*

The answer to the question with which we began this rapid survey (p. 203) is that, so far as extant sources indicate, no one else took equivalent interest in the laws of menstrual uncleanness, uncleanness after childbirth, and the uncleanness of the *Zabah*. Indeed, it is difficult to adduce evidence that anyone outside of the circles behind the law of Mishnah-Tosefta took the matter seriously. Clearly, the laws were known. I assume they were kept. The story about Jesus's healing of the *Zabah* leaves little reason to suspect otherwise. The accusation that the priests of the Jerusalem Temple did not observe these same laws tells us that the Essenes of Qumran assumed they should be kept. But, observed or not, the Levitical laws attracted no interest whatsoever. They were left undeveloped. Their silence on secondary issues provoked no one outside the Pharisaic and later rabbinical movement to raise any questions, so far as I can see.

iv. Conclusion

All sects read the Torah. That same Torah, moreover, formed the center of the religion of the Israelite part of the Land of Israel, the core of the world-view common to all. Niddah, for its part, does not present conceptions which, on the surface, are distinctive to Pharisaism. Our tractate in no way expresses a conception absolutely essential to, and definitive of, the Pharisaic viewpoint, so strikingly present at the very beginnings of Kelim, Parah, Tohorot, very probably Miqvaot and Negaim, and (only) possibly, Ohalot as well. We have now seen that what separates the work on our topic by the rabbis after 70 and by Pharisees before that time from the consideration of the same topic in all other literature known to us is susceptible to remarkably simple definition. The Pharisees and rabbis turned to the particular chapters of Torah which deal with the stated topic, devoted time and attention to their elucidation and extension. They took the matter seriously. Others do not seem to have done so. And that fact too must be definitive of Pharisaism: detailed attention to matters of uncleanness which others either took for granted or ignored entirely. What makes Pharisaism and later rabbinism Pharisaic and rabbinic is not only distinctive, characteristic, or even unique conceptions, but the very selection of topics for serious attention and continuing, rigorous thought. The tractate's agendum itself, without regard to its principles and detailed contents, is Pharisaic.

It presently appears, therefore, that what marks our tractate, as to its beginnings, as Pharisaic solely is its very keen interest in matters of no special interest to other groups. We recall in this connection the theory (*Rabbinic Traditions about the Pharisees before 70*, III, pp. 304-306, *From Politics to Piety. The Emergence of Pharisaic Judaism*, pp. 90-92), that at the time of Herod, the Pharisaic group, formerly a political party in Hasmonean politics, begins to reshape itself into something quite different, a sect devoted to, and defined by, table-fellowship. The sect develops conceptions and laws of cleanness in this regard. If, as seems clear, the laws of Niddah go back to the times of Shammai and Hillel, then Niddah should represent one of the earliest topics to which the Pharisees of that period devoted attention. Why should that have been the case? First, because, in the inquiry into matters of cleanness, menstrual and comparable uncleanness bulks large in the Scriptural account, and second, because meals are prepared by women, who, in consequence, should be given a sizable corpus of law for the protection of the cleanness of food. Scripture itself, furthermore, declares that chairs and beds and analogous objects on which menstruating women sit are unclean. Someone who wanted to preserve cleanness outside of the Temple will have had to take care not to sit where menstruating women sit, nor sleep in a bed in which she has slept. The ramifications are considerable. Accordingly, the primary and generative notion of our law, as of much else in our Order, is that we shall keep clean outside of the cult. That is the Pharisaic problematic, from which, here as elsewhere, all else flows.

When someone with the Pharisaic problematic in mind opens Scripture, moreover, attention naturally is drawn to that conception common to the Priestly Code and to Pharisaism, that cleanness in respect to unclean bodily discharges must be kept so that the tabernacle will be clean (Lev. 15:31): *Thus you shall keep the people of Israel separate from their uncleanness, lest they die in their uncleanness by defiling my tabernacle that is in their midst.* But the menstruant, *Zab*, *Zabah*, and woman after childbirth do not go to the Temple. The Priestly Code is explicit that a rite of purification must be undertaken by the last three named (Lev. 15:13-15 for the *Zab*, Lev. 15:28-30 for the *Zabah*, and Lev. 12:6-8 for the woman after childbirth). Accordingly, someone reading the Scripture will have asked himself, How are the unclean people going to make the Temple unclean, when, in point of fact, before they are able to enter its precincts, they undergo the rite of purification Scripture itself specifies? And, he will have answered, the people Israel itself, *in whose midst is the tabernacle*, is to be kept clean, so that the tabernacle which is in their midst will be in a clean setting. It will follow that the rules of cleanness in general pertaining to the Temple must apply as well to the people outside of the Temple.

The rules of menstrual uncleanness and comparable uncleanness in the beginning, before the revision accomplished by P, had nothing to do with the cult. Menstrual taboos are not associated with the cult even in the very pericopae of the Priestly Code which refer to them. It is only in the subscription that the Priestly Code naturally insists upon an integral and necessary relationship between menstrual taboos and the cult, and this, as I said, is even redactionally claimed only after the fact. We assume that everyone avoided having sexual relations with menstruating women, without regard to whether or not he intended to go to the Temple, indeed to whether or not he even lived in the Land of Israel. That fact then invites the conclusion, reached by the Pharisaism known to us in the Gospels and in the rabbinical traditions attributed to authorities before 70 whom we assume to be Pharisees, that the people must be kept clean for life in the land which is holy.

Land, people, Temple—all form an integrated and whole realm of being, to be kept clean so as to serve as the locus of the sacred. If the laws of Niddah are as old as they seem, then out of the studied consideration of those laws in particular, much else will have come, many conclusions reached in consequence. To put matters simply:

Pharisaism apparently emerges from thought on the menstrual taboo, specifically by taking most seriously, and therefore utterly reversing, the view that Israel must be clean because of the tabernacle in their midst. *Because the tabernacle is in their midst, Israel must be clean, even when not in the tabernacle*, which is exactly what Lev. 15:31 says—to a Pharisee.

IX. Zabim Before 70

i. Introduction

As our understanding of the character of the data has changed, we have tended to take diminished interest in the problem of the validity of attributions. We have learned to recognize that the logical structure and sequence of laws are to be discerned in their own terms, to be discovered within the conceptions of the laws themselves. Attributions therefore have proved interesting primarily as a way of checking upon the alleged sequences of logic. They form an external, therefore valuable if not probative, test of the correctness of our claim that one principle is prior to, and developed by, some other. Attributions also are important in proposing the point, in the unfolding of the law, at which an idea entirely lacking in antecedents or posterior development may belong. But in the main, our history of the law in no way depends primarily upon the allegation that a given authority, who is supposed to have lived at one or another of the periods into which the history is divided, really said what is assigned to him.

The present tractate poses a problem because of its disjointedness. The Houses' materials lead nowhere; the conceptions of Chapters Three and Four are not based upon substantial antecedent notions attributed to Yavneans. Chapter Five is curiously unconnected with what has gone before. Attributions by themselves do not give us evidence of the same reliability as is to be claimed in behalf of attributions which, in temporal sequence, correlate with sequences of interconnected and mutually contingent legal-logical principles.

ii. Attributions

1. *Unattributed Pericopae*

In the following list are contained all items not clearly assigned to a specific authority, as well as entries in which the role of a named master is minor and primarily important in helping us to find a location for the larger pericope in a given stratum. Items presented in smaller type and in brackets are of the latter sort and are included for the sake of completeness. There we specify the reasons for assigning to a given stratum pericopae which do not bear clear and major attributions to some specific authority.

> [1-3. M. 1:3-5: This set is certainly Ushan, attested by Yosé, M. 1:5H, Simeon, T. 1:10, Yosé, T. 1:12.]
> [4. M. 1:6: Attested to Usha by Yosé, T. 1:13.]

5-8. M. 2:1, T. 2:1-3: This set, on who is susceptible to become a Zab and on the status of *tumtom* and androgyne, is wholly unattributed.

> [9. M. 2:2A-E: In seven ways they examine the Zab. Attested to Yavneh by ʿAqiva, etc. + T. 2:5.]

10. T. 2:4: Difference between flux and semen.

> [11. T. 2:7: Cites M. 2:3C, part of an Ushan construction.]
> (12. T. 2:8-9: Not relevant to Zabim.)

13. M. 2:4: Zab imparts uncleanness to bed in five ways, bed imparts uncleanness to man in seven.

> [14-18. T. 3:1-5/M. 4:6B-J: This major construction is certainly post-Ushan, since it depends upon (inter alia) M. Nid. 5:1, Simeon vs. sages. But the laws obviously are much older.]
> [19. M. 4:1E, 4:2-3/T. 4:5-7: This set bears many Ushan attestations for the distinction between knocking or vibration and shifting or moving by a Zab.]
> [20. M. 4:4: Simeon attests the principle of M. 4:4A-G. T. 4:4B leaves no doubt of the matter.]
> [21. M. 4:6A/T. 4:9A: This matter carries forward M. 4:5, which is Ushan.]
> [22. M. 5:1A-D, 2, 3, 6-9 + 10/T. 5:2B/A-G, 5:3, 4, 5A: So far as these items stress the difference between touching a source of uncleanness and letting go of the source, they apply Joshua's principle, M. 5:1E-M.]
> [23. M. 5:2-3/T. 5:1A, 5:2B, H-K: So far as these items deal with different modes of transferring uncleanness, they build upon scriptural references. Eliezer attests.]
> (24. T. 5:7-8, 9-12: Not relevant to Zabim.)

There are only two major problems, Nos. 5-8 and No. 13. The latter lays the foundations for the shank of the tractate, Chapters Three-Four and Five. Clearly, the Scriptural references to diverse ways in which objects become unclean are taken very seriously and generate much of the law of No. 13. We do not know when the exegetical work produced principles on the modes of transfer of uncleanness, or how these principles unfolded. I am inclined to think the entire matter belongs to the period before 70. The former set, Nos. 5-8, is not attributed. The secondary question on those of unclear sexual characteristics or of dual sexual characteristics in general interests Ushans, but that is not decisive. No. 10 is fundamental to the tractate, and I cannot suggest the point at which that definition was supplied.

2. *Attributions*

For convenience' sake, we now catalogue all the references to specific authorities.

Before 70

Houses of Shammai and Hillel

1. M. 1:1: He who sees one flux, or, on one day, one, none the next day, then two on third, etc. + T. 1:1, 2, 3.
2. M. 1:2: Status of semen on days of counting + T. 1:8, 9A.

Yavneh

Joshua

1. M. 4:1A-D/T. 4:4A: Menstruating woman who sat with a clean woman on a bed—the cap which is on her head is unclean with *midras*.
2. M. 5:1: A general rule did Joshua state: distinction between uncleanness while still in contact with the source and that after one lets go of the source. M. 5:6-8 + 9, 10 depend on this same distinction.

Eliezer/Eleazar

1. M. 2:2M-Q: Gloss of M. 2:2A-L. Examine Zab before confirmation only after first, second flux. Eliezer: After third, because of sacrifice.
2. M. 5:3, 7: *Re* carrying and moving.
3. T. 5:2B: Semen of Zab *re* carrying.

'Aqiva

1. T. 1:4-6: *Re* Houses dispute, M. 1:1.
2. M. 2:2G-I: If person ate any food, semen is attributed to it, *vs.* Judah b. Beterah, No. 1.
(3. T. 5:6 = M. A.Z. 3:6)

'Aqiva vs. Ishmael

1. M. 1:2: Re Houses + T. 1:8.

Eleazar b. Judah

1. M. 1:1K-T: Revises Houses' dispute.

Eleazar Ḥisma
  1. T. 1:7: Eleazar b. R. Yannai before Rabbi in the name of Eleazar Ḥisma *re* M. 1:1's Houses.

Judah b. Beterah
  1. T. 2:5 [see ʿAqiva, No. 2]: Seven foods cause semen.

Usha

Simeon
  1. T. 1:5-6: *Re* Houses, M. 1:1, + ʿAqiva.
  2. T. 1:10: Sufficient time to divide fluxes defined.
  3. T. 2:6: Simeon reads M. 2:3 into M. 2:2.
  4. M. 3:2I, T. 4:1C/T. 4:3/T. 4:1A: Transfer of *midras* uncleanness takes place if clean person merely shifts the weight of the Zab.
  5. M. 4:4I/T. 4:4B: If chair bears the bulk of Zab's weight, it is unclean. But if the weight is evenly distributed, it does not. + M. 4:5: One chair must bear the bulk of Zab's weight. + T. 4:8 + M. 4:7A-B.
  6. M. 5:4-5/T. 4:3, 5:1B (5:2A): This set carries forward Simeon's stress on bearing the greater part of the Zab's weight.

Yosé
  1. M. 1:5H/T. 1:12: Profusion produces three fluxes, not two.
  2. T. 1:13/M. 1:6: Passage of days at sunset distinguishes a flux into two fluxes.
  3. M. 2:3: He who sees semen does not produce flux for twenty-four hours. Yosé: That day alone.
  4. M. 4:2B: Yosé augments the lists of firm objects + T. 4:7B-D.
  5. M. 4:7E-F: House imparts uncleanness with hindlegs, etc.

Judah
  1. M. 2:2F: Glosses M. 2:2D-E *re* fantasy.
  2. M. 3:1/O/T. 4:1B/M. 3:2C-D: Transfer of Zab's uncleanness as *midras* to the clothing of a clean person takes place only when the latter clearly raises up the weight of the former.
  3. T. 4:7A (following Sens' reading): Judah adds to M. 4:2A.

Meir
  1. T. 4:1A/M. 3:3L-P (+ M. 3:2A): Transfer of Zab's uncleanness to clothing of a clean person takes place with any sort of shift of weight of former by latter.

Neḥemiah and Simeon
  1. M. 4:3F-G/T. 4:6: Re shifting box, chest, cupboard.

Neḥemiah
  1. M. 4:7G-I: Zab on fuller's press,

After Usha: None

iii. THE WEAVING OF THE LAW

Our tractate deals with two questions pertinent to the Zab, first, how a man becomes unclean as a Zab, and, second, how a Zab imparts uncleanness. The intellectual structure of the tractate is remarkably abbreviated. A far richer agendum is available, e.g., doubts in connection with the character of flux, with whether a Zab has imparted uncleanness to someone or something, with the retroactive uncleanness imputed to an object discovered to have been contaminated by the Zab, and the like—that is to say, Niddah's equivalent structure. By contrast to its counterpart, Niddah, Zabim pays close attention to the rules of transfer of uncleanness, which apply to the menstruating woman, the Zabah, and the woman after childbirth, just as much as to the Zab and meṣoraʿ. It cannot be claimed that, because matters of doubt are investigated at Niddah, the complementary tractate, Zabim, need not attend to them. The reason is that Zabim goes over ground familiar at Kelim and Tohorot, e.g., on the difference between one's status as to uncleanness while he is actually touching the source of uncleanness and that which pertains after he has let go of the source of uncleanness. We have already observed, moreover, that Niddah and Tohorot dwell upon the matter of doubts and principles applicable to their resolution. Accordingly, there is no substantive, editorial or redactional reason for the truncated agendum of Zabim, just as we could find none for the limited intellectual repertoire of Makhshirin.

We review the law of Zabim contained within the limits of Mishnah-Tosefta, with attention to Sifra as well.[1] Division of pericopae among the four periods within which we are able to work, Before 70, Yavneh, Usha, After Usha, in the first instance is based upon the presence of attributions of sayings to masters generally assumed to have flourished in these periods. It then is tested against the materials attributed to other periods, on the one side, and against the evident sequence of principles—uncontingent, contingent; primary, secondary; or logically prior, logically posterior—contained within the pericopae. In order to show how materials interrelate, I have cross-referenced the entire repertoire. Items bearing an * either generate, or are generated by, conceptions in other entries. Items bearing

---

[1] Pertinent materials of Sifra Meṣoraʿ Zabim are cited only when they deal with substantive issues, not when they attempt to prove that established laws derive solely from Scripture and not from reason.

≠ stand alone, that is, with neither precedents nor developments. The triangular mode of discussion has already been explained. Further exposition of the theoretical basis for this exercise is at Part III, pp. 237-244, 273-276, V, pp. 158-160, VIII, pp. 138-139, X, p. 135, XIV, pp. 110-111, XVI, pp. 114-117, 127-128, and XVII, p. 173.

There is one major change in established procedures. When we come to the second major theme of the tractate, the Zab's uncleanness and how it is transferred to men and diverse utensils, we immediately observe that many conceptions, particularly in Chapter Five, are without attributions. These same conceptions, moreover, clearly relate to, and, I shall argue, are secondary or tertiary developments of, Scripture's clear and plain statements on the same subject. Rather than postpone the question of the relationship of Zabim to Scripture until after we have considered the evidence of named pericopae and their logical sequences, I have therefore dealt first with Scripture, then with the unassigned pericopae, and finally with the sequences of assigned ones. The result is to show that, just as at Niddah and Negaim, our tractate consists of secondary and derivative developments of conceptions laid forth in Scripture (Lev. 15:1-15) and contains no ideas or principles fundamentally autonomous of, and distinct from, those readily discerned in, or logically derived from, the relevant verses.

1. *Becoming a Zab*

A. *Before 70*

The Zab falls midway between the Zabah and the one who has had a seminal emission. Since what makes a man into a Zab is flux (*zob*), the verbal analogy to the Zabah is demanded. Since flux is like semen, the substantive analogy to the one who has a seminal emission and is unclean on that account is invited. The first entry explores the former, the second, the latter, analogy.

*1. M. 1:1: He who sees one flux — the House of Shammai: Like a woman who awaits day against day. House of Hillel: Like one who has had a seminal emission. If he saw one and none on the next day and two on the third— House of Shammai: He is confirmed as a Zab. House of Hillel: He imparts uncleanness to bed and chair and must

*1. The issue is in two parts. First, what is the analogy which applies to the Zab? Is he like a Zabah? If so, if he sees one appearance of flux, he is in the status of the woman who awaits day against day. Is he like the one who has had a seminal emission? If so, he is unclean and immerses, but then is clean in the evening.

immerse in running water, but brings no offering.

Second, what is the affect of a clean day upon the original flux? If he is like a woman who awaits day against day, then the clean day annuls the affects of the unclean. But here the case is different. He has a double flux on the third day. The Shammaites see him as entirely unclean, and the Hillelites say he nonetheless is not confirmed so as to have to bring a sacrifice.

Eleazar b. Judah: The issue is a case in which there are two appearances of flux, then none, then on the third day, one. The opinions are as above. + T. 1:1, 2, 3.
Sifra Meṣoraʿ Zabim 1:5-6: One who saw two appearances of flux imparts uncleanness to bed and chair. Sifra Meṣoraʿ Zabim 5:1B-3: One who sees two appearances of flux has to count seven clean days, imparts uncleanness to bed and chair.
See *Yavneh, No. 1, Usha, No. 3.*

Once there are two appearances, the man is certainly unclean. Now the issue is limited to the status of the man who had the two, then a clean day, then one.

The Houses clearly agree that a single appearance of flux is insufficient to impose upon the man the status of the Zab. Three appearances of flux confirm that status. Two appearances mean the man is unclean, and the sole difference is whether he brings an offering as well. Accordingly, prior to the dispute must be the following principles:

1. A man is confirmed as a Zab if he has suffered three appearances of flux.
2. A man furthermore imparts uncleanness as a Zab if he has suffered two appearances of flux.

On these matters the Houses are in agreement. Concerning what do they differ? Concerning a clean day between the time that one, or two, appearances of flux have taken place, and between the time that a third appearance of flux should confirm his status as a Zab even in respect to the requirement to bring a sacrifice. But, as we shall see, the definition of the case is subject to Yavnean dispute. Accordingly, we must regard as primary to the Houses' dispute solely the matter of the interrupted sequence of the appearances of flux, the stated matter, whether it is one, a clean day, then two, or two, a clean day, then one, being secondary to the fundamental point at issue.

*2. M. 1:2A-C: He who sees semen on the third day of counting after flux —House of Shammai: He loses the two clean days before it. House of Hillel: Loses only that day.
(M. 1:1I-L: But if he sees flux, even on the seventh day, he loses all.)
See *Yavneh, No. 2.*

*2. The issue is the comparison of semen to flux. The Hillelites do not deem semen equivalent to flux in causing the loss of the clean days. The Shammaites hold that, once the man is confirmed as a Zab, there is reason to refer whatever semen that comes to the original uncleanness. The matter is stated in terms of the third day, since the dispute could not be phrased in respect to the second. That is, if it were the second day, then the Houses would have to agree on the loss of that day, and there would be no room in which to clarify the Shammaite position. The Hillelites cannot ignore the semen, since Lev. 15:16-18 declares it a cause of uncleanness for a day. The man thus must lose the day on which the semen appears. But semen is not flux.

Semen which appears once the man is deemed unclean as a Zab and further has begun to count clean days is at issue. The Hillelite view is that the semen marks the man as unclean in any event; he hardly has a claim on a clean day in that case. But what is the affect of the semen on the clean days already counted? The Shammaites hold that whatever semen appears is attributed to flux; the semen accordingly costs two clean days. There is no reason to suppose the House of Shammai would take up a different position in respect to semen on any later day in the period. The agreement, M. 1:1I-L, therefore, is important primarily from the viewpoint of the House of Hillel.

B. *Yavneh*

Pericopae assigned to Yavneans carry forward the Houses' disputes, particularly, the definition of their protases, and introduce one important, new conception.

*1. T. 1:4-6: 'Aqiva: Houses disagreed on the case of the man who had one flux on the first day, then none, then two. Simeon cites Eleazar b. R. Judah.
See *Before 70, No. 1.*

*1. Simeon's interpretation is the interesting side. When the man sees one at the outset and then has a clean day, then has two, the clean day annuls the affects of the first day, and the man is unclean because of the two on the third day, but then is not entirely a Zab.

> But if he has a double flux on the first day, he has to count seven clean days, and so the clean day does not annul the double flux of the first day.

If there is flux on the first day, then none, then two, the Houses can have a disagreement. Why? Because the two fluxes mark the man as unclean, and now the sole issue is, What is the requirement for purification? In any event, the Houses agree, the man imparts uncleanness to bed and chair and must wait out seven clean days. Accordingly, the Houses, in 'Aqiva's view, are in agreement that the clean day annuls the affects of the unclean day. The man after a single flux is like the woman who awaits day against day, and the appearance of the clean day, not followed by unclean days, accordingly annuls the former flux. The dispute therefore is possible only in the single flux-clean day-double flux sequence. But if that is the case, then at issue, 'Aqiva maintains, is simply the effect of the double flux. The matter of the single clean day intervening between two fluxes is not under dispute at all. When we look back at M. 1:1, we find that the Houses dispute the single flux in its own terms. The Shammaites compare the man who has had one flux to the woman who awaits day against day, that is, 'Aqiva's position. The House of Hillel see the man as equivalent to one who has had a seminal emission, just as is their position at M. 1:2A-C. 'Aqiva's position at M. 1:2D-H is identical to that of the House of Hillel at M. 1:1, in respect to the single flux. It appears, therefore, that the Yavneans assign to the Houses a dispute on a point moot at Yavneh, in which case all the Houses can have debated is, as observed above, the effect of a clean day on the sequence of unclean ones, with or without regard to the question of the double-flux on the first or third day. This is made still more obvious by the next entry.

*2. M. 1:2D-H: *Re* M. 1:2A-C, Ishmael says, He who sees semen on the second day loses the day before it. 'Aqiva: All the same is the second and third day: if a man sees semen on the second or on the third day, the Shammaites hold he has lost the days before it; the House of Hillel say he has lost only that day.
+ T. 1:8. T. 1:9A: Any semen which imparts uncleanness in the case of priests causes the loss of a day in the

*2. Ishmael attempts to revise the Houses' dispute. 'Aqiva maintains that the issue is semen, not the day on which it occurs.

T. is not assigned, but it simply restates the position of 'Aqiva.

case of a Zab. The Zab may have sexual relations on the days of the completion of purification, losing that day alone, etc.

The Houses's dispute and the present one are parallel, but sufficiently distinct from one another that we cannot propose the Houses' names simply replace those of Ishmael and 'Aqiva. 'Aqiva of course is consistent in insisting that the Hillelites deem semen and flux to be essentially different. If, therefore, during the days of counting, the Zab has a flow of semen, the Hillelites and 'Aqiva maintain that that day is unclean—as it would be if the man were *not* a Zab at all! Perhaps Ishmael wants to read M. 1:1 into M. 1:2. That is, if the man has been confirmed as a Zab, then has had a clean day, then produces semen, we link the appearance of semen to the status of the confirmed Zab, just as the Shammaites maintain. If this takes place once the clean days have been under way, that is, on the third or later days, however, the semen is not assigned the status of flux, the intervening passage of clean days having confirmed that the process of purification is underway.

*3. M. 2:2A-E, J: In seven ways do they examine the Zab before he is confirmed as to flux: eating, drinking, carrying, jumping, illness, fantasizing, etc. M. 2:2G-I: Any sort of food. T. 2:5: Eliezer b. Pinhas in the name of Judah b. Beterah: Seven kinds of food.

*3. The attestation of the seven ways is in 'Aqiva's story, with the contrary opinion of Judah b. Beterah, on whether any sort of eating constitutes a sufficient reason, or whether we ask what sorts of food he has eaten. I am inclined to think that the conception of the pericope, that we attribute the flux to some external cause and therefore deem it to be semen, not flux, is attested in the dispute, which surely is secondary and contingent upon the main principle. Judah, M. 2:2F, further attests a different aspect of the list, the fantasy.

The principle, as I said, is that the flux must be entirely natural and not caused by some source other than the body's own mechanism.

M. 2:2M-Q: They examine (in the above regard) after the first, second flux, but not after the third. Eliezer/Eleazar: After the third, too, because of the sacrifice.

I am not sure that this is an Eliezer/Eleazar of Yavneh. But the point rests on M. 1:1, the distinction between two fluxes, at which point the Zab imparts uncleanness to bed and chair, and three, at which point the sacrifice is required as well. The principal point is that once

> the man is confirmed as a Zab, there is no reason to doubt that further flux derives from the same unclean cause, and we do not attempt to attribute it to some secondary and external one.

Sifra Meṣoraʿ Zabim 1:7: Cites M. 2:2.
See *Usha, Nos. 1, 2 (+3)*.

The principle behind the final Yavnean item seems to me well attested by the dispute of ʿAqiva and Judah b. Beterah. We do not take for granted that flux means the man is unclean. We attempt to attribute it to some external cause, rather than to an internal, bodily origin. If there is reason to suppose that something has made the man produce a flow of semen, then that is not deemed to be flux. Only if we cannot find some extenuating circumstance do we deem the flow of semen to be flux. With this matter the definition of the nature of flux begins. The Ushans develop the point in two ways. First, they continue the process of glossing the basic pericope. Second, they define the matter of lengthy fluxes, introducing a further consideration into the process of defining flux.

C. *Usha*

All entries bearing Ushan attributions or attestations carry forward Yavnean materials. The first set simply presents glosses of established principles. The second, by contrast, extends the problem dealt with by Yavneans, but raises its own considerations.

*1. M. 2:2F: Judah says, Even if he saw cattle, beast, fowl, engaged in sexual relations, we attribute the flow of semen to that cause and do not deem it to be flux.
See *Yavneh, No. 3*.

*1. Judah attests M. 2:2D7-E.

Judah simply refines and augments the principle stated at *Yavneh, No. 3*.

*2. M. 2:3A-B: He who sees semen does not become susceptible to uncleanness by flux for the next twenty-four hours. Yosé: That day alone.
+ T. 2:4: Difference between flux and semen. M. 2:3C/T. 2:7: Gentile who converted forthwith is susceptible to uncleanness by flux.

*2. The principle of M. 2:2 is extended. Once there has been a flow of semen, then we have good reason to suppose flux over the next twenty-four hours is clean. Yosé, consistent with his view at M. 1:6, limits the matter to the same solar day. The gentile is deemed to begin life afresh and so

T. 2:6: We impose the twenty-four hours' consideration on fantasy, but not upon food, drink, carrying, jumping, so Simeon b. Judah in the name of Simeon. See *Yavneh, No. 3, above, No. 1*.

Simeon introduces M. 2:3 into the interpretation of M. 2:2 and again attests the latter to Usha.

The secondary development of the principle, that if we can find extenuating circumstances, we do not deem a flow of semen to be flux, is before us. Once we have found reason not to deem semen to be flux, we add that that reason may pertain for a full twenty-four hours. Simeon's and Judah's quibble confirms the fact that the Yavnean notion has generated this secondary development.

*3. M. 1:3-5: If there was flux on one day, then two on the next, or three on three successive days or nights, this is entirely a Zab.

If there was one, and it ceased for sufficient time for immersion and drying, then two, or one as profuse as two, etc., he is entirely a Zab.
If there was one flux profuse as three, which is time enough for two immersions and dryings, he is entirely a Zab. One as profuse as two imparts uncleanness to bed and chair, imposes the requirement of immersion, but does not indicate a sacrifice must be brought (− Hillelites, M. 1:1D-T). Yosé: An issue profuse as two has no affect; only one profuse as three. + T. 1:9B, 10-12.

*3. The main point is that the flux which marks the man as a Zab does not depend upon its appearance on three successive and contiguous days, but on three distinct appearances. But it may come on three days. The fluxes must be separated by an appropriate interval, or they form one continuous flux.
We take account of a flux as profuse as three. T. adds there must be appropriate intervals between the prolonged flux.

T. I:9B: Simeon: Sufficient time to circumambulate the Temple mount on the inside.

M. 1:6/T. 1:13: If one saw one flux by day and one at twilight, one at twilight and one on the following day, if it is known for sure that part of the appearance was on one day, and part on the next, he is certain as to the sacrifice and as to uncleanness. + Variations.
See *Yavneh, No. 3*.

The principle is that fluxes are divided not only by intervals but also by the passage of a day. That is, the rule of the Zabah, for whom a day can divide one flux into two, applies here also. Accordingly, if there is one flux by day, and then at twilight another, then that second flux is deemed divided by the passage of time into two days, and we have three fluxes, so certainty as to

	uncleanness and sacrifice. This point is important to Yosé in particular, as T. shows.
Sifra Meṣoraʿ Zabim 1:1-2: Uncleanness of Zab depends upon discharge, not on days. That is, unlike the Zabah, the Zab can be confirmed as unclean if there are three fluxes in a single day.	This view is taken for granted at *Before 70, No. 1*, as well as at the present unit.
Sifra Meṣoraʿ Zabim 1:3-4: M.1:5A-D, T. 1:11E-J cited. If there was one flux as large as three, the man is confirmed as a Zab. See *Before 70, No. 1*.	This is Yosé's view, but the opposition of course concurs.

The problem is familiar, but the conception is fresh. We continue the definition of the flux and its effects. But now we ask about the "flux as profuse as two" or "the flux as profuse as three." While glossed into the Houses' dispute of M. 1:1, in fact the conception that a single flow of flux may be subdivided into two or three parts seems to begin at Usha. The connection to the materials assigned to earlier authorities is through the conception that three appearances of flux are required to confirm a man as a Zab. The secondary consideration is whether these appearances may be comprised of one long, but interrupted flow. There are two complementary ideas. First, the Zab is different from the Zabah in that, while the latter must produce flux on three successive days, the former may be confirmed as a Zab even if the three appearances of flux take place on one day only. It is this notion which generates the second. We impose distinctions even upon a single appearance. If it is profuse and yet demarcated, then it constitutes two or even three appearances. Yosé contributes the view that the passage of a day certainly demarcates even a brief flux into two. He preserves this aspect of the analogy to the Zabah, therefore, and the other authorities most certainly concur. The consideration is important chiefly to Yosé, because, so far as he is concerned, an issue profuse as two otherwise is of no effect. It is also important to observe that the Ushan materials take for granted the Hillelite position at M. 1:1D-T; that is hardly surprising.

D. *After Usha*

*1. T. 1:7: Eleazar b. R. Yannai in name of Eleazar Ḥisma before Rabbi:	*1. The tradition is the same as ʿAqiva's.

Houses disagree on the one who sees a double flux, then none, then one. See *Before 70, No. 1, Yavneh, No. 1.*

E. *Unassigned*

#1. M. 2:1/T. 2:2; 1-3: All Israelites are susceptible to uncleanness through flux, even converts, slaves, etc. The *ṭumṭom* and androgyne are subject to the strict rules of the Zabah and the Zab. Red or white flow marks them as unclean, but their status as to uncleanness remains in doubt.
T.: The problem of heave-offering, contamination of the sanctuary is worked out.

Sifra Meṣoraʿ Zabim 1:1: Only Israelites are susceptible to uncleanness through flux. This includes, however, converts, women, and children. Ishmael b. R. Yoḥanan b. Beroqah proves this last point.

2. Sifra Meṣoraʿ Zabim 1:2: The law on Zabim does not apply before the giving of the Torah.

#1. This rule bears no clearcut attestations at M.-T. But Sifra supplies one: Ishmael the son of Yoḥanan b. Beroqah.

The equivalent conception for Negaim (Part VI, M. Neg. 3:1A, 11:1A-D, 12:1A-B) seems to be Yavnean, since it is attested by Ishmael. Judah, M. Neg. 13:10/T. 7:9, is clear that gentiles are not susceptible to uncleanness through *ṣaraʿat*. I see no reason to doubt that the present item is later than Usha, and, as at Negaim, I think it likely that by Yavnean times the law had excluded gentiles from consideration.

Reconsiderations

The basic issue in respect to the rules governing a man's being declared a Zab devolves upon the conflict of two available analogies:

(1) The Zab is governed by the rules applying to the Zabah.

(2) The Zab is made such by the flow of a kind of semen, and, therefore, is subject to the rules applying to one made unclean by semen (Lev. 15:16-18).

The conflict between the two analogies is inaugurated at the stratum of the Houses, and that debate is carried forward. The unfolding of the law is through concrete and discrete pericopae. These interrelate in a tight pattern. The Houses' dispute (*Before 70,*

No. 1) on the rule which applies to an interrupted flow of flux, that is, the case of a man who has a flux, then a clean day, then more flux (in whatever profusion) generates *Yavneh, No. 1*, defining the sequence. The Houses' dispute (*Before 70, No. 2*) on the affect upon the clean days of a flow of semen, stands behind—and is not an effect of—'Aqiva's and Ishmael's dispute (*Yavneh, No. 2*).

The second major development in this aspect of the law is at *Yavneh, No. 3*, the principle that flux must be natural and not produced by external causes, which is carried forward at *Usha, Nos. 1 and 2*. *Usha, No. 3* presents an augmentation of the definition of flux, thematically related to the foregoing. It perhaps is intended to develop *Before 70, No. 1*. Once we assume, as do the Houses, that the flux may occur all on a single day, then we have to define how we distinguish one from two, and two from three, appearances of flux.

The only item which seems to me not tightly woven into the existing, unfolding fabric is the rule that Israelites are susceptible, and gentiles are not susceptible, to Zabim, a principle familiar at the Yavnean and Ushan strata of Negaim, as noted.

Accordingly, the proposed sequences of themes and principles exhibit close correlation with the available sequences of attributions and reciprocally confirm one another. It follows that, in line with the mode of falsification and consequent verification herein applied, the history of this segment of the law may be regarded as firm and reliable. It in no fundamental aspect depends solely upon the names to which sayings are attributed or the attestations supplied by these same names.

2. *Transferring the Zab's Uncleanness: Scripture*

Once a man is in the status of the Zab, he imparts uncleanness (1) through diverse means of the transfer of uncleanness (2) to various objects: to man, to clay utensils and utensils which are cleaned in an immersion pool and, by contrast to clay utensils, not solely by breaking; to utensils used for sitting and lying; and utensils not used for sitting and lying (= *maddaf*), inclusive of food, and drink. Further, various body-fluids are deemed equivalent to flux in their capacity to impart uncleanness, and others are not. Finally, the transfer of uncleanness is deemed to take place in two distinct aspects: (1) while a person or object actually is subject to the mode of transfer of uncleanness; (2) after a person or object has ceased to be subject to the mode of transfer of uncleanness. Our tractate presents a rich discussion of all of these matters, even extending its interest beyond the matter of the Zab himself. We shall limit our discussion to the Zab.

We cannot investigate the second principal conceptual unit of our tractate without first examining the Scriptural legacy. The reason is that a sizable and important group of pericopae stand wholly without clearcut attestations, not to mention attributions. This group furthermore makes distinctions and takes for granted concepts which, I think, derive from a reading of Scripture. Accordingly, as in the case of Niddah, with Zabim it is simply impossible to undertake the description of the stages by which the law unfolded without paying close attention to Scripture. If we were to follow our established procedure, which has been to consider the tractate as a self-contained unit and to lay out the presuppositions of the earliest strata therein, we should have to treat many items as unassigned which, in fact, simply state in the form, language, and context of Mishnah what Scripture already has told us. Accordingly, we avoid much needless confusion by turning first of all to Lev. 1:1-15.

Having studied our tractate, we shall find it extremely difficult to attempt to read Scripture as if we had no familiarity whatever with the great principles of Zabim. Eisegesis need not be intentional and rarely is. We must, nonetheless, attempt to ask, What rules or principles will anyone discern in the pertinent verses? We thereby exclude any consideration of the affects of various sorts of uncleanness and modes of transfer of uncleanness upon heave-offering and unconsecrated food. Scripture knows nothing of that consideration. The notion that under some circumstances, what is unclean renders something else unclean in such wise that that which is made unclean imparts uncleanness to still another object or substance, by contrast, is assuredly to be discerned in the verses before us. Whether or not the person who wrote the verses meant to emphasize that matter, of course, we do not know. Someone who wanted information on the topic, however, will readily have found it in Scripture. The eisegetical act is to deem the detail, perhaps stated tangentially and without intended significance by the original author, to be portentous, and to draw consequences from it. But the exegetical process, consequent upon the prior and originally eisegetical program, is now to be described. We know in consequence of our study of Niddah that what is striking and distinctive in our tractate is nothing other than its remarkable interest in developing laws plainly laid down in Scripture itself. What is not before us is a single genuinely new and original idea, not to be located in, or spun out of, Scripture itself.

In order to distinguish among the layers of meaning, I lay matters out in a way meant to be visually striking. At the outset, I cite the verse and opposite it restate what it says in simple language. This is given in italics. The secondary meaning of each verse, given in regular type, is attained simply by generalizing upon the plain and unadorned statement in, and restatement of, the Scriptural verse itself. There is then the tertiary meaning, distinguished from the secondary generalization of Scripture by bold face type. This tertiary meaning is the point at which I introduce conceptions drawn from our tractate. I believe that, in the main, principles at a second level of exegesis from Scripture, that is, tertiary meanings, represent little more than a *further* generalization of what Scripture says, on the one hand, and the (now surely eisegetical) introduction of a few simple and obvious distinctions necessitated or invited by that generalization, on the other. In some instances there is yet a fourth level of meaning, and this invariably is drawn by me from Mishnah-Tosefta. That too is represented in bold face type.

The exercise is meant to demonstrate that each and every proposition of Mishnah-Tosefta derives either directly or indirectly, through processes of close reasoning, generalization, and secondary logical exegesis, from Scripture itself. At each point at which our abstract exercise produces a principle found in Mishnah, the appropriate pericope is of course designated. The relationship of Mishnah's unattributed pericopae to Scripture is then spelled out in detail in the following section. The net result is hypothetically to demonstrate in close detail that this aspect of the law of Zabim is little more than a logical expansion of Scripture, and that each such expansion stands in close logical relationship to the foregoing, so that the result, at the end, is a very tight sequence of logical-exegetical steps.

In this exercise we do not follow the path of Sifra and its greatest exegetes, Rabad, Qorban Aharon and Rabbenu Hillel, who tell us the principles of *formal* exegesis by which laws are derived. I do not find it difficult to concede that their account of formal principles is valid. But my interest is not in the technology of exegesis, but rather in the hypothetical logic by which a rule produces a principle, and by which the principle generates further developments, only at the end inviting formal-exegetical linkage to Scripture. That is, I offer, by way of supplement of the accounts of the admirable exegetes in Sifra and of Sifra, a hypothetical-logical exegesis of what I conceive to have been the intellectual processes by which the results of our tractate have been achieved. Whether or not my account of these processes is deemed valid depends upon the cogency and persuasiveness of my hypothesis of how people thought, and, in particular, of the successive and demarcated stages by which the processes of logic unfolded.

Scriptural Verse
Lev. 15:4: *Every bed on which he who has the discharge lies shall be unclean. And everything on which he sits shall be unclean.*

Clear Implication (Plain meaning)
The Zab imparts uncleanness by lying on a bed or by sitting on a chair.

Secondary Meaning

1. The Zab imparts uncleanness to objects which can be used for lying or sitting.
2. The Zab imparts uncleanness to objects used for lying or sitting by exerting the pressure of his weight on said objects.

Tertiary Meaning

A. **The uncleanness of the Zab is transmitted by pressure.**
B. **Pressure is exerted through lying and sitting.**
C. **Other modes of exerting pressure, standing, leaning, being suspended, by analogy to lying and sitting, likewise transfer the uncleanness of the Zab to another object.**
D. **Pressure exerted by a clean person upon an object made unclean by a Zab will in like manner transfer the uncleanness from the object or the Zab to the clean person.**

Mishnah

C: M. 2:4 (3:1-3, 4:1-7).
D: M. 3:1-3, 4:1, 5, 5:1-5.

Lev. 15:5: *And any one who touches his bed shall wash his clothes and bathe himself in water and be unclean until the evening.*

Touching the Zab makes a person unclean. His clothes are unclean.

Secondary Meaning

3. The Zab's uncleanness is transferred by contact,
    a. either a clean person's touching the Zab
    b. or the Zab's touching a clean person.
4. One who is made unclean by the Zab imparts uncleanness to his clothing.

Tertiary Meaning

E. **One made unclean by the Zab makes utensils unclean.**
F. **Said utensils are cleaned by immersion.**
G. Since Scripture specifies that touching the bed or the Zab (Lev. 15:7) effects the transfer of uncleanness, and since Scripture specifies that sitting or lying also effects the transfer of uncleanness, it follows that these are distinct modes of the transfer of uncleanness, and therefore touching without exerting pressure or exerting pressure without touching imparts uncleanness.

Mishnah

E: M. 2:4
G: M. 5:1-9

Lev. 15:6: *And whoever sits on anything on which he who has the discharge has sat shall wash his clothes and bathe himself in water and be unclean until the evening.*	*Sitting on the bed or chair made unclean by the Zab makes a person unclean. His clothes are unclean.*

Secondary Meaning

5. The object used for sitting or lying to which the Zab has imparted uncleanness is unclean in exactly the same measure as the Zab himself.

Tertiary Meaning

H. **Since said object is unclean exactly as the Zab is unclean, it therefore transfers uncleanness as does the Zab, that is, if one exerts pressure on it** (the plain meaning) **or if one touches it, or if it touches the clean person or exerts pressure on the clean person.**

I. One made unclean by the unclean bed of the Zab makes utensils unclean. Said utensils are cleaned by immersion.

Mishnah

5: M. 2:4C-D.
H: M. 2:4C-D (3:1-3, 4:1-7).
I: M. 2:4C-D.

| Lev. 15:7: *And whoever touches the body of him who has the discharge shall wash his clothes and bathe himself in water and be unclean until the evening.* | Touching the person of the Zab imparts uncleanness. The clothes are unclean. |

Secondary Meaning

6. There is no difference between touching the bed of the Zab (Lev. 15:5) and touching the person of the Zab (Lev. 15:7). The consequences are the same in all regards.

Mishnah

6. M. 5:1.

| Lev. 15:8: *And if he who has the discharge spits on one who is clean, then he shall wash his clothes and bathe himself in water and be unclean until the evening.* | The spit of the Zab is unclean exactly as is the Zab or his bed. The clothing of the person spat upon by the Zab is made unclean. |

Secondary Meaning

7. Fluids which exude from the Zab are unclean exactly as is his body or the bed he sits upon, etc.

Tertiary Meaning

J. The ways in which the Zab and the bed made unclean by the Zab transfer uncleanness apply also to the body fluids, so far as these modes of transfer are relevant: 1. touching, 2. carrying (below, Lev. 15:10b).

Mishnah

7: M. 5:6, 5:7.

| Lev. 15:9: *And any saddle on which he who has the discharge rides shall be unclean.* | The saddle ridden upon by the Zab is unclean. |

Secondary Meaning

8. Since the saddle is dealt with apart from the bed and chair, it is subject to a distinctive set of rules.

Mishnah

8: M. 5:8.

Lev. 15:10a: *And whoever touches anything that was under him shall be unclean until the evening.*

An object located underneath a Zab is unclean.

Secondary Meaning

9. I take it that the simple meaning is derived by treating Lev. 15:10a as a continuation of Lev. 15:9, which is to say, "A saddle on which a Zab has ridden is unclean, and whoever touches anything on which a Zab rides (or: has ridden) is unclean."

But if we read the verse disjunctively, then it bears a different meaning. Mere *location* of an object beneath a Zab—even if he is not touching it, and even if he is not riding on it—imparts uncleanness to the object. Accordingly, we take account of the spatial relationships of objects to a Zab.

10. And this yields the clearly required notion (L) that an object used for sitting, lying, or riding which is located beneath a Zab is unclean, even though the Zab has not sat, lain, or ridden on said object.

Tertiary Meaning

K. **Touching or carrying the saddle produces uncleanness, as specified.**

L. **Touching an object located underneath a Zab, even though said object is not touched by the Zab and even though said object is not directly sat, lain, or ridden upon by the Zab but merely bears the weight of his body, imparts uncleanness so that the formerly clean person is made unclean and furthermore makes his clothing unclean, and, by extension, imparts uncleanness to utensils in general.**

Fourth Level of Meaning

1. **An object used for sitting and lying which is located underneath the Zab is subject to the uncleanness imparted by**

the Zab to objects upon which he has sat or lain, etc. It follows that the same sort of object located above the Zab is *not* subject to the uncleanness imparted by the Zab to objects used for sitting and lying.

ii. An object not used for sitting and lying located *beneath* the Zab (but not touched by him or subjected to the pressure of his body-weight) is *not* unclean.

iii. And, it follows in the rule of opposites, an object not used for sitting and lying which is located *above* the Zab *will* be unclean in some way or degree, not specified.

Mishnah

9-10: M. 5:1-3.
K: M. 5:8.
L: M. 5:1-3.
 i: M. 5:1-2.
 ii: M. 5:1.
 iii: M. 5:1-2.

| Lev. 15:10b: *And whoever carries such a thing shall wash his clothes and bathe himself in water and be unclean until the evening.* | *Carrying an object used for riding, sitting, or lying, and made unclean by the Zab makes the clean person who carries said object unclean. He makes his clothing unclean.* |

Secondary Meaning

11. The uncleanness of the Zab is conveyed through carriage. Specifically, if one carries an object, such as a bed or chair, made unclean by the Zab, one is made unclean as if he touched the Zab or as if he was subjected to the weight or pressure of the Zab or of an object made unclean by the Zab. This seems to me to follow naturally from the concept of pressure, since it is not possible to carry something without bearing its weight.

Tertiary Meaning

M. A person or an object which a Zab carries is made unclean. That is, just as there is no difference between touching the Zab or being touched by him, placing pressure upon the Zab or having the Zab's pressure applied to a clean person, so there is no difference between carrying the Zab and being carried by him.

N. The person made unclean in this way imparts uncleanness to his clothing, therefore to utensils.

Fourth Level of Meaning

iv. The person made unclean in these several ways makes his clothing unclean. Clearly, that is the case when the uncleanness of the Zab is transmitted to the person. It will follow, therefore, that when the Zab touches or exerts pressure on a clean person, the person is made unclean, and the clothing on the person is made unclean. Accordingly, it is when the clean person is subject to the uncleanness of the Zab, etc., that his clothing is made unclean: "he renders utensils unclean." When the person is no longer subject to the uncleanness of the Zab, he (of course) remains unclean. But he no longer will make his clothing unclean.

Mishnah

As above, Lev. 15:10a.
iv: M. 5:1, Joshua.

| Lev. 15:11: *Any one whom he that has the discharge touches without having rinsed his hands shall wash his clothes and bathe himself in water and be unclean until the evening.* | *The unclean person imparts uncleanness through touching. The person made unclean thereby transmits uncleanness to clothing.* |

Secondary Meaning

I see nothing in this verse which is both relevant to Zabim and new.

| Lev. 15:12: *And the earthen vessel which he who has the discharge touches shall be broken. And every vessel of wood shall be rinsed in water.* | *Earthen, or clay, utensils cannot be cleaned by rinsing, but only by breaking. Wooden utensils can be cleaned by immersion.* |

Secondary Meaning

12. Wooden vessels are subject to a different rule from earthen ones. That rule, moreover, will be the same as affects any other utensil which is cleaned through immersion.

3. *Transferring the Zab's Uncleanness: Unassigned Pericopae*

Unassigned pericopae are those units of thought which contain no trace of attribution and bear no direct attestations. These pericopae lack also the indirect, and therefore probative, attestation which follows when the fundamental presupposition of an attributed or well-attested pericope clearly depends upon the datum of an unattributed and unattested one. The unassigned entries clearly relate to, and I think are generated by, the primary allegation of Scripture or its logical developments, as specified.

1. M. 2:4: The Zab imparts uncleanness to the bed in five ways so that the bed imparts uncleanness to man and garments: standing, and sitting, lying, suspended, and leaning. The bed imparts uncleanness to man in seven ways so that he makes clothing unclean: standing, sitting, lying, suspended, leaning, contact, and carrying. (Compare M. Kel. 1:3.)

Sifra Meṣoraʿ Zabim 3:1-3: Pressure exerted by Zab, even if he sits on top of a heavy stone, imparts uncleanness.

Sifra Meṣoraʿ Zabim 2:7: If Zab lay down on chair, sat on bed, stands or is suspended, they are unclean = M. 2:4.

2. Sifra Meṣoraʿ Zabim 11:1-2: Man who touches bed imparts uncleanness to clothing, but bed which touches bed does not impart uncleanness to clothing. Bed imparts uncleanness when under the Zab to impart uncleanness to man and clothing, but man under the Zab does not impart uncleanness to man and clothing.

1. The rule is specific, that the Zab imparts uncleanness to the bed in the specified five ways. The second component is distinct. How does the bed transmit uncleanness to the clean man? Omitted from consideration: How does the Zab impart uncleanness to the clean man? In point of fact, the Zab transmits uncleanness through touching and through being carried (= exerting pressure).

2. The Zab imparts uncleanness when he touches a bed. The bed touching a bed does not impart uncleanness to clothing. The bed under the Zab imparts uncleanness as a bed, man does not.

Perhaps the several contrasts are based solely upon those established in Scripture, specifically, objects used for lying and sitting located underneath the Zab impart uncleanness to clothing, Lev. 15:10a. Man is not used for sitting and lying, therefore when located under the Zab, he does not. Along these same lines, Scripture is clear, Lev. 15:5, that man who touches the bed washes his clothes—therefore imparts uncleanness to clothing (= utensils). Scripture is silent on the affect upon clothing of a bed which touches a bed made unclean by a Zab. It will have followed that what is stated explicitly at Lev. 15:5 then deliberately means to exclude what is omitted, which is the status of the bed which touches the bed. This is, of course, rather acute, since Scripture speaks of common occurrences, and it is difficult for a bed to reach out and touch another bed; Scripture's use of touching naturally is in the context of animate creatures.

3. M. 5:2: Whatever is carried above the Zab is unclean. Whatever the Zab is carried upon, but which is not touched by him, is clean, except for something used for sitting and lying (Lev. 15:10a) and except for man who carries the Zab (Lev. 15:10b).
+ T. 5:1.
Sifra Meṣora' Zabim III:3-7: Food, drink, utensils not used for sitting and lying which are above the Zab are made unclean on that account, proved by Simeon.

3. The important point here is the distinction between what is carried *above* the Zab and what is carried *below* him, without touching him. In the former case, there is uncleanness, and this applies, specifically, to food, drink and objects not used for lying and sitting (*maddaf*). If these are carried below the Zab, they are clean. Only man and bed and chair below the Zab are made unclean because of their serving to carry his weight even without directly touching him.
The illustration, M. 5:2L-M. further indicates that what is unclean above the Zab—food, drink, *maddaf* (an object not used for lying and sitting)—is unclean in the first remove.

The principle is dual: (1) What is carried *underneath* the Zab is unclean, except for an object used for lying and sitting. (2) What is carried *above* the Zab is unclean. The relationship to Scripture is not self-evident. On the one side, we may readily account for the first principle. That an object used for lying and sitting which was under the Zab is unclean is specified at Lev. 15:10a. But the rule excludes objects not used for lying and sitting. Perhaps the distinction begins at Lev. 15:9. The saddle on which the Zab rides is unclean. Lev. 15:10a, continuing this point, then specifies that whoever touches anything that was under him—thus, that has served him for sitting—is unclean. And, by exclusion therefrom, whoever touches something which has been located under the Zab but which the Zab has *not* used for sitting is not unclean. Accordingly, the object itself, if not used for sitting, does not become unclean if the Zab is located above it.

But whence the notion of *maddaf*? That is, how do we know that an object *not* used for lying and sitting and located *above* the Zab is unclean? At first glance, it appears that we come to the fourth level of meaning imputed to Lev. 15:10a (i, iii). (1) What is unclean beneath the Zab is not unclean above him. (2) Then: What is not unclean beneath the Zab *is* unclean above him. Objects not used for sitting and lying, food and drink (2) are unclean above, because they (1) are clean below, the Zab. Thus: Objects used for sitting and lying are clean above, because they are unclean below, the Zab.

But the problem of *maddaf* is not so readily settled. We have to ascertain the meaning associated with the word in the earliest assigned pericopae. With the help of Kasovsky (Chayim Yehoshua Kasovsky, *Thesaurus Mishnae* [Jerusalem, 1958], IV, p. 353a), let us rapidly review the several meanings assigned to the word *maddaf*. The word is familiar as the name of an object, which we have translated *bird trap* at M. Kel. 23:5 (Part II, p. 220); as *the smoker of the bees* (M. Kel. 16:7, Part II, p. 78), required by context in both cases. Our tractate, by contrast, knows that word to mean "an object, not used for lying or sitting, located above the Zab," and we need not review the passages in which the word appears in that meaning (M. Zab. 4:6, 5:2). The third meaning is "a status as to uncleanness," a definition to be made more precise when we return to M. Par. 10:1-2, and M. Toh. 8:2. The former (Part X, pp. 164-171) requires the meaning, "A status as to uncleanness related to *midras* but of lower degree of uncleanness than *midras*." Thus M. Par. 10:1 states: "Whatever can become unclean with *midras*-uncleanness is regarded as actually unclean with *maddaf*-uncleanness so far as the purification-rite is concerned." (There is a further dispute, M. Par. 10:1, assigned to Yavneans, on what can be made unclean with corpse-uncleanness and whether that sort of object likewise is unclean with *maddaf*-uncleanness)

Accordingly, in the context of M. Par. 10:1-2, *maddaf* can only mean, "a status of uncleanness," which, we know, is uncleanness in the first remove, effecting uncleanness for food and liquid. This same meaning is absolutely required at M. Toh. 8:2 (Part XI, p. 186): If someone deposits with an '*am ha'areṣ* a box full of clothing, Yosé says, "When it is tightly packed, it is unclean with *midras*-uncleanness, and if it is not tightly packed, it is unclean with *maddaf*-uncleanness." Accordingly, once more, *midras*-uncleanness is set into contrast with *maddaf*-uncleanness. In this instance the point is that the '*am ha'*-*areṣ* is unclean as a Zab. If a Zab shifts an object not used for sitting or lying, we know, the object suffers *maddaf*-uncleanness and renders food and drink unclean. M. Ed. 6:2 (*Eliezer b. Hyrcanus. The*

Tradition and the Man [Leiden, 1973, 1, p. 339-340) further has a dispute of Joshua and Neḥunya b. Elinathan with Eliezer, in which it is taken for granted, tangentially and within the structure of argument: "The uncleanness of living beings is greater than the uncleanness of corpses, for a living being imparts uncleanness, by lying and sitting, to what is underneath him, so that it conveys uncleanness to man and utensils, and also conveys *maddaf*-uncleanness to what is above him, so that it conveys uncleanness to food and liquid, a mode of transferring uncleanness which a corpse does not convey." The same authorities—Joshua and Eliezer—are at M. Par. 10:1-2, and, moreover, Yosé continues the matter, at M. Toh. 8:2, taking the rule for granted, just as do Joshua and Eliezer. We need not review in detail Tosefta's usages of the same word, since all occur in the context of the correlative Mishnaic pericopae (T. Par. 10:2, 3, T. Toh. 9:4, T. Zab. 3:3, 5:1).

The two senses in which the word is used (now omitted: references to the occurrences in M. Kel.) of course are complementary. M. Par. and M. Toh. know *maddaf* as a status as to uncleanness contrasted to *midras*, and M. Zab. uses the word to refer to objects which can enter that very same status as to uncleanness. Our translation in the present tractate has been required by its context. But the meaning in point of fact is complementary to that necessitated by the context of M. Par. and M. Toh.: What can become unclean with *maddaf*-uncleanness— an object not used for lying and sitting and hence not susceptible to *midras*-uncleanness (a point familiar throughout our order e.g., Kelim Chapter Twenty-Four)—here is called *maddaf*. And M. Par. and M. Toh. know *maddaf* as that uncleanness imparted to something which can become unclean with *maddaf*-uncleanness, as distinct from something (used for lying and sitting) susceptible to *midras*. Our tractate, moreover, hastens to add: The status of *maddaf*-uncleanness is attained when an object not used for lying or sitting (also food or drink, explicitly included as well) is located above a Zab. *Maddaf* as the opposite of *midras*, of course, is contained in the pericopae of M. Toh. in particular, but also, with slight eisegesis, at M. Par.

The contrast between *midras* and *maddaf*, strikingly, is precisely the same the contrast as I have hypothetically imputed to the exegetes of Lev. 15:10 A at i, iii. Indeed, *midras* and *maddaf* express exactly the same idea as is spelled out in the circumlocutions above (p. 182). Our invocation, at that point, of the rule of opposites therefore is justified by the result of the present analysis of the consistent contrast, drawn in M., between *midras* and *maddaf*. The concept of *maddaf*, in its two, complementary senses, most certainly is attested by Joshua and Eliezer at M. Ed. and M. Par. Because of the givenness of the idea of M. Par., at both pericopae assigned to Eliezer and Joshua, I am inclined to suppose that the concept of *maddaf*-uncleanness and of objects susceptible not to *midras*, because they are not used for lying and sitting, but, under the specified circumstance, to *maddaf*-uncleanness, hence *maddaf*-objects, originates before 70.

4. M. 5:6: He who touches the Zab, Zabah, menstruating woman, woman after childbirth, meṣoraʿ, or a bed or chair on which any of these have lain or sat. Touching and shifting, carrying and being carried, are equivalent.
+ T. 5:3: utensils are in the first remove.

4. The pericope so far as it deals with modes of transfer makes two points.
First, while one is touching these sources, he is able to impart uncleanness at two removes, unfitness at one. That is to say, just as at M. 5:1, he is like a Father of uncleanness, so far as food for heave-offering is concerned.
Second, touching is deemed equivalent to shifting, carrying, and being carried.

That the uncleanness of the Zab is transferred to one who touches the Zab (etc.) is stated explicitly at Lev. 15:5. That one who carries such a thing is made unclean is stated at Lev. 15:10b.

The sole new point has to do with the inclusion of shifting as a mode of transfer of uncleanness. This is probably generated by the analogy to bearing the weight of the Zab, that is, carrying. The inclusion of shifting as a mode of transfer of uncleanness derives simply from the extension of Scripture's stated modes. One can hardly carry without shifting the object. The sole open question is whether we include even derivatives of the pressure of the Zab or of pressure upon the Zab, that is, vibration, movement which takes place indirectly and not directly. We do not, as the Ushans state.

5. M. 5:7: He who touches the flux of the Zab, his spit, his semen, his urine, and the blood of the menstruating woman (imparts uncleanness at two removes, etc.). All the same is touching and moving. Eliezer: Also carrying.

5. 1. The specified excretions are unclean just as the Zab is unclean.
2. They transfer uncleanness just as the Zab transfers uncleanness, that is, through contact.
3. Shifting is equivalent to contact.
4. Eliezer: Carrying is equivalent to contact.

Touching the spit of the Zab effects the transfer of the Zab's uncleanness, so Lev. 15:8. The secondary point is the inclusion of other substances. The issue of carrying as equivalent to contact of course is not of equivalent antiquity.

6. T. 5:2B: Phlegm, mucous, saliva, and snot of Zab are like his spit. Tear, blood of wound, milk of woman, blood of mouth and penis are unclean only in the first remove. Flux, spit, urine are unclean as Fathers. Semen of Zab: Eliezer—does not impart uncleanness when carried; and sages—imparts uncleanness when carried, because urine is contained therein.

Sifra Meṣoraʿ Zabim 1:7-8: Zab imparts uncleanness through white flux, not through red flow (blood from penis).

Sifra Meṣoraʿ Zabim I:9-13: Flux itself is unclean. Blood which exudes from the penis is not unclean as flux. His urine is unclean. Sweat, rancid moisture, excrement are not unclean. Nine liquids apply to Zab: secretion, putrid sweat, excrement are clean in all respects; tear, blood, milk impart susceptibility to uncleanness as liquids; flux, spit, urine are unclean as flux.

Sifra Mesoraʿ Zabim 3:8: Phlegm, slaver, and snot are equivalent to spit.
Sifra Meṣoraʿ Zabim 1:3: Flux derives solely from the genitals, not from the nose or mouth.

There are two issues in the present set, first of all, the notion that the transfer of the Zab's uncleanness takes place not solely through touching the Zab, but also through touching other substances which exude from him. Second, other modes of transfer besides direct contact are of the same effect as direct contact. The matter of touching the Zab's spit is explicit at Lev. 15:8. Accordingly, not only the flux, but also spit is unclean. Then spit supplies an analogy for other such substances which are like it. Flux is like semen; urine derives from the same location. Phlegm, mucus, saliva, snot, all are treated as analogous to spit. The second issue is the analogy between touching and moving, on which all parties agree. Eliezer wishes to treat carrying as equivalent mode of transfer of uncleanness. His basis, surely, will be the diverse rulings which treat touching, shifting, and carrying as equivalent. At T. 5:2B, an Eliezer wishes to exclude semen of the Zab. If this is the same Eliezer, then M. 5:7 should contain the equivalent qualification, that is, adding *carrying* as a mode of transfer of uncleanness, and detaching *semen* from the opening list. We do not know which Eliezer is before us, one of the Yavneans or one of the Ushans. That is why we cannot adduce the present set as evidence that discussion of the interrelationships of the diverse modes of transfer of uncleanness was carried forward at Yavneh, with the secondary notion that the issues were still live at that time. This is suggested by the pointed claim, intruded at M. 5:6, 7, etc., that the diverse modes do produce equivalent effects, or are the same as one another, which suggests that in the background are efforts seriously to distinguish among them. But the main point in Mishnah is that there are diverse modes, and that point derives from the obvious sense of Scripture, which specifies touching or contact, carrying, lying or sitting, generalized into exerting pressure.

7. M. 5:8: He who carries saddle, is carried on it, and moves it, etc.	7. Carrying, being carried on, and moving, the saddle imparts uncleanness as if one were made a Father of uncleanness.
Carrying carrion, purification water sufficient for sprinkling. + T. 5:5A.	Here, too, the man is as if he were a Father of uncleanness.
M. 5:9: He who eats carrion of clean bird, while it is in his gullet, etc. + T. 5:10-12.	This item is not relevant to Zabim.
Sifra Meṣoraʿ Zabim 4:2-3: Bed and chair impart uncleanness when they are carried.	
Sifra Meṣoraʿ Zabim 4:1: Whoever touches saddle is unclean, but whoever touches what is under the saddle is not unclean on that account.	

Carrying the saddle or being carried on it make a person unclean, so Lev. 15:10 states explicitly. That the bed and chair which are carried impart uncleanness is also at Lev. 15:10b. Touching the saddle produces uncleanness, so Lev. 15:10a. Lev. 15:10b then specifies that whoever carries something which has been underneath a Zab is unclean, which then is exclusive of merely *touching* the saddle. Nothing in this set brings us significantly outside the boundaries of Scriptural meaning, so far as I can see. (We omit reference to the matter of carrion, which is not within the thematic limits of our tractate.)

8. M. 5:10: He who touches a dead creeping thing, semen, one made unclean by corpse-uncleanness, meṣoraʿ during period of counting clean days, purification water insufficient for sprinkling, carrion, and saddle ...
This is the general rule: Whatever touches any of all the Fathers of uncleanness listed in the Torah imparts uncleanness at one remove and renders unfit at one. Man in contact with a Father of uncleanness, imparts uncleanness at two removes, unfitness at one. Or: except for man, who, as a corpse, makes that which touches it into a Father of uncleanness and so that which is in contact with a corpse imparts uncleanness at two removes and unfitness at one more.

M. 5:11: He who has a seminal emission is like one who has touched a dead creeping thing. He who has sexual relations with a menstruating woman is like one who is unclean by reason of corpse-uncleanness, but he also imparts uncleanness to bed and chair so that they render food and drink unclean, which the former does not accomplish.

M. 5:12: Ten items which are in the second remove of uncleanness and therefore render heave-offering unfit. Sifra Meṣoraʿ Zabim 2:8-13: Seminal emission does not cause uncleanness. Person unclean through *negaʿ*, corpse, does not impart uncleanness to bed and chair.

8. In all these cases, the one who touches the source of uncleanness is unclean only in the first remove, not functioning as if he were a Father of uncleanness.

Any object, other than man, in contact with a Father of uncleanness, is in the first remove of uncleanness.

The last units, M. 5:10-12, complete the construction of M. 5:6-9 by specifying sources of uncleanness, touching which leaves a person unclean only in the first remove, then in the second. The set contains no attestations, but in fact goes over the specifications of Scripture. What is pointed is the distinction between "whatever touches any of the Fathers of uncleanness" and *"man* who touches a Father of uncleanness," which is to say, the important point of M. 5:1, 6-9, upon which Joshua's further observation, about the difference between one's state while touching such a Father and after one has ceased to touch the Father, is based. It is, of course, the specification at Lev. 15:5, for the Zab, Lev. 15:21, for the menstruating woman, Lev. 15:27, for the Zab, and the comparison of the woman after childbirth to the menstruating woman, Lev. 12:2, 5, that the person who touches things on which the aforenamed have lain or sat washes his clothes, which leads to the stated conclusion.

If one has to wash his clothes in consequence of touching these people or objects made unclean by them, it is because he has made his clothes unclean. It follows that the man who touches the specified sources of uncleanness, as well as other sources or Fathers of uncleanness analogous to them, renders utensils (clothes) unclean. Accordingly, in the language of the authorities beginning with Joshua, such a person "renders uncleanness at two removes and unfitness at one—a third," a notion certainly attested to early Yavneh at M. Toh. 2:3-6 + 7. Accordingly, the secondary development upon which the present massive set of materials external to Zabim is based begins at Yavneh, though it is not, either in formulation or conception, necessarily so early as the time of Joshua.

4. *Transferring the Zab's Uncleanness: Mishnah*

Having dealt, in connection with the present theme, with the Scriptural rules and the unattested materials of our tractate which restate the data of Scripture, we come to the more familiar territory of Mishnah and its sequences of legal conceptions. Our interest is not only in the established agendum of questions, that is, the interplay between the conceptions and attributions of pericopae and the correlation of temporal and logical sequences, but in yet a second matter. We want to see at what point, in our account of the logical unfolding of Scriptural rules, the assigned conceptions of Yavneh and Usha find a place. The satisfying result may be stated in advance. All of the materials before us turn out to stand in direct relationship to Scripture, and no important conception lies outside the secondary or tertiary conceptions thereof. Accordingly, from Scripture to the conceptions of the last strata of Mishnah-Tosefta, we move in a perfectly straight line, step by step, stage by stage.

A. *Before 70*

No pertinent materials are assigned to the authorities before 70. This accords with (but obviously does not prove) our larger theory that the matter of removes of uncleanness comes under intensive study in the time of Yavneh (Part XII, pp. 202-206), as well as with the evidence before us that Joshua's ideas on the related topic of Niddah predominate in our tractate.

B. *Yavneh*

Joshua, the primary authority of Zabim, does not refer to the Zab at all. His two major rulings stand behind the problems of Chapters Three-Four, and Five, respectively.

*1. M. 4:1A-D/T. 4:4A: Joshua says, If a menstruating woman sat with a clean woman on a shaky bed, the cap on the clean woman's head is unclean with midras-uncleanness. (+ Two more examples.)	*1. Joshua's point is that an object need not actually be used for lying and sitting. It must be something which might be used for that purpose, even though it presently is not so utilized, to be susceptible to *midras*-uncleanness. This item is not directly relevant, in its current terms, to Zabim; but the Zab of course imparts uncleanness exactly as does the menstruating woman.

See *Usha, Nos. 1, 2, 3*.

Joshua's position is in two parts. First, an object need not be regularly used for lying and sitting. It must be potentially available for that purpose, that is, the cap on the head. Second, the object need not actually be sat upon, but if it is merely in some way or other subjected to the movement or pressure of the Zab, it is made unclean thereby. The former point, "the cap on the head," is not at issue. That is taken for granted, perhaps along the lines of *Lev. 15:4, Secondary Meaning No. 1*. In any event we can hardly imagine that the conception of *midras*-uncleanness begins with Joshua (!). The real issue, as is obvious, is the extent of the transfer of *midras*-uncleanness. Since the menstruating woman and the clean woman have sat on the shaky bed, the clothes on the latter are made unclean by the effects of the shaking of the former, as at *Lev. 15:4 Tertiary Meanings A-D*. The connection to the Ushan materials at *Usha No. 1* cannot be missed, since we have at the latter set the very same shaky bed. Accordingly, Joshua stands behind the diverse Ushan developments of the issue of secondary and derivative pressure. His mode of thinking demands either the interesting distinction between derivative pressure, which does impart uncleanness, and vibration, which does not, or the rejection of such a distinction. For limits to the matter must be set.

*2. M. 5:1E-M: A general rule did Joshua state: Whoever imparts uncleanness to clothes when in contact with the source of uncleanness imparts uncleanness to food and drink, putting them in the first remove, hands in the second; but does not impart uncleanness to man or clay utensils. After he separates, he imparts uncleanness in the first remove to liquid, but uncleanness only in the second remove to food (and hands); and in any event he does not impart uncleanness to clothes.

*2. The important point of Joshua's ruling is the difference between imparting uncleanness while one is in touch with the source of uncleanness and doing so after he lets go. In the former instance one imparts uncleanness as if one were a Father of uncleanness, so far as food is concerned, but not so far as man or clay utensils are concerned. In the latter instance he imparts uncleanness solely by reason of his former contact with the Father of uncleanness and so is in the first remove. Accordingly, food which he touches is in the second remove.

M. 5:1A-D: He who touches the Zab or whom the Zab touched, he who moves the Zab or whom the Zab moves, while in contact with the Zab imparts uncleanness to food, drink, utensils cleaned through rinsing. But he does not do so when he carries them without touching them.

The opening unit of the pericope states the matter in terms of the Zab only, as against the more general statement of Joshua, which does not specify the source of uncleanness or the mode of its transfer but only the difference between the state of affairs while one is in contact with "whoever imparts uncleanness to clothes" and after one lets go. Thus once more Joshua's ruling omits specific reference to Zabim in particular. Important at M. 5:1A-D is the specification of modes of transfer of uncleanness: touching, moving; also the addition of utensils which may be cleansed through rinsing; and the specification of contact as against carrying without contact.

M. 5:2F-P: If the finger of the Zab is under the course of stones and the clean person is above, he (since he is sitting on the Zab, exerting pressure even through the stone) imparts uncleanness at two removes and unfitness at one more. When he separates, he imparts uncleanness at one remove and unfitness at one.

This set illustrates Joshua's proposition, combining his principle with the modes of transfer at M. 5:2A-D.

M. 5:6, 7, 8, 9: He who touches, etc., imparts uncleanness at two removes and unfitness to heave-offering at one more. If he let go (etc.), he imparts uncleanness at one remove and unfitness at one remove.

The point of the apodosis of the construction is the same as that of Joshua, that distinction between the uncleanness which prevails while one is subject to the transfer of uncleanness and that which prevails after he is no longer subject to the transfer of uncleanness but merely suffers its effects. In the latter case, in all instances, the man is unclean in the first remove.

Sifra Meṣoraʿ Zabim II:9: M. 5:1's distinction, between uncleanness imparted while one is touching the bed and that imparted after he separates from the bed, is repeated.

Sifra Meṣoraʿ Zabim II:10-11: M. 5:1 is cited.

Joshua's saying, amplified at M. 5:6-9 by reference to diverse modes of the transfer of uncleanness, in point of fact is not centered on modes of transfer, but on the difference between the time that one is subjected to the transfer and the time after the transfer has concluded. Joshua's point accords with *Lev. 15:10 b Fourth Level of Meaning iv*. Self-evidently, the same distinction proposed at that point is to be drawn at all the equivalent statements that the person who touches, carries, lies, or sits upon the objects made unclean by the Zab must wash his clothes. He therefore has made his clothes unclean, meaning, I assume, fresh clothes which he has touched after he has taken off the former, since he has not made them unclean. It is this reasoning which stands behind Joshua's conception, I believe.

The formulation of the whole may be held to take for granted that we speak of heave-offering. The heave-offering is governed by the rules stated at M. Toh. 2:3-6, that is, heave-offering in the first and second removes is unclean and renders other heave-offering unclean at one further remove. Accordingly, Joshua will maintain that the Father of uncleanness imparts uncleanness at two removes and unfitness at a third—solely to heave-offering. Nonetheless, Eliezer/Eliezer of M. Toh. 2:7 need not differ, since he holds that holy things, heave-offering, and unconsecrated food at the first remove of uncleanness impart uncleanness at two removes and unfitness at one further remove. If we insist that under discussion is ordinary, unconsecrated food and not heave-offering, then the position before us cannot be articulated in the way of Joshua at M. Toh. 2:2 + 3-6. Certainly excluded is the position of ʿAqiva at M. Sot. 5:2 (compare Part XI, pp. 50-68).

#3. M. 5:3: Whatever carries or is carried on top of a bed is clean, except for man; whatever carries or is carried

#3. Man alone, and not utensils, contracts uncleanness through carrying something. Man alone is made unclean

on top of carrion is clean, except for him who moves it. Eliezer: Also: he who carries it. Whatever carries or is carried on top of the corpse is clean, except for that which overshadows and except for man when he shifts it.

M. 5:7: He who touches the flux of the Zab, spit, semen, urine, blood of menstruating woman ... All the same is the one who touches and who shifts. Eliezer: Also: the one who carries. + T. 5:4.

by carrying a bed or other object used for lying by a Zab. (The matter of carrion and corpse is irrelevant to our tractate.)

There are again two points.
First, while touching these sources, it is as if he was touching the Zab, Zabah, and so on.
Second, in the present regard, touching and shifting are equivalent. Eliezer deems carrying to be in the same category as touching and shifting, just as at M. 5:6.

Sifra Meṣoraʿ Zabim 4:4: Eliezer's position, M. 5:7, is formulated: one who *carries* flux of Zab, spit, urine, semen, blood of menstruating woman is unclean.

At M. 5:3, Eliezer's point is that one who carries the carrion (not moving it) is unclean; at M. 5:7, one who carries the flux, Zab, spit, etc., is unclean. It is the latter item which is relevant to Zabim. Carrying is equivalent to touching flux. On what basis will Eliezer have come to such a conclusion? Perhaps it is by analogy of Lev. 15:10b, "Whoever carries such a thing will wash his clothes," to Lev. 15:5, "Whoever touches the bed of the Zab," and Lev. 15:8, "Whoever is touched by the spit of the Zab." In both cases the person made unclean in that way is required to wash his clothes. Accordingly, there is no difference in the affects upon the man who has carried something made unclean by the Zab and who has touched something made unclean by the Zab. In both cases one must wash his clothes—the result is the same. Therefore in both cases the *modes* of transfer are equivalent to one another: *post hoc, ergo propter hoc*. If that is his reasoning, then sages will reject his position for the obvious reason. We do not know that the present Eliezer is a Yavnean, nor are there continuators of the dispute, on the one side, or logical developments of it, on the other.

C. *Usha*

All pericopae assigned to Ushans begin in the principle attributed to Joshua that if the menstruating woman (hence: the Zab, whose uncleanness is equivalent) and the clean woman sit on a shaky bed, even the cap on the clean woman's head is made unclean as a Father of uncleanness (Joshua: *midras*-uncleanness), as if the menstruating woman had sat, lain, or exerted pressure upon the little cap. What the Ushans accomplish is, first, to extend Joshua's principle from the menstruating woman to the case of the Zab, which self-evidently is demanded by Scripture, and second, to explore the limits of the notion of pressure.

*1. M. 3:1: Zab and clean person who sat on boat or raft, etc.—even if clothes do not touch—the clothes of the clean person are unclean with *midras*-uncleanness.
If they sat on a plank or chair, etc., which is infirm, the clean man and his clothes are made unclean.
Judah declares clean.
T. 4:1B: Judah's position restated. The principle is at the following.

1. The point is that it is as though the clean person has been shifted by the man with flux.

M. 3:2A-B: They open or close a door [and both are unclean]. Sages: Uncleanness is transferred only if one opens and the other closes.

The view is that any pressure, even on a common object from the same side, involves the transfer of uncleanness. Sages hold that only if one presses from one side and the other from the other is there a transfer of uncleanness.

M. 3:2C-D: If one lifts the other out of the pit, they are unclean. Judah: Only if the clean raises the unclean.

Judah's point is that if we know the clean person has borne the weight of the unclean, then the person and his clothing are unclean with *midras*-uncleanness. But if the unclean raises the clean, there is no transfer of *midras*-uncleanness; all we have is shifting.

M. 3:2E-I: Twist ropes together, etc. Weave together. Simeon: Clean in the case of all except for when they grind with a handmill. + T. 4:1C, 4:2.

M. 3:3A-K: Zab and clean person who sat on large ship, firm plank, etc.—clean.

There is no transfer of uncleanness since the objects on which the clean and unclean person sat are firm and do not shake.

M. 3:3L-P: If the clean person hits the unclean, he is clean. If the unclean hits the clean, he is unclean, for if the clean person should draw back, lo, the unclean person would fall down.
T. 4:1A: Unclean person who hits clean and clean person who hits unclean—clothes of the clean person are unclean, so Meir. Sages: As at M.

Now the clean person is holding up the unclean, who thus leans upon him and therefore imparts his uncleanness.

Now we see that Meir stands behind sages of M. 3:2A, because he rejects the distinction important to sages and Judah at M. So far as he is concerned,

Simeon: If he hits him with knuckles, he is unclean; with the back of the hand, he is clean. See *Yavneh, No. 1.*	whether the clean hits the unclean or *vice versa*, there is a transfer of *midras*-uncleanness. Accordingly, he deems shifting of the one by the other, without distinction, as capable of transferring *midras*-uncleanness. Sages' view is verbatim that of M. 3:3L-P. Judah is not so far from sages. He simply adds to their distinction a further consideration. Simeon distinguishes a hard push from a light one, so in accord with sages of M. 3:2B. Accordingly, we have Meir at M. 3:2A, Simeon at M. 3:2B, and Judah's position is articulated at M. 3:2D, I assume as against Simeon or Meir at M. 3:2C.

The first unit does little more than to restate Joshua's position. The boat or raft or whatever is deemed equivalent to the shaky bed (or the shaky bed is interpolated into Joshua's ruling to bring it into conformity to the Ushan cases). The clothes are unclean even if they do not touch. Why? Because they have been subjected to something made unclean by the pressure of the Zab. That is, the Zab has sat on the boat, which has been subjected to his weight; so too has the clean person; and the rest follows. This is the case when the object on which the Zab and the clean person have sat is infirm.

The secondary issue, M. 3:2, is spelled out in the tripartite positions of Judah, Meir, and Simeon. Judah is clear that the only situation in which there is a transfer of *midras*-uncleanness is when the clean person bears the weight of the unclean. But if the unclean person bears the weight of the clean person, Judah maintains, then we have shifting. This then is not equivalent to carrying, as against the view of Eliezer. But we do not have pressure, that is, bearing the weight of the Zab. Judah accordingly imposes a narrow construction both on the matter of shifting, on the one side, and the exertion of pressure, on the other.

Meir takes the opposite position. The Zab imparts *midras*-uncleanness if he exerts pressure on something, and the person who exerts pressure on the Zab is equivalently unclean. Meir's position surely is based upon Lev. 15:6: Whoever sits on anything on which he who has the discharge has sat shall wash his clothes. He will reason: just as the Zab imparts uncleanness by sitting on the bed, and just as the clean person is made unclean by sitting on the bed, therefore the clean person who sits—that is, exerts pressure—upon the Zab becomes unclean. Once more the construction of a secondary analogy is based upon the primary analogy produced by Lev. 15:4 and Lev. 15:6. (This analogy still further yields the principle that touching is equivalent to exerting pressure, e.g., carrying or being carried.) *If* that is how Meir has reached his conclusion, then his reasoning is parallel to that of Eliezer. Once again, the contrary view, here represented by Judah, is to discern the underlying fallacy: *post hoc, ergo propter hoc*. Simeon, of course, accords with Judah's view. He wants the clean person to bear the weight of the unclean. We shall now see that Simeon makes his own contribution as well.

*2. M. 4:4-6A/T. 4:4B, 8, 9A: A Zab on five benches—lying lengthwise, unclean; breadthwise, clean. Lying on six seats, with hands on two, feet on two, head on one, body on one—unclean is only the one under the body. Standing on two chairs: Simeon, If they are far from one another, they are clean.

T. 4:4B to M. 4:4A-B: If chairs are set lengthwise, they are clean, for no one of them bears the greater part of his weight. Simeon: If the middle one is higher than the others, it is unclean, because the greater part of his weight is borne on it.

T. 4:5: Ten cloaks, one on top of the other, if he slept on top, all are unclean. Zab on one side of balance, bed or chair opposite, if Zab went down, they are clean [of *midras*]. If they went down, they are unclean [with *midras*]. Simeon: If there was one place and it went down, it is unclean. If there are many, they are clean, for no one of them bears the weight of the greater part of the Zab. M. 4:6A: If Zab is on one side of scale, food and drink are on the second, they are unclean.

*2. The main point is that something is made unclean by the Zab's lying or sitting on it only if it bears the greater part of the weight of the Zab. Simeon concurs in this principle and applies it. Food and drink shifted by the Zab are unclean, so it does not matter whether or not they outweigh him or he outweighs them. The issue is important only for *midras*-uncleanness, e.g., bed and chair.

M. 4:7/T. 4:4C, 4:9B: If Zab was sitting on the bed and cloaks were under the four legs, they are all unclean, because the bed cannot stand on three legs. Simeon declares clean.

We regard each leg as if it bears the greater part of the weight of the Zab.

If a Zab was riding on a beast, and four cloaks were under the four hooves, they are clean, because the beast can stand on three. If there was a single cloak under two forelegs, etc., it is

The greater part of the weight of the Zab is not located upon any one leg. The principle is clear.

unclean. Yosé: The horse imparts uncleanness with the two hindlegs, ass with the forelegs, for the horse leans on the hind legs, the ass on the forelegs.

M. 5:4-5/T. 4:3, 5:1B, F:2A: If part of one who is unclean is on him who is clean, or part of one who is clean is on him who is unclean, and the same with connectors, the clean one is made unclean. Simeon: If part of one who is unclean is on one who is clean, he is unclean. If part of one who is clean is on top of one who is unclean, he remains clean. If the unclean person is on part of the bed and the clean person is on part of the bed, he is unclean.

Simeon's principle now is qualified. We require the greater part of the weight of the Zab's body only when he is lying on an object. But if a clean person lies on the unclean, then even if less than the greater part of the unclean person is on the clean, the clean person is made unclean. Uncleanness enters and leaves the bed through only part of the bed. Simeon obviously will accept this further qualification of his position that we require the greater part of the weight of the Zab's body on top of an object or person for the object or person to receive the Zab's uncleanness.

Sifra Meṣoraʿ Zabim 3:5: Excrement, entangled hair, chains, finger-rings, earrings, etc. do not impart uncleanness. Hair and fingernails do (= T. 5:2A to 5:4-5).
Sifra Meṣoraʿ Zabim 4:5 = 3:5.
See *Yavneh, No. 1.*
(Sifra Meṣoraʿ Zabim I:6: Zab is not unclean until flux exudes from the penis. *Vs.* Simeon, M. Nid. 5:1.)

Once we insist that the clean person bear the weight of the unclean, it is natural to add that the clean person must bear the greater part of the weight of the unclean, and that is Simeon's contribution to the position inaugurated by Judah. The matter of beds and chairs in the scale, of course, is an embellishment of Simeon's view with an issue not intrinsic to the statement of that view. If the objects are suitable for sitting and lying, then, when they bear the weight of the Zab, even as transferred through a balance, they are made unclean with *midras*-uncleanness. Simeon's basic position is repeated. One chair or one bed is deemed to have borne the greater part of the weight of the Zab, but several beds in the opposite scale from the Zab self-evidently do not. The shifting of the food and drink, whether they are carried upward or downward, of course, means the objects are unclean, having been carried by the Zab.

*3. M. 4:1E: A Zab who knocked against the balcony and a loaf of heave-offering bread fell down—it is clean.

*3. Vibration, not direct pressure, caused the bread to fall. Accordingly, we distinguish between pressure direct-

M. 4:2-3/T. 4:5-7: If a Zab knocked against a firm object and a loaf of heave-offering fell from it, it is clean. If the Zab knocked against an infirm object and the loaf fell, it is unclean. See *Yavneh, No. 1, above, Nos. 1, 2*.

ly applied and that which derives indirectly, e.g., from the vibrations of the Zab's pressure.
If something falls by the force of the Zab's shifting, it is unclean, but if by the force of the tremor, it is clean.

The final Ushan entry completes the development of the line of thought inaugurated by Joshua. The matter of pressure now is fully worked out by Judah, Meir, and Simeon. What are the limits of pressure? They are set by the distinction between direct and indirect consequences of the Zab's shifting. The balcony has borne and absorbed the pressure of the Zab. The loaf of heave-offering which fell down did not fall because of the direct pressure of the Zab, but only as a secondary consequence of that pressure, vibration. The Ushan attestations for the present set are confirmed by the secondary and derivative character of the principle herein expressed.

D. *After Usha*

No pertinent rulings are attributed to Rabbi and his contemporaries.

Reconsiderations

The relationship between Joshua's general rule and the refinements accomplished by the several Ushans is clear. What is begun in an item attributed to Yavneh is refined and developed in items attributed to Usha. This unit is a model of the way in which principles assigned to earlier authorities generate refinements or applications assigned to later authorities.

iv. THE STAGES OF THE LAW

We now review the foregoing results, this time grouping all materials we have assigned to the several periods, without regard to their division among the diverse topics. We therefore see how the law seems to have evolved by the end of the several periods among which we divide it. Zabim comprises three major themes. Two of them exhibit the traits of expansion and refinement over time; the third is complete before 70 and produces only a minor improvement thereafter. The sequence beginning with the Houses on becoming a Zab is characterized by a tight interplay between one stratum and the next. That is all the more the case with the named pericopae commencing with Joshua on the matter of *midras*, spelled out by Ushans for Zabim in terms of the pressure exerted by the Zab. The modes of transfer of uncleanness, by contrast, begin in Scripture, with such development as they are subjected to complete by 70. (The refinement of an Eliezer/Eleazar, possibly Yavnean, possibly Ushan, is minor and yields only some glosses of established rules, and the purpose of the rules is not to set forth the conflict with Eliezer/Eleazar.) This third item is handsomely intertwined with the conception of Joshua that when one is subject to the transfer of uncleanness, he imparts uncleanness to food at two removes, and when the uncleanness is no longer under transmission, he imparts uncleanness to food at one remove. That matter, of course, is part of the larger Yavnean inquiry into the greater susceptibility to receive uncleanness of heave-offering and Holy Things, on the one side, than of ordinary food, on the other. The removes of uncleanness are integral to the development of that theme. Description of the law as it existed in the several stages requires only rapid review.

Before 70

The Scriptural legacy upon which our tractate is based already has been described in detail (pp. 175-183). Part of the legacy to the authorities before 70, and, we have no reason to doubt, to the authorities who come even before the Houses after the turn of the first century A.D., certainly has been specified in our account of the clear implication of Scripture; another part is likely to be contained within what we have deemed the secondary meaning of Scripture. (The origin of the terminology, e.g., *midras* and *maddaf*, is not equivalently clear, nor can we be certain that the homogenization of diverse forms of pressure under the term, *midras*, and its differentiation, as at M. 2:4, into diverse acts, all of which produce *midras*-uncleanness, are equally early.) In any event so far as we claim to account for the history of the legal ideas of Zabim, we simply allege that whatever Scripture states explicitly and much that is derived from Scripture merely by generalizing on details given in Scripture form the fundamental antecedents to the work of the Houses and others in the period before 70. Of greater weight, as at Niddah, Zabim commences its development not in Scripture but among that group which determined to take seriously, therefore to study with great care, Scripture on the subject of the Zab. That group or circle self-evidently takes shape before the turn of the first century A.D., but we have no way of estimating the time at which it did its work on this tractate or on any other.

    1. 1A1: The Houses agree that three occurrences of flux confirm a man as a Zab. Two appearances confirm that he is unclean as a Zab. The third is needed to impose the requirement to bring a sacrifice. They disagree on the rule which applies if a clean day interrupts the sequence of the three occurrences. Underlying the disagreement seems to be a conflict on the determinative analogy, Zabah or semen.
    2. 1A2: The Houses agree that any flux which occurs during the counting of the seven clean days causes the man to lose the clean days already counted. The issue has to do with semen. Is it deemed unclean as if it were flux? Yes, the Shammaites maintain, and therefore the man loses the antecedent clean days. No, the Hillelites hold. The man is unclean on that day—Scripture says so explicitly, Lev. 15: 16-18—but not by reason of flux.

There is no relationship whatever between the unattributed conceptions developed from Scripture and the Houses' materials. The interest of the Houses, as we observed, is in a secondary matter in regard to confirming the beginning of the uncleanness of the Zab, which means that, before their time, the basic conception that three fluxes are required for the sacrifice, but two (merely) to impart uncleanness to bed and chair, had been established. The second ruling, on the relationship of semen to flux, deals with the opposite aspect, the end of uncleanness. As we now see, both rulings generate secondary developments at Yavneh.

Yavneh

    1. 1B1: Clarifications of 1A1's protasis: Do we there deal with one flux, then a clean day, then two, or two fluxes, a clean day, then one? All parties concur that two fluxes confirm the man as to uncleanness.
    2. 1B2: He who sees semen on the second day loses the day before it, so Ishmael. 'Aqiva: All the same is the second or third day, the Shammaites say the man loses both days, the Hillelites, only that day.
    3. 1B3: The flow of semen is deemed unclean only if it cannot be attributed to some external cause, such as eating, drinking, fantasizing, or the like. Semen which flows as if it were flux but caused by constraint of that sort is not unclean as flux.
    4. 3B1: What can be used for lying or sitting is made unclean through *midras*-uncleanness, even though such an object is not actually used for lying or sitting, so Joshua, in the context of the menstruating woman.

5. 3B2: Uncleanness imparted under the affect of the mode of transfer of uncleanness makes the person so contaminated unclean as a Father, and that uncleanness remaining after the cessation of transfer leaves the person in the first remove of uncleanness, so Joshua.

[6. 3B3: Eliezer on the equivalence of carriage to moving, touching, etc. (May not be Yavnean.)]

Yavneh witnesses three developments. First, the Houses' materials undergo refinement and definition, Nos. 1-2. Second, the definition of semen which is deemed to be flux is greatly improved by the consideration of constraint, No. 3, an entry which thematically is a continuation of the foregoing but in principle is new. Finally, Joshua's ruling at No. 4 stands behind the whole Ushan component on the same theme. No. 5 is intertwined with the diverse modes of transfer of uncleanness (M. 5:1-12), but I see no development of the principle, merely a highly elaborate restatement, through weaving together with a quite separate set of rules.

Usha

1. 1C1: Refinement of 1B3.
2. 1C2: Refinement of 1B3.
3. 1C3: Expansion of the principle of 1B3.
4. 3C1: The Zab and clean person who sat on a boat, raft, etc., even if their clothes do not touch, produce *midras*-uncleanness for the clothes of the clean person. This restates Joshua's principle, with diverse positions on refining it.
5. 3C2: Something is made unclean by the Zab's sitting or lying only if it bears the greater part of the weight of the Zab.
6. 3C3: The vibration, not direct pressure, caused by the Zab does not constitute shifting and does not impart uncleanness to a loaf of bread made of heave-offering of flour.

Self-evidently, all the Ushan materials develop antecedent conceptions.

v. The Two Torahs: Scripture and the Sources of Uncleanness of Mishnah Negaim, Niddah, and Zabim

We have now to appreciate the striking fact that Zabim is nothing more than a compilation and extension of principles of uncleanness laid down in Scripture. To do so, we must distinguish the three tractates which deal with sources of uncleanness, Negaim, Niddah, and Zabim, from those which deal with the locus of uncleanness and with the removal of uncleanness, Kelim, the shank of Ohalot, Parah,

Miqvaot, and the rabbinical tractates, Tohorot and Makhshirin. When we review the first four, we see that their fundamental and generative conceptions bear no resemblance to anything laid down in the Priestly Code, although the articulation of details of the law responds to specific verses of Scripture. The last two, Tohorot and Makhshirin, in any event begin after 70 and either ignore Scripture or utterly reverse its implications by introducing considerations undreamt of in the Priestly Code. Zabim. Niddah, and Negaim, by contrast, all spin out Scriptural conceptions, with scarcely a single generative idea, let alone fundamental presupposition, not explicitly stated within the Priestly Code.

Kelim begins in the original conception that utensils not in the Temple and not for use in the cult are subject to uncleanness. Neither Scripture nor the exegesis of Scripture generated that revolutionary conception (Part III, pp. 383-4). The prologue of Ohalot (M. Oh. 1:1-3:5) deals with things which contaminate in the tent, or through overshadowing, and the epilogue (M. Oh. 16:3-18:10) with graveyards, thus grounds or substances which contaminate as does the corpse. Nothing in these sections on sources of uncleanness equivalent to the corpse does more than extend and fill out the Scriptural rule of corpse-uncleanness itself. Accordingly, laws on sources of corpse-uncleanness in the opening and closing parts of Ohalot stand upon the foundation of Scripture, with remarkably little exegesis. When, however, we deal with the shank of the tractate, M. 3:6-16:2, and turn to the subtle interplay between the Tent and the utensil, we leave the Scriptural domain entirely. Not a single concept or presupposition derives directly or indirectly from the exegesis of Scripture. The proposition that corpse-uncleanness passes through a handbreadth of open space and its passage may be prevented by a handbreadth of closed space, which stands behind every major and formative conception of the shank of Ohalot, is autonomous. The obvious difference is that the prologue and epilogue deal with sources of uncleanness, and the body of the tractate, with the locus, the definition of the Tent affected by the corpse (Part V, pp. 225-234).

Parah presents a noteworthy contrast to Scripture. Num. 19:1-20 take for granted that the rite of burning the red cow is conducted in a state of uncleanness, since it is not performed in the tent of meeting. Participating in the rite makes a person unclean. Parah by contrast assumes that a high degree of cleanness characterizes all those who participate in the rite as well as utensils used therein.

The tractate spells out the requirements of cleanness in preparing the ash, drawing the water, and participating in the cult (Part X, pp. xi-xii). Parah deals not with sources of uncleanness, but with the locus of cleanness (Part X, pp. 220-222). The cleanness-rules of Parah create in the world outside the cult a place of cleanness analogous to the cult. The main point of the Priestly Code is that for cultic purposes purification is attained through the application of blood, or through immersion in living water, or through sunset. But for purification Miqvaot speaks only of immersion in the appropriate pool, or, self-evidently, a flowing stream. Miqvaot accepts immersion in a pool of water, the natural properties of which have not been affected by human agency. Since the purpose of immersion is the attainment of cultic purity, they take a position quite outside that imagined in Scripture. In Parah we create a place for a sacrifice outside of the Temple, a place of cleanness and holiness. In Miqvaot we call into being a means of attaining cleanness outside of the Temple, a kind of water not used for the Temple described in the Priestly Code. Spring water (which serves as well) is different from rain water. The one is exceptional, the other ordinary, the one flows with force, the other stands still, the one (Miqvaot says) cleans in any amount, the other serves the body or the utensil only in the volume of forty *seahs*. The spring water, which can purify for the cult and for the table alike, therefore has traits quite distinct from the sort of water which serves for the table. That is as it should be, for the difference between the altar of the Temple and the table of the home, both to be clean, to be sure, is not to be obscured (Part XIV, pp. 193-205).

Two tractates deal not with the sources of uncleanness but with the processes, the affects *upon* food and drink, of the several sources of uncleanness. Both begin their history after 70 and both express deeply rabbinical concerns. Tractate Tohorot bears no close tie to Scripture at all (Part XII, p. 2). True, an effort is made to ground rules on removes of uncleanness, in particular of unconsecrated food, in Scriptural exegesis. But the exegesis is blatantly *post facto*; no claim is made that the exegesis goes back to hoary antiquity. It is difficult to see that the legal achievements of Yavneh and Usha rest upon a considerable antecedent corpus of laws or even of principles. It looks to me as though the primary contribution of the authorities before 70 to Tohorot is the general notion that cleanness applies to foods and liquids consumed outside of the Temple. In the matter of removes of uncleanness as related to degrees of sanctification of such food, the clear evidence is that the issue is first investigated after 70. Opinions attributed to Yavneans contain the basic suppositions, and these are under dispute. Most of the pericopae of Tohorot on doubts in connection with uncleanness are assigned to Ushans. Similarly, with respect to how people who keep cleanness-rules deal with those who do not, we may suppose that before 70 some sort of corpus of principles may have existed, for the problem begins when a few people undertake to keep the laws among many who do not. But the systematization of principles is not all that the Ushans have accomplished. They also appear to set down principles, because they debate the most fundamental questions on the relationship between the 'am ha'areṣ and the ḥaver.

While Makhshirin depends upon the datum of Scripture (Lev. 11:24, 38) that produce is susceptible to uncleanness only when it is wet, that tractate begins in an interest absent in Scripture, which is in the character of the liquid which imparts wetness, therefore susceptibility to uncleanness, and in the way in which the liquid happens to come upon produce. In fact, the tractate's first principle, its distinction between liquids which do and do not impart susceptibility to uncleanness, derives from circles including 'Aqiva, and its second principle, the distinction between intentional and unintentional wetting down, assuredly comes to us from 'Aqiva, in a direct line from Abba Yosé-Joshua. The tractate as a whole begins its major conceptual development with 'Aqiva. What forms its center and unifies its diverse pericopae into a single, remarkably coherent document is the thought of 'Aqiva on the principal role of human intention in activating the supernatural forces of uncleanness, a view which does not begin in, and is not produced by exegesis of, Scripture (Part XVII, pp. 1-6, 178-222). We therefore notice once more that what the foregoing tractates have in common is an interest in the locus of uncleanness and the processes by which uncleanness affects and is removed from that locus.

We now come to the three tractates which give laws of *sources* of uncleanness. Negaim contains not a single generative idea except for the distinction between *negaʿ* and *ṣaraʿat*, which, once drawn, makes no difference whatsoever in the articulation of the law (Part VIII, p. xii). Negaim, which provides an account of one source of uncleanness, follows, except where it improves upon, the thematic agendum of Leviticus Chapters Thirteen and Fourteen (Part VI, pp. 2-18, Part VIII, p. 221). No primary theme or supposition of Mishnah diverges from what is explicit in Scripture. True, *nega'* and *sara'at* are separate diseases, with the former laid under the examination of the rabbi. But in no way does *nega'* as a source of uncleanness differ from *sara'at* as a source of uncleanness (Part VIII, pp. 244-250). When we first encountered the fact that Scripture and Mishnah simply go over the same ground, we found it difficult to account for because of contrary results for Kelim and Ohalot (Part VIII, pp. 257-8). Negaim then seemed to present an exception to a well-established rule of the autonomy of Mishnah, Oral Torah, from the Priestly Code, Written Torah. The law of Niddah begins in Scripture and rises in necessarily sequential and logical stages therefrom. Accordingly, the laws of that tractate clearly begin at the point at which someone determined to undertake a careful reading of Scripture on the matter of Niddah and draw practical consequences from the results of that reading. There is not a single principle which Scripture does not supply. In Niddah we do not discover a single central conception of Mishnah which stands apart from, let alone at variance with, the Written Torah. Mishnah serves essentially to fill out areas opened, but left undefined, by Scripture (Part XVI, pp. 1-6, 194-211).

Accordingly, the three tractates, Negaim, Niddah, and Zabim, devoted to the materials of Leviticus Chapters Twelve, Thirteen, Fourteen, and Fifteen, those chapters of the Priestly Code which specify sources of uncleanness apart from unclean creatures, and M. Ohalot Chapters One-Three and Sixteen-Eighteen, bear a single relationship to Scripture. All begin in the Scriptural conceptions as to the uncleanness of the *mesora'*, the menstruating woman, the Zabah, the Zab, the woman after childbirth, and the corpse. Among the sources of major uncleanness mentioned in the Priestly Code, Mishnah treats these at great length and in much detail. What the tractates have in common is that none of them innovates in any regard. All of them draw out tendencies and implications of Scripture. In their fundamental and generative conceptions, they constitute little more than secondary and derivative developments of the conceptions of the Priestly Code. By contrast, the tractates which define objects susceptible to uncleanness, areas in which, and processes by which, uncleanness takes place, and modes of purification from uncleanness contracted by such objects and in such areas, all have in common the simple fact that Scripture contributes little of generative consequence.

The Oral Torah therefore is autonomous and distinct from the written Torah in respect to two dimensions of the tripartite realm of purity: (1) sources of uncleanness (including modes of transfer of uncleanness), (2) objects of uncleanness (including food and drink), and (3) means for the removal of uncleanness. The Oral Torah is entirely dependent for its principles upon the written one in regard to sources of uncleanness. The Oral Torah—Mishnah Seder Tohorot—does not contain a single new source of major uncleanness. Apart from adding analogous substances and the idol, it scarcely specifies any object or substance or person or status which generates major uncleanness. Nothing causes major uncleanness which Scripture itself does not declare to be a major source of uncleanness. (M. Zab. 5:10-12 are clear on this point.)

The Oral Torah, despite the diverse traits of the relationship of various tractates to the Written Torah, is whole and harmonious. A single conception accounts for the differences characteristic of the several tractates, explaining why some begin in exegesis of Scripture and others, in autonomous and original conceptions. The reason that Mishnah, the Oral Torah, does not innovate in respect to major sources of uncleanness is that its primary focus lies elsewhere.

What Oral Torah wishes to say in completion of the whole Torah of Moses, our Rabbi, is that the locus of cleanness, therefore also of uncleanness, is in the world beyond the cult. World completes cult. The lines of structure emanating from the Temple encompass all reality. The table at home must be clean as the altar in the Temple must be clean. Domestic utensils have therefore in principle to be divided between those susceptible, and those insusceptible to uncleanness. The utensils subject to corpse-uncleanness (Num. 19:15) are distinguished from the Tent of the corpse. Means of attaining cleanness outside the cult, water, and a locus of cleanness even for sacrifice outside the cult, the place in which the rite of the red cow is conducted, are beautifully constructed. The complex rules governing food and drink are worked out at Tohorot and Makhshirin. (The contribution of the last tractates, Tebul Yom, Yadayim, and Uqsin, will be spelled out in due course.)

The Written Torah's system of uncleanness and cleanness by the Oral Torah is augmented and enriched, not revised or overturned. Nothing declared by the Written Torah to be a source of uncleanness is held to be clean in the Oral Torah. The Oral Torah adds to the sources of uncleanness specified in the Written one only analogous substances (excluding the idol, about which P knows nothing). The difference in the relationship to Scripture of the two groups of tractates, Negaim-Niddah-Zabim, on the one side, Kelim, the shank of Ohalot, Parah, Tohorot, Miqvaot, Makhshirin, on the other, accordingly begins in the distinctive and fresh perspectives of the authorities who, some time before the turn of the first century A.D., brought to the Priestly Code a peculiarly priestly interest in the analogy between sacred and secular, Temple and world, cultic altar and domestic table. Aptly might a Pharisee have said, "Think not that I have come to abolish the (priestly) Law. I have come not to abolish but to fulfil and complete it." And appropriate to the Order of Purities is the later rabbinical view of Mishnah as a whole: the Oral Torah indeed forms the complement and completion of the Written Torah, the dual Torah which is the *one* whole Torah of Moses, our Rabbi.

X. The Formation of the Mishnaic Law of Purities: The Cases of Kelim and of Ohalot

i. Definition

We have now made sufficient progress to ask larger historical questions. First, precisely what sort of history of Mishnaic law of purities is made possible by the materials in hand? Second, in exact detail, what historical results have we now achieved? Having completed the analysis—dissection and reconstruction—of Mishnah-Tosefta Kelim and Ohalot, forty-eight of the one hundred twenty-six chapters, nearly 40% of the Order of Purities, we now review the results.

The sort of history our sources make possible in general terms may be called history of ideas, and, more particularly, history of religious and legal-philosophical ideas. We cannot specify *when* particular intellectual events took place, but we can fairly reliably propose the order of such events. To the extent that history must be synchronic, arranging historical events, personalities and ideas so as to indicate coincidence or coexistence, our success is modest. For in only a few instances can we show the interplay between a major idea, on the one side, and a particular personality or event, on the other. The sole event, the destruction of the Temple, and the few really formative personalities—ᶜAqiva and his disciples in the second century —explain and relate to a modest part of the larger corpus of laws and conceptions. To be sure, history as diachrony, the analysis of changes extending through time, also is attempted, with the qualification that we do not know much about the length of time under discussion. On the other hand, as stated (pp. 158-160), we have a fair picture of the sequence of ideas, confirmed by the relationship between the sequence suggested by logic, on the one side, and that suggested by the attributions of sayings and the consequent assignment of pericopae to particular authorities or periods, on the other.

In describing what I conceive to be the history of the Mishnaic law of purities in Kelim and Ohalot, I shall treat as conclusive the results of the commentaries and studies now completed. That requires the omission of the qualifying language implicit throughout. All that follows should be understood as introduced by, "in my opinion" and

"I think," not to mention "may have been," "perhaps," and other necessary language. I believe it is legitimate to state as a matter of fact, and to describe, the various substantive results of our inquiry to date.

Finally, I have repeatedly to stress the purpose of this study, which is to describe the history of the *Mishnaic* law of purities, to analyze data already firmly in hand. That history has a pre-history, the state of the law prior to the earliest evidences now contained within Mishnah-Tosefta, the law prior to pericopae which derive from or are attributed to the earliest named authorities. The pre-history of Mishnaic law commences (in a chronological, but not thematic or logical way) with the Priestly Code, contained in Leviticus and Numbers. What goes into, and before, that Code is hardly our problem. The ancient rabbis solved the difficulty of supplying a history to the law in their hands by assigning the title, "Torah," to what they had, just as what they had received in Scripture also was called by them "Torah." The one was Oral, the other Written, Torah.

At the end we shall ask about the logical and conceptual relationships between the one Torah and the other. The interrelationship between Mishnah = Oral Torah and the Priestly Code = Written Torah for our Order must be described from an other-than-historical perspective.

ii. INTRODUCTORY OBSERVATIONS

Neither Kelim nor Ohalot begins in the Priestly Code. Neither tractate develops the lines laid out therein. Indeed, the most fundamental convictions of both tractates lie wholly outside of Scripture. For Kelim the issue is the susceptibility and insusceptibility to impurity of various utensils. For Ohalot the issue is the nature and functioning of Tents (and utensils). Scriptural law knows little of either issue. The Mishnaic conception that we must ask about the susceptibility of one object as against that of another is utterly alien to those few references to Scripture which are even relevant to the laws of Kelim. The question, what is a Tent? would be ludicrous to the authority behind Num. 19:11-22, for he takes for granted that a Tent is a tent.

Proof of the irrelevance of Scripture to the two Mishnaic tractates is contained in the exegetical compilations which purport to link the Oral Torah to the wholly Written one. Sifra has virtually nothing which, in conception, let alone in articulation, does not correlate with Mishnah-Tosefta as completed compilations. Sifré on Numbers does have exegeses which clearly seem in conception prior to, and in formulation autonomous from, anything in Mishnah. But these accomplish virtually nothing in linking Scripture to the underlying conceptions of the Tent (which are far, far earlier than our tractate's inquiry). And even if, for both tractates, we had considerably richer collections of exegesis, we can hardly claim that many specific laws have been worked out in response to the exegesis (let alone eisegesis) of the Scriptures. The contrary is the case. Perhaps the exegetes took for granted that the bed-rock convictions of the laws also were assumed by the Scriptures. But they still have not shown us where, in Scripture, they locate those laws or principles, and I think the probable explanation is that they could not. That is why they remind us that Ohalot has much law but little Scripture.

When, therefore, we refer to Scripture in seeking the beginnings, the pre-Mishnaic history, of Mishnaic law, we commit an error of gross anachronism. To put it very simply: Kelim begins somewhere, but not in Leviticus. At some stage in its early history, however, the law responded to such verses in Leviticus as seemed relevant to it, though the law's datum, its basic assumption, comes before the inquiry into Scripture. The problem of Ohalot, of course, is somewhat different, for the appended tractates, fore and aft, M. 1:1-3:5, M. 16:3-18:10, do little more than add some clarifications and explications to what Scripture tells us about corpse-contamination and modes by which corpse-contamination is conveyed. Yet the Tents, the processes of overshadowing, of which Ohalot speaks, bear no relationship whatever to the tent, the real tent, in which a person has died, mentioned by Numbers 19:11, 14-16, etc. We have, consequently, to address ourselves first to what is everywhere taken for granted, and only second to what is found pertinent in the Priestly Code to that datum of the law, its primary conception.

Implicit in the contents and concept of Oral Torah therefore is the notion of the independence and autonomy of that Oral Torah. If, as I have suggested, the Mishnaic law is separate and autonomous from Scripture, though in its unfolding it is made to interrelate, where it can, to Scripture, then we must wonder whether we have not simply stated in historical language what the ancient rabbis meant in speaking, to begin with, of two Torahs, one in writing, the other transmitted orally. It certainly is a drastic misstatement of the facts to see these two Torahs as interrelated in their beginnings, so far as the pertinent and reciprocally relevant segments of Leviticus and Numbers, Kelim and Ohalot, are concerned. It is an accurate statement of the fact to regard Leviticus and Numbers as a Torah, Kelim and Ohalot as another, separate but correlative one. The authorities of Mishnah-Tosefta do not derive their laws from Scriptures. On occasion they do twist Scriptures to make them fit preconceived conclusions. The implicit question of the exegetical compilations on the law is, "How do we know X from the Torah," with X the given law or belief, and the problem being to justify it from Scripture, not to find out what Scripture teaches about that subject. If we started with Scripture and asked what it taught, we should never, *never* discover even the simplest datum of rabbinic law. When we start with the answer—the rabbinic law—and ask how Scripture can be made to justify that law, the answers are anything but perspicuous. That the authorities of Mishnah-Tosefta understood these facts full well seems strongly implied by their mythic view of two Torahs, one written, the other oral.

iii. History of Kelim

The pre-history of the Mishnaic law of Kelim begins with the assumption that the status as to uncleanness of utensils outside of the cult is consequential. That is, extra-cultic utensils should be kept clean for any purpose whatever. If we have no reason to consider the status of the utensils, we also have no cause to begin with to investigate whether they are susceptible to uncleanness or insusceptible to uncleanness. Since only the Pharisees, among those known to us, thought someone who was not a priest had to keep pure outside of the cult (the Essene community at Qumran is a special case), we need not doubt the fundamental conception of Kelim is part of the primary structure of Pharisaism. The laws of Kelim do not begin before Pharisaism in the formulation given it by lay people pretending to be priests.

The one specific concept characteristic of the Mishnaic law of Kelim, beginning to end, is that a utensil which is susceptible to uncleanness is one which is whole, complete, useful—normal. *That* notion is to be discovered in Scripture (III, p. 368). Leviticus 11:33 tells us that to clean an unclean utensil, one has to break it, make it useless. Then a utensil which can become unclean is one which is not broken, which is useful. The same exegete can have understood a utensil—a KLY—to be defined in the same place, "Every KLY made of any material" refers to anything at all; "any KLY used for any purpose" limits the foregoing to useful objects only. Autonomy, distinctiveness follow in the wake of purpose.

A second important, early concept is that utensils are regarded as divided into their inside or inner part and their outside or outer part. The first implication of that division is that something which has a 'midst' or an inner part or a receptacle is susceptible to uncleanness, and something which does not—which is flat—is insusceptible. Lev. 11:33 readily generated that concept. To be sure, that Scripture in the first place need not have brought the idea into mind. The importance of a receptacle in containing uncleanness may have derived from the larger notion of uncleanness. If one conceived uncleanness as a kind of gas of heavy viscosity, which will flow every which way unless it is contained within some receptacle—a utensil or a Tent—but which then will be kept in that one place, then the importance of the receptacle depends not upon Lev. 11:33 but upon a quite separate conception of the material qualities of uncleanness. Accordingly, the first major development in the formation of the law of the susceptibility of domestic utensils stresses two points, usefulness as the definitive criterion of what is a utensil which can be made unclean, and the presence of a receptacle as the requisite for the containment of uncleanness. Other early rules or conceptions cannot be so readily formulated.

If we stand back from this first stage and ask what the Written Torah has contributed to the Oral Torah, the question may be simply answered. The Written Torah has said that those things which break the natural rhythm of life are unclean. The Oral Torah has said that those things which, among all objects, serve, or are part of, the normal course of life are susceptible to becoming unclean. The abnormal affects what is normal.

The Yavneans raise the further, still fundamental questions on the susceptibility of utensils. These begin with the simple one: At what point does a utensil become susceptible to uncleanness? And in regard to a random and insusceptible object, must we process it for use in order to subject it to uncleanness? And if we must, then how much adaptation must be carried out? The principle is that an object must have a specific and distinctive purpose and must be irrevocably processed for that particular purpose. These are most basic matters indeed.

The Ushans then raise the matter of the processing of various distinctive materials: wood, leather, bone, matting, a tube, gourd, horn, glass, and the like. Thus while the Yavneans do not seem to differentiate among various materials, but treat all objects in a single theory as to the general traits of utensils of any substance, i.e., presence or absence of a receptacle, the Ushans go on to differentiate one sort of material from another, e.g., whether or not the receptacle is made of a substance which lasts permanently. The matter of adaptation is further developed. Among the Ushans, intention is the criterion. Intention alone is insufficient to render an object insusceptible; we require some form of permanent and irrevocable adaptation.

The Yavnean rulings on the susceptibility of specific materials are of little consequence. As we saw, those on the susceptibility of objects come down to a single issue: Does the object have a receptacle? If it does, it is susceptible, and if it does not, it is insusceptible. A second criterion, for metal objects, is whether they are autonomous or are part of some other object. Do they have a 'name' of their own? Clearly, an object also must function properly. If it is broken, it is clean.

Yavneh also produces long lists of specific objects which are or are not susceptible. These lists yield the principles already stated. A utensil to be susceptible must have a receptacle, be fully processed and available for routine use, have a distinctive and permanent character. A broken object is useless and clean; a whole and distinctive object is useful and unclean. To these principles the Ushans add the concept that use is defined in terms of intention or human needs, a refinement of the idea of use by supplying the criterion: to whom must the object be useful? A further refinement concerns the receptacle. We require a receptacle, but what if it serves only imperfectly? Again, what criterion determines distinctive character, shape, or purpose? Is it function or form? Do we depend upon a formal trait or the use to which the utensil is put? If an object must serve man, must it serve man all the time? If we have two materials, how do we know which is primary? Is it that which is fundamental to the function or the form of the utensil? Time and again we observe the mode of thought characteristic of Ushans: to improve, refine, discern complexity and subtlety. Even their innovations are dependent, in the final analysis, upon available conceptions. Much as we may admire the genius of the Ushans, it is a fundamentally derivative genius which is theirs. The Yavneans, both those known to us by name as well as others whose ideas are subsumed into the law as a whole, laid the foundations and set forth the outlines of the law. And when we do know the name of the Yavnean responsible for the most fruitful developments in the law, it is, time and again, ᶜAqiva.

The matter of connection for the transmission of uncleanness from one part of an object to another and for the completion of the processes of purification is treated at Yavneh in a fairly simple way. Yavneans (ᶜAqiva) see the important question as whether the materials of which an object is composed firmly adhere to one another. If they stick together, they are connected for contamination or purification. The Ushans refine this conception, holding that form (adherence), that is the nature of the material alone, is not decisive. The question is, how do the materials function together. If the connector functions normally is tandem with the primary object, it is connected. Yavneans (Eliezer) also stress that we have to have a permanent, physical connection to produce shared susceptibility. Ushans refine the matter. They lay particular stress on whether the attached object functions along with the primary one, that is, whether the normal functioning of an object is permitted with the attachment. If not, then we do not regard the attachment as connected.

As to dividing utensils into inner and outer parts, the Yavneans are clear that such division is taken for granted. It also seems clear that the Hillelite conception, that the status of the inside of a utensil determines the condition of the whole, is taken for granted in the Yavnean rulings, even though in the period before 70, the question was moot. The Ushan improvement is to distinguish between formal and functional differentiation. The part which carries out an object's primary function is "inner," and that which does not is outer. Or the part which is, in form, on the inside, is inner.

Susceptibility comes to an end when an object is broken. The Yavneans do not move beyond the Scriptural principle. But one important improvement occurs. If we change the function of an object, we change its status as to susceptibility. The Ushans turn attention to the end of susceptibility of objects made of leather, wood, bone, and other materials. As before, so now they speak not of the traits of objects in general but of the qualities of specific materials. The Ushans refine matters in another respect. Once we hold the useless object is clean, the Ushans ask about the case in which the broken object or sherd still works more or less as it did before. If it does, it is not "useless." So the meaning of "breaking" or damage is refined. We consider not only a break in form, but whether the break prevents functioning. Ushans also hold that if a utensil can carry out a secondary function even though it cannot perform its original one, it is still susceptible. Other Ushans reject this viewpoint. If an object serves, but not in a normal or comfortable way, it is no longer susceptible.

The Ushans take account of the intention of the maker. Intention alone will not annul the effects of an action. The change must be marked and irreversible.

The Ushans make several highly suggestive but minor refinements as well. They ask whether the completion of process of manufacture can be carried out by an ordinary person, or whether only a skilled craftsman can do it. Second, they ask whether an object is useful only to a poor person or to anyone, poor or rich. They ask about whether one must actually carry out a deed or merely intend to do so before an object becomes insusceptible. And, finally, they ask about changing one object into another sort of object.

Sherds and remnants fall, for Yavneans, within the generalization that "breaking is purifying." If a remnant of a utensil works as the whole utensil did, it is still susceptible. How do we know it continues to be functional? Eliezer says the matter is relative to the original use. Then the Ushans reject a fixed measure, following ʿAqiva who rejects that notion. They offer two criteria, either that of a relative measure, or that of the function of the utensil. Sherds are susceptible when serviceable, or sherds are never susceptible. The Yavneans leave open two issues. How to determine uselessness? And what to do with the useful sherds? As we see, the Ushans split on this second matter, one holding a useful sherd is susceptible, the other denying the sherd is susceptible at all, seeing it as fully broken.

In general, the Ushans will do one of the following to materials received from Yavneh: (1) continue the received principles without alteration or development, but apply them in many new cases; (2) develop and apply established principles; or (3) introduce subtleties and refinements.

iv. History of Ohalot

The main lines of the history of Ohalot are somewhat confused. The reason is that we have two separate conceptions of what we mean by "tent," the one, a real tent, in which someone can live or die, the other a figurative or imaginary "container," a Tent of sufficient size not for a human being but for that which exudes from the human being upon death. Our tractate clearly speaks sometimes of the one, at other times of the other.

The history of Mishnaic rules on the real tent is relatively simple to outline. We have a few somewhat complex inquiries into the parts, e.g., projections, of such a tent, the divisions of the sides or cover-fabric of such a tent, and related matters, along with some slight clarifications of what Scripture means by the corpse which contaminates in a tent. The history of the Mishnaic rules on the imaginary Tent and on overshadowing is of course far more difficult, occupying the bulk of our tractate. We have two major notions. First comes the Tent as a real, formal container, with a door and walls. Second we have the Tent as anything with requisite size which overshadows a corpse, the Tent as "that which overshadows" or interposes.

The Tent as a formal container, that which can hold what exudes from the corpse upon death, which must be a cubic handbreadth, produces the further question about the relationship between the Tent, with its rules, and the utensil, with its own laws. That this conception arises early in the history of the Mishnaic law is shown by Eliezer's importance in the development of the latter matter. Ushans, moreover, investigate the consequences of the conception of the Tent-as-a-house.

Both notions—the Tent as that which overshadows, or interposes against corpse-uncleanness, and the Tent as that which contains corpse-uncleanness—begin in a conception wholly alien to Scripture. This idea is that corpse-uncleanness ("the soul" for Philo) is sufficiently thick to pass through an area of a square handbreadth, on the one side, or to be contained by a cover of that same size, on the other. Scripture knows nothing about the space required to contain or to prevent the passage of that effusion. When we leave the realm of the real tent in which real people live and begin to define the matter in terms of the standard measure, the squared or cubic handbreadth, then the tent becomes the Tent, and the pre-history of our tractate commences. We have seen abundant evidence that that conception lies far, far earlier than the pericopae attributed to the earliest authorities in our Mishnah-tractate.

We can hardly be surprised by the evidences of the relatively greater antiquity, the longer pre-history of Ohalot, as compared to the pre-history of Kelim. Kelim, after all, cannot have started before someone supposed domestic utensils may be subject to uncleanness, and that uncleanness matters so far as the use of such utensils in the home is concerned. By contrast, corpse-uncleanness was immensely significant for the cult, as Num. 19:11ff. states explicitly. The laws and conceptions concerning the Tent can have arisen in any group to which uncleanness produced by being overshadowed by a roof over a corpse, or by being in the same house with a corpse, was important. It goes without saying that that sort of uncleanness, important specifically to the priests, will have been subject to much reflection from the promulgation of the Priestly Code onward. The relative difference in the depth of the antecedent exegetical materials and of the earlier conceptions, the deep layers of profound thought which seem to lie underneath even the earliest Mishnaic rules, are hardly surprising. But the facts we have thus far adduced simply do not lead us beyond that simple observation. Further conjecture or speculation seems without purpose. Domestic utensils mattered only to Pharisees to whom the table at home was like the altar of the cult. Corpse-uncleanness was important to the priesthood. The two tractates therefore probably arise in quite different circumstances. They are linked solely by the concept of uncleanness, a homogeneous notion which links together many quite separate phenomena.

In Ohalot we find hardly any development in Scriptural conceptions of sources of uncleanness, rather a refinement of the sole important principle: a corpse contaminates what is with it in the Tent. What the Oral Torah adds is that things which are like a corpse function as does the corpse, not much of an advance. The specification of burial areas and other land which is unclean as is the corpse changes little. These additional sources of uncleanness can come from any source; the process is agglutinative.

To this matter the Ushans add one major innovation, consideration of the principle of connection, which, as in regard to connection in Kelim, seems to have been the contribution of Ushans in particular. For Ohalot what is important is that with materials deriving from a corpse, connection applies only when it is natural, not man-made.

A further Ushan contribution is the set of distinctions so handsomely constructed in M. 18:2-4, the three kinds of grave-area, together with what one may and may not plant in them and do with their dirt. This construction is what one would expect from Ushans: architectonically brilliant, but in no way ground-breaking. The larger Ushan contribution is to introduce secondary issues about who owns a field, the owner's intention, the possibility of creating one grave-area out of another, and the like. The Houses know only "the grave-area," while the Ushans tell us about three, a formal progression revealing a deepening of logical tools but not logical expansion or innovative conceptions.

The Houses take for granted that what lies outside of the exit of a Tent will be contaminated by the effusion of corpse-uncleanness.

This is the foundation of their dispute in M. 7:3. The size of the egress, a handbreadth, is of course taken for granted. The secondary conception of the contamination effected through the exits clearly is based upon the exegesis of Sifré Num. The Houses assume that conception as well, their only problem being *when* the exit has to have been created which will channel all the uncleanness through itself and leave the other exits unaffected. Here we have five stages in logic: (1) the standard measure, (2) the egress of the standard measure, (3) the affect upon what is subject to the exit, (4) the notion that if we are sure the corpse-matter will exude through one exit, other exits are unaffected, and finally (5) the idea that if we have such a designated exit, it has to have been designated at an appropriate time. Yet if we consider this last item, it hardly is a natural outcome of the earlier ones. After all, at stage four, we have nothing to require us to impose the matter of intention (the issue of stage five) upon the law. And even stage four is problematic. Why should the designation of a single exit have any affect upon the uncleanness? All we know is that it naturally exudes. Why should it naturally also respond to our actions, let alone our intentions or wishes, as to its means of effusion?

The primary conception of Ohalot, as I said, the view of a tent as a Tent, that which can contain what exudes or effuses from a corpse, begins the processes by which our tractate took shape. ᶜAqiva's view that the Tent combines the contaminating effects of all that is in its shadow supplies to the Tent an active role in the spreading uncleanness, treats the Tent as a positive, transitive force, which, as it were, takes over the effusion and shapes or moulds it (much as the body takes an active role in containing the soul). Perhaps what he has done is penetrate the deepest implication of interpreting tent as Tent. For once tent becomes Tent—the dimension of the standard measure, with all that that implies—then the next stage is to attribute to the Tent a formative force in the process of contamination. That is to say, with ᶜAqiva what becomes important is the meaning of ᵓHL as (active) *overshadowing*, rather than as (passive) *Tent*. That meaning imposes its own logic. Once something affirmatively acts by overshadowing, that active or transitive force dominates matters. The two names for our tractate, *Ohalot* and *Ahilot* (Goldberg, p. 9), therefore appear in retrospect to contain within themselves the two large, conflicting (or, at least, not wholly harmonious) notions, the one, *Tent* as a formal entity, the other *overshadowing* as process or function, or, more simply still, a noun as against a verb, a structure or thing as against a process. That will account for the two conceptions' existing side by side in the tractate, the one built upon the formal structure and traits of a building, with projections, flaps, and so forth, the other formed upon the way in which materials, however formed, either interpose against, or permit the transfer of, uncleanness.

Along the same lines we may interpret ᶜAqiva's reworking of the inherited dimensions: movables *contaminate* through overshadowing if they are a handbreadth in size. That is, after all, what establishes the viability of a material for interposing or permitting the transfer of uncleanness. Movables *become unclean* whatever their size. That is, they are objects of uncleanness, not agents of contamination, by virtue of their status as utensils or objects. This is nothing more than the fundamental notion of Kelim. Finally, they serve to bring uncleanness on the person who carries them if they are as thick as an ox-goad, an intermediate stage, depending upon a mode of uncleanness other than Tent. The distinction underlying ᶜAqiva's definition, therefore, is between carrying and Tent. Contact is subsumed in the second dimension, "bring uncleanness on themselves through *contact* over any surface whatever." The combining of separate sources of uncleanness, clearly an issue for Yavneans, therefore derives directly from ᶜAqiva's conception of the Tent.

The Ushans take up ᶜAqiva's mode of thinking about the Tent as an active force and follow the next issue to its foundation: Do modes of contamination work together, as ᶜAqiva has said sources of contamination may be brought together? But the issue is not logically parallel, not at all. For it is the Tent which combines the several sources of contamination. Whether or not we attribute to the Tent that active force, the result of the argument bears no implications whatever for the combining of separate *modes* by which contamination is spread. This is parallel formally, but not substantively.

The Ushans' conception of the Tent as that which interposes carries within itself the requirement to define what will interpose or diminish the requisite handbreadth, and what will not interpose but permit the passage of uncleanness. The stress of Chapter Eight is on the traits of materials, rather than the quality of objects. Materials which are permanent may serve as Tents; so too those which are insusceptible. The main point of Chapter Eight is insusceptibility. In Chapter Thirteen our interest also is in the secondary question, the combination of various sources of contamination to produce a contaminating substance.

This is a development and revision of ᶜAqiva's conception of combining through the affects of the Tent. We have the combination—but now without consideration of the Tent's active power at all.

The matter of projections from a Tent-as-a-house is worked out by Joshua and Eliezer. The primary principle is whether we create an imaginary union between an upper Tent and a lower one. I find it difficult to account for this conception, which does not appear in Mishnah and is introduced only by Tosefta. Perhaps it is read later on into the simple issue of whether a projection is part of a door or window from which it projects or regarded as entirely separate. What is of special interest here is the way in which Yavneans treat the Tent-as-a-house. The dominant tendency of Ushans, by contrast, is to dwell upon problems of Tent-as-overshadowing and Tent-as-interposition (the same thing). But we cannot claim that Tent-as-overshadowing begins in Usha and Tent-as-house ends in Yavneh. All we can propose is that the movement from the latter to the former is through ᶜAqiva's pivotal conceptions.

The Ushan case of M. 7:2 treats Tent-as-house. I think the purpose is to make two points. First, we distinguish the surfaces of the Tent and treat them as two separate objects, in contact with one another, for the purposes of uncleanness. Second, we wish to ask about whether a Tent must be a tent in form or only in function, with Simeon demanding the form of the tent, Yosé speaking solely of the function of interposition. In this instance, therefore, Ushans have revised the case in accord with the principle they wish to work out. A further instance of Ushan thought on the Tent-as-house is in M. 6:3ff., the conception of dividing the walls of a house in terms of the location of the corpse-uncleanness. Here Tent is seen in its most material, concrete, and natural guise, as a real house in which real people live. Or perhaps the use of "house" here is equivalent to "burial niche," as seems clear in some of the specific discussions, e.g., the house wall created by excavating two "houses," one on either side. If that is so for M. 6:6, then why should the remainder of the pericope not have in mind the same conception? The Ushans further deal with the problem of the relationship between two Tents and that between the space enclosed by a Tent and the space round about it. The Ushans also work out the partitions of a Tent, whether this be a whole house, as in Chapter Fifteen, or a large cabinet, as in Chapter Four.

The Ushan capacity for high abstraction is best revealed in the spelling out of the concept of the Tent-as-interposition and the working of the Tent—overshadowing—as the absence of interposition in the problem of the pot and the hatchway (M. 10:1-7). Here all that constitutes a non-"Tent" is the opening of a handbreadth, and all that constitutes "overshadowing" or Tent is the closing of that opening to less than a handbreadth. Tents no longer have walls (to be divided), flaps, entry, or projections. A Tent is now "that which has a covering of a handbreadth and egress of a handbreadth." A Tent has come to mean an *autonomous domain* signified by adequate egress and that alone. Thus what is striking in the Ushans' contribution is their working out various problems around the theme of the standard measure. This appears, for instance, in their interest in problems of egress, on the one side, and of the establishment of an autonomous domain, on the other. With the Tent so abstract as "something which interposes against, or permits the passage of, uncleanness," little is left of the classic concept of Tent except the standard measure. It is the Ushans, therefore, who take the concept of ᵓHL as Tent and show its meaning when it is understood as *overshadowing*, a major transformation.

The relationship between the pot and the Tent seems to be a problem discerned and solved primarily by Ushans. But the matter begins long before Usha, with a case which is later interpreted as a statement of a principle. Then that principle generates a whole new set of cases. The case is the Houses', and concerns the capacity for interposition of a pot. Does a clay pot protect all of its contents, as the Hillelites maintain, or only those contents which cannot be purified in a ritual pool, as the Shammaites hold? This is primary to Kelim and secondary to Ohalot. Once we ask about the clay pot in the context of Tents, we have to posit that the pot itself protects the *upper room*, the notion of the pot's "contents" thus being drastically revised. That, after all, is the only situation relevant to Ohalot in which we can impose the inherited problem. Then we are confronted with the problems of Ohalot, to which the original case was not meant to address itself. We wonder how the pot, to begin with, functions in relationship to the Tent. This produces the rule that the pot does so in "conjunction with the walls of the Tent," a classic principle based upon the conception of the Tent-as-a-house.

Once we have gone that far, what is left for the Ushans, but the effort to render the whole matter into a set of total abstractions? These begin with the question: When is a pot a pot and when is it a Tent? Clearly, that question begins with the assumption that a tent is a Tent, that is to say, something is a Tent when it measures a handbreadth. So the Ushans revise the earlier case by turning the conception of the Tent-as-a-house into that of the Tent-as-that-which-contains-the-standard measure, thus once again: the Tent is that which interposes against what exudes from a corpse or contains it.

Here, interestingly, the three stages with which we have worked, Houses, Yavneh, Usha [(1) M. 5:1-4 + ʿAqiva, (2) B. 5:5-7, (3) M. 9:1-14] correspond to the three major stages in the development of the pot/Tent relationship: (1) the Houses state their problem; (2) the Yavneans derive a principle from that problem; and, finally, (3) the Ushans treat the principle in the most abstract possible framework, thereby revising the problem and supplying it with an entirely new set of illustrations. To summarize: Once the pot protects its "contents" in the hatchway between a lower and an upper room, it is going to follow that the pot has conjoined to the hatchway, and the final stage will be to see the "pot" as some sort of Tent.

Chapter Nine, finally, lays out the several principles consequent upon the Ushans' conception of the Tent/pot relationship. When an object is a utensil, it spreads contamination but does not interpose as a Tent. When it is *not* a utensil ("pot"), it serves as a Tent. Uncleanness inside a pot is compressed and breaks forth perpendicularly, which is the same as the first point. That is, when a hive is a utensil, it is not a Tent and does not diffuse the uncleanness across its upper surface. To the contrary, the compressed uncleanness, not diffused, has the power to surge forth upward or downward through the side of the pot.

Eliezer's position about the pot as equivalent to the Tent also stands in midcourse between the Houses and Usha. Had his position, instead of ʿAqiva's, prevailed, we could not have asked about the relationship between a pot and a Tent. For so far as he was concerned, the one indeed was the equivalent of the other. If of requisite size, both Tent and pot could either interpose against, or spread, uncleanness. This matter requires that we return to Eliezer's position in M. Kel. 8:1. There Eliezer's position is that if a broken, then patched, hive is hung down into the airspace of an oven, and an insect is in the oven, food in the hive is clean, not affected by the insect in the oven. The sages say it is unclean. Now M. Kel.'s debate's formulation of Eliezer's reasoning makes his position depend upon mere consistency: "If the hive affords protection in the Tent of a corpse, which is a serious source of contamination, it surely will afford protection in the case of a clay utensil, which is a minor source of contamination." The sages say, "They divide Tents and do not divide utensils." This is the view of M. 6:1-2: Tents and utensils do differ. That reply however suggests the real—and different—basis for Eliezer's position in M. Kel. The utensil is no different from a Tent, both being divisible. In other words, M. Kel. 8:1 repeats the position of Eliezer in M. 6:1. Accordingly M. Kel. 8:1 represents Eliezer's position as a matter of logic, but M. Oh. 6:1 suggests that position is a matter of law. As noted, GRA (I, p. 185) understands Eliezer's position in exactly this way. When the hive is broken, it ceases to constitute a utensil and *then* can form a Tent. GRA is on firm grounds, for Yoḥanan b. Nuri in T. Kel. B.Q. 6:3-4 rephrases the matter exactly in terms of Tents and utensils. To which tractate is the matter of Eliezer's opinion on utensils/Tents primary? Clearly it belongs to Ohalot, to which it is integral. Repeating it in Kelim is logical, but requires an explanation of Eliezer's opinion divorced from the facts of the case and allows only the sages to tell us what really is at issue. It goes without saying that the spelling out of issues common to Kelim and Ohalot is prior to the division of materials on common problems into the separate, thematic tractates, and the working out of cases "appropriate" to each of the two tractates follows that division. Way back in the Yavnean period or even before that time will come the grand problems and conceptions of law. These most basic conceptions will then have been applied to cases relevant to the theme and subject-matter of the several tractates.

When we come to the history, within the Mishnaic law, of the prior conception of the standard measure for the Tent, we find no development, but a major, and, to me, ultimately insoluble problem. Whether man or utensils give passage to uncleanness is made to depend upon whether we have the standard measure, the hole sufficient for the passage of corpse-uncleanness. The Houses assume that corpse-uncleanness will pass only through a space at least as large as a handbreadth. A further assumption (M. 11:2-3) is that some sort of passage way has to be constructed. The corpse-uncleanness will evaporate upward, not be transferred from one domain to another, unless some sort of enclosed space of a handbreadth is provided, e.g., a reed, below the split in a roof, a handbreadth above the ground. (It is difficult to reject MA's observation that the reed is assumed a handbreadth in breadth, although the pericope contains no such suggestion.) The sole argument between the Houses in respect to men or animals is whether they contain an empty space, that is, how we regard the abdomen.

The imposition of *intention* upon the standard measure in M. 13:1ff., therefore, is exceedingly odd. The attribution to the Houses can be set aside, perhaps, with the claim that here Ushans assign as a datum of the Houses' conceptions what in fact is characteristically an Ushan concern. But what are we to make of ᶜAqiva and Ṭarfon, who assume the same? If a hole serves a useful, intended purpose, it will permit the passage of uncleanness whatever the size of the hole. This notion contradicts the (inherited) supposition of the remainder of the tractate. It furthermore has no impact whatever on any other pericope or composite. Everywhere else the standard measure alone prevails. And ᶜAqiva's and Ṭarfon's assumption, further, is that a hole made by nature will afford passage to uncleanness however small it is, while the one made by man has to be a standard measure. What Ṭarfon here tells us is that the standard measure applies to holes made by man, but nature's apertures will allow uncleanness to pass whatever their size—a strange distinction indeed. We are not going to be helped by either authority, ᶜAqiva because here he does not see the handbreadth measure as standard, Ṭarfon because he supplies us with an impossible distinction. This is a most perplexing pericope. Yet there is one *possible* solution. Judah's view that a tent made by nature is no Tent, carried to its logical end, contradicts the assumption of the Houses, M. 13:1ff., that a holes made by nature or one by man serve equally for the passage of uncleanness. Perhaps Judah's view depends upon the distinction, attributed to the Houses, between the hole made by nature and the one made by man. Or perhaps the construction at M. 13:1ff., even including Ṭarfon's and ᶜAqiva's item, is wholly Ushan, with its stress on intention, on the one hand, function (of the hole) on the second, and the distinction between man and nature, on the third.

Finally, we note that Yosé challenges the notion that, since uncleanness is bound to exude at some point, it inevitably will contaminate what is in the Tent and therefore should be regarded as already having done so, an extraneous issue, imposed on Ohalot, but congenial to our tractate.

v. Two Torahs—One Whole Torah

Having carefully distinguished Mishnaic from Pentateuchal conceptions in respect to utensils and Tents, Kelim and Ohalot, we now see that there is virtually no further fundamental and reciprocal relationship whatever. True, a few verses in Leviticus prove not only relevant to Kelim but also formative of elements in the basic stratum of laws, and the same seems so for Numbers and Ohalot. But the generative concept, the mythopoeic event or force, from which the Mishnaic tractates emerge is not Scripture, precisely as the rabbis of the second and later centuries claim, but an entirely separate "Torah"—"revelation" in theological language.

We have, therefore, to ask about the relationships between the two "Torahs," Scripture and Mishnah, just as did the third-century exegetes behind much of Sifra and Sifré. We eliminate two closely related theoretical relationships at the outset: historical and exegetical. The Scriptures and the Oral Torah will obviously have originated at different times, and because of their utter disparity, I cannot see how the two Torahs relate in some causal and sequential way. And, it follows, exegesis of the Written Torah, the Pentateuch, did not create, and does not stand behind, the fundamental conceptions of the Oral one, the Mishnah, although once those primal conceptions were in being, the Pentateuch obviously would shape their articulation.

The sole reciprocal relationship we can describe, therefore, is conceptual, or, in a loose sense of the word, metaphysical. And here the relationship is amazingly close. The two Torahs complement one another, are necessary to one another, balance and complete the conceptions of one another. The world-view of the one invites and instigates the reflections which lay the foundations of the other.

Specifically, in the case of Kelim, we noticed that the sources of uncleanness specified in Scripture are things which break the natural and normal course of life, the unusual or the abnormal (or, that which was perceived in remote times of antiquity to be unnatural or abnormal). Objects which are abnormal or useless are not affected by these processes. Susceptible to the unusual and abnormal are things which are commonplace, normal, everyday, and useful. The negative, the out-of-the-ordinary and disharmonious, affects the positive, that which is whole and complete. There is a striking correspondence between the priestly conception, in Leviticus, of the sources of uncleanness and the Mishnaic conception, in Kelim, of objects susceptible to the uncleanness imparted by those sources.

For the problem before us, we may discern parallel correspondences. When someone dies, a change affects the economy of nature. The body which has housed the person lies lifeless. Scripture is clear that

that body produces "uncleanness," specifying the various ways in which the uncleanness is transferred and the things affected by it. (This imbalance specified by Scripture uses the language "uncleanness" to refer to that which has taken place, and we do not have to diverge from that language.) What then happens to the uncleanness released from the body? Where does it go? What is it?

The Oral Torah's answer, suggested above, is that that uncleanness now will find a new container, something which will keep and contain it as the body has done. What will do so? Something a handbreadth in height, breadth, and depth, with adequate entry (thus: egress) for the effusion of the corpse to find a way in. This new 'house', the Tent, takes the place of the old, thus restoring the natural economy and order. It may be envisioned as a 'house'/Tent, or it may be seen as something far more abstract, simply as that which will prevent the passage of uncleanness, keeping it in ("bringing the uncleanness") or preventing its entry ("interposing against the uncleanness"). The two processes, interposition or containment, are one and the same thing. The point of interest of the Oral Torah, therefore, is in righting the imbalance specified by the written one, in explaining how the whole, complete order or economy of reality is to be conceived. The Written Torah tells about the unbalancing, the Oral Torah records the restoration of the wholeness and completeness, the order and perfect form, of reality. This is so for both Kelim and Ohalot.

I therefore affirm the view of Mary Douglas (stated in my *Idea of Purity in Ancient Judaism*, pp. 138ff.) who sees the total structure of purity laws as a "symbolic system." She says, "A symbolic system consists of rules of behavior, actions and expectations which constitute society itself. The rules which generate and sustain society allow meanings to be realized which otherwise would be undefined and ungraspable... In the case of the Bible, purity and impurity are the dominant contrastive categories leading to holiness. As in any social system, these rules are specifications which draw analogies between states. The cumulative power of the analogies enables one situation to be matched to another, related by equivalence, negation, hierarchy and inclusion... The purity rules of the Bible... set up the great inclusive categories in which the whole universe is hierarchized and structured. Access to their meaning comes by mapping the same basic set of rules from one context to another." Douglas argues that each set of purity rules matches the next: "In this exercise the classification of animals into clean and unclean, the classification of peoples as pure and common, the contrast of blemished to unblemished in the attributes of sacrificial victim, priest and woman, create in the Bible an entirely consistent set of criteria and values. The table, the marriage bed, and the altar match each others' rules, as do the farmer, the husband and the priest match each others' roles in the total pattern..."

Unintentionally and in a very circuitous way I have found the relationship between the conceptions of purity, the respective articulations of the rules, of the Written and the Oral Torahs, to supply an apt illustration of Douglas's proposition. She has argued that the purity laws are a set of expressions, in discrete materials, of a single set of cogent and coherent categories, each parallel to the next, all necessary for a complete, whole conception of reality. In much the same way, the two Torahs, Written and Oral, create an entirely cogent and consistent set of conceptions. If we had one without the other, our structure, our metaphysics, should be incomplete. We can say what constitutes the incompleteness of the one Torah without the other, just as Douglas can say what constitutes the uncleanness of the unclean animals and the cleanness of the clean. Just as she has told us about a whole symbolic system, so we have been able to discern elements in a vast expansion and completion of that same whole symbolic system, though only through discerning what must be a very tiny part of the metaphysic.

Yet that is not the whole story. Clearly, the people who stand behind those segments of the metaphysic we discover in Kelim and Ohalot (and expect to see elsewhere) have done a great deal of selection. Why, after all, should a handful of verses in Leviticus have produced so vast a tractate as Kelim? The uncomplicated picture of Numbers 19:11ff. has been made to yield the extraordinarily complex laws of Ohalot. So what has been selected is not merely the Scriptural themes. Someone at some point has seen as terribly important what Scripture at best alludes to, and then not in a conceptual framework remotely resembling what is before us in Oral Torah. A world-view is contained within the laws of the Oral Torah. As I said, that world-view not only corresponds to, but also complements and completes, the conceptions, such as they are, of the Written Torah. Yet the disproportions, the disequilibrium, are such as to prevent our claiming anything like balance and correspondence.

Two massive and all-encompassing conceptions of reality—the one now in the Priestly Code, the other far in the background of Mishnaic law—existed, each with its areas of emphasis, special obsessions, deep concerns. These are seen by us to be complementary, but this is only after the fact. To begin with, they were not. Why not? Because to the Priestly legislator, what is in the center of things is the cult. Utensils made unclean are not used in the cult. That is nearly the whole story, and a very minor story at that. In like manner, the person made unclean by a corpse cannot enter the cult. The predicate expressing the ultimate value in both cases is cultic. For the Oral Torah, by contrast, the obsession is not with the cult, which rarely explicitly occurs, but with the *fact* of cleanness or uncleanness itself, as affecting pots or houses, as contained or released, as creeping through windows and doors or kept out. The laws before us see cleanness and uncleanness not as contigent, dependent upon the cult for their importance, but as important in and of themselves. That does not mean that for the Priestly legislator uncleanness was relative and not absolute, immaterial and not material. To him it was very real. But its *importance*— not its reality—depends upon the cult. For the Mishnah, by contrast, at times uncleanness may seem relative and immaterial, e.g., dependent upon a person's intention or conception of usefulness or upon time and circumstance. But uncleanness always is a given, a datum, assumed to affect *all* of one's affairs, not solely the cult or equivalent cultic activities. The Priestly legislator homogenizes all sorts and sources of "uncleanness" within a single term, *ṭum’ah*. The Mishnaic legislators differentiate that simple "uncleanness," assigning to it a rich vocabulary of highly articulated and definitive words.

Working with the same themes, and, I think, working partly with the inherited materials of Scripture, the minds behind Mishnaic law have given us something quite different from those Scriptural materials. What is it?

It is the picture of the relevance and importance of uncleanness as it must have existed before [1] the Priestly lawyers took all modes and forms of uncleanness and turned them into a single cultic concern. In Mishnah, as in the time before the Priestly Code, uncleanness is everywhere consequential, not merely in the cult. It is highly differentiated both as to causes and as to effects. Mishnaic law seems, therefore, to carry us back to the situation prevailing before the Priestly reformulation of purity. It not merely complements Scripture but reverses and revises Scripture's basic assumptions.

---

[1] On the diverse origins and meanings of the sources of uncleanness, see Baruch A. Levine, *In the Presence of the Lord. Aspects of Ritual in Ancient Israel* (Leiden, 1974), in particular Part Two, Sacrifices of Expiation, and especially pp. 77-91.

So far as the second and third century rabbis were concerned, both Torahs, written and oral, came down from Sinai as one whole Torah. In a strange way we agree that the Oral Torah, contained in Mishnah-Tosefta, beginning as it seems in the mid-first century and reaching its present condition, in a proximate way, by the beginning of the third, not only corresponds to and completes the Written Torah of the sixth or fifth century B.C. The Oral Torah returns us to the conceptual world prevailing long before that time, restoring what was reformed by the priests of the Second Temple. Perhaps a certain logic, inherent in the subject matter, dictated that there should have to be two Torahs, the written one for the cult, the oral other one for the world outside the cult, one for the place of the holy, the other for the realm of the ordinary and profane. If indeed there is such an inherent logic, then it is that which we may conclude—to speak in the language of rabbinic myth—was revealed to Moses at Sinai, one whole Torah indeed, completing the sacred with the profane.

BROWN JUDAIC STUDIES SERIES

140001	*Approaches to Ancient Judaism I*	William S. Green
140002	*The Traditions of Eleazar Ben Azariah*	Tzvee Zahavy
140003	*Persons and Institutions in Early Rabbinic Judaism*	William S. Green
140004	*Claude Goldsmid Montefiore on the Ancient Rabbis*	Joshua B. Stein
140005	*The Ecumenical Perspective and the Modernization of Jewish Religion*	S. Daniel Breslauer
140006	*The Sabbath-Law of Rabbi Meir*	Robert Goldenberg
140007	*Rabbi Tarfon*	Joel Gereboff
140008	*Rabban Gamaliel II*	Shamai Kanter
140009	*Approaches to Ancient Judaism II*	William S. Green
140010	*Method and Meaning in Ancient Judaism*	Jacob Neusner
140011	*Approaches to Ancient Judaism III*	William S. Green
140012	*Turning Point: Zionism and Reform Judaism*	Howard R. Greenstein
140013	*Buber on God and the Perfect Man*	Pamela Vermes
140014	*Scholastic Rabbinism*	Anthony J. Saldarini
140015	*Method and Meaning in Ancient Judaism II*	Jacob Neusner
140016	*Method and Meaning in Ancient Judaism III*	Jacob Neusner
140017	*Post Mishnaic Judaism in Transition*	Baruch M. Bokser
140018	*A History of the Mishnaic Law of Agriculture: Tractate Maaser Sheni*	Peter J. Haas
140019	*Mishnah's Theology of Tithing*	Martin S. Jaffee
140020	*The Priestly Gift in Mishnah: A Study of Tractate Terumot*	Alan J. Peck
140021	*History of Judaism: The Next Ten Years*	Baruch M. Bokser
140022	*Ancient Synagogues*	Joseph Gutmann
140023	*Warrant for Genocide*	Norman Cohn
140024	*The Creation of the World According to Gersonides*	Jacob J. Staub
140025	*Two Treatises of Philo of Alexandria: A Commentary on De Gigantibus and Quod Deus Sit Immutabilis*	David Winston/John Dillon
140026	*A History of the Mishnaic Law of Agriculture: Kilayim*	Irving Mandelbaum
140027	*Approaches to Ancient Judaism IV*	William S. Green
140028	*Judaism in the American Humanities*	Jacob Neusner
140029	*Handbook of Synagogue Architecture*	Marilyn Chiat
140030	*The Book of Mirrors*	Daniel C. Matt
140031	*Ideas in Fiction: The Works of Hayim Hazaz*	Warren Bargad
140032	*Approaches to Ancient Judaism V*	William S. Green
140033	*Sectarian Law in the Dead Sea Scrolls: Courts, Testimony and the Penal Code*	Lawrence H. Schiffman
140034	*A History of the United Jewish Appeal: 1939-1982*	Marc L. Raphael
140035	*The Academic Study of Judaism*	Jacob Neusner
140036	*Women Leaders in the Ancient Synagogue*	Bernadette Brooten
140037	*Formative Judaism: Religious, Historical, and Literary Studies*	Jacob Neusner
140038	*Ben Sira's View of Women: A Literary Analysis*	Warren C. Trenchard
140039	*Barukh Kurzweil and Modern Hebrew Literature*	James S. Diamond
140040	*Israeli Childhood Stories of the Sixties: Yizhar, Aloni, Shahar, Kahana-Carmon*	Gideon Telpaz
140041	*Formative Judaism II: Religious, Historical, and Literary Studies*	Jacob Neusner

BROWN JUDAIC STUDIES SERIES

140042	*Judaism in the American Humanities II: Jewish Learning and the New Humanities*	Jacob Neusner
140043	*Support for the Poor in the Mishnaic Law of Agriculture: Tractate Peah*	Roger Brooks
140044	*The Sanctity of the Seventh Year: A Study of Mishnah Tractate Shebiit*	Louis E. Newman
140045	*Character and Context: Studies in the Fiction of Abramovitsh, Brenner, and Agnon*	Jeffrey Fleck
140046	*Formative Judaism III: Religious, Historical, and Literary Studies*	Jacob Neusner
140047	*Pharaoh's Counsellors: Job, Jethro, and Balaam in Rabbinic and Patristic Tradition*	Judith Baskin
140048	*The Scrolls and Christian Origins: Studies in the Jewish Background of the New Testament*	Matthew Black
140049	*Approaches to Modern Judaism I*	Marc Lee Raphael
140050	*Mysterious Encounters at Mamre and Jabbok*	William T. Miller
140051	*The Mishnah Before 70*	Jacob Neusner
140052	*Sparada by the Bitter Sea: Imperial Interaction in Western Anatolia*	Jack Martin Balcer
140053	*Hermann Cohen: The Challenge of a Religion of Reason*	William Kluback
140054	*Approaches to Judaism in Medieval Times I*	David R. Blumenthal
140055	*In the Margins of the Yerushalmi: Glosses on the English Translation*	Jacob Neusner
140056	*Approaches to Modern Judaism II*	Marc Lee Raphael
140057	*Approaches to Judaism in Medieval Times II*	David R. Blumenthal
140058	*Midrash as Literature: The Primacy of Documentary Discourse*	Jacob Neusner
140059	*The Commerce of the Sacred: Mediation of the Divine Among Jews in the Graeco-Roman Diaspora*	Jack N. Lightstone
140060	*Major Trends in Formative Judaism I: Society and Symbol in Political Crisis*	Jacob Neusner
140061	*Major Trends in Formative Judaism II: Texts, Contents, and Contexts*	Jacob Neusner
140062	*A History of the Jews in Babylonia. I: The Parthian Period*	Jacob Neusner
140063	*The Talmud of Babylonia: An American Translation. XXXII: Tractate Arakhin*	Jacob Neusner
140064	*Ancient Judaism: Debates and Disputes*	Jacob Neusner
140065	*Prayers Alleged to Be Jewish: An Examination of the Constitutiones Apostolorum*	David Fiensy
140066	*The Legal Methodology of Hai Gaon*	Tsvi Groner
140067	*From Mishnah to Scripture: The Problem of the Unattributed Saying*	Jacob Neusner
140068	*Halakhah in a Theological Dimension*	David Novak
140069	*From Philo to Origen: Middle Platonism in Transition*	Robert M. Berchman
140070	*In Search of Talmudic Biography: The Problem of the Attributed Saying*	Jacob Neusner
140071	*The Death of the Old and the Birth of the New: The Framework of the Book of Numbers and the Pentateuch*	Dennis T. Olson

BROWN JUDAIC STUDIES SERIES

140117	*The Talmud of Babylonia: An American Translation.*	
	VII: Tractate Besah	Alan J. Avery-Peck
140118	*Sifre to Numbers: An American Translation and Explanation,*	
	Vol 1: Sifre to Numbers 1-58	Jacob Neusner
140119	*Sifre to Numbers: An American Translation and Explanation,*	
	Vol 2: Sifre to Numbers 59-115	Jacob Neusner
140120	*Cohen and Troeltsch: Ethical Monotheistic Religion and*	
	Theory of Culture	Wendell S. Dietrich
140121	*Goodenough on the History of Religion and on Judaism*	Jacob Neusner/
		Ernest Frerichs
140122	*Pesiqta DeRab Kahana I:*	
	Pisqaot One through Fourteen	Jacob Neusner
140123	*Pesiqta DeRab Kahana II:*	
	Pisqaot Fifteen through Twenty-Eight	Jacob Neusner
140125	*Comparative Midrash II*	Jacob Neusner